**Advance Praise for**

# THE BUDDHA'S WIFE

---



"A beautiful imagination of the feminine and relational side of the Buddha's tale."

—**Jack Kornfield**, author of *The Wise Heart*

"Though I'm not a Buddhist, I sense that this account deepens and adds beautiful shadings to the story of the Buddha's life. I know that in its focus on relationship, it's a powerful antidote to the hyper-individualism that marks our world."

—**Bill McKibben**, author of *The Comforting Whirlwind*

"An imaginative tour de force, this book lets the Buddha's central teaching of dependent co-arising shine through with fresh relevance for our lives today. Acknowledging the meagerness of scriptural references to Yasodhara, Surrey and Shem are equally open about their motivation in creating a story for her that will meet the needs of contemporary men and women. Along with the engrossing story, you'll find guidance on mindful practices that help us awaken to and through our relationships."

—**Joanna Macy**, author of *Coming Back to Life*

"*The Buddha's Wife* is a gripping telling of an amazing 2,500-year-old story, followed by a collection of contemporary inspirational stories, and specific reflections and practices collected from the lives and work of 'relational activists' all over the world. A great read and a practical guide for anyone who wants to 'wake up' and walk a path of healing with others."

—**Martin Sheen**

"Janet Surrey and Samuel Shem have written a remarkable book, both as a work of literature and a work of spiritual teaching. Through their moving personal story and their beautiful imagining of the life of Yasodhara, the Buddha's wife, they describe a 'relational path' to awakening, one that contrasts with that of the heroic solitary seeker we see so often in religious texts and myths. *The Buddha's Wife* comes at a time of distress and conflict in our culture and offers hope that we might learn to live together in a new way, founded in an understanding of our shared struggle for happiness and freedom."

—**Kevin Griffin**, author of *One Breath at a Time* and *Recovering Joy*

"*The Buddha's Wife* carries us beyond any one religious tradition to launch us gently into streams of a universal wisdom. Therein is its spiritual power. This is a beautifully written book for all who know, at least intuitively, that our liberation—as people and as a planet—is rooted in our shared commitments to more radically relational and mutual ways of being than any of the major world religions (including Buddhism) either teach or practice."

—**(The Rev) Carter Heyward, PhD**, professor emerita of Theology, Episcopal Divinity School, Cambridge, MA

"A brave and life-changing book, *The Buddha's Wife* speaks to perhaps the greatest challenge of our time, our false sense of separateness. For all people of all faiths, this book shifts perception and thus opens us to possibility. It touched me deeply."

—**Frances Moore Lappe**, author of *Diet for a Small Planet*

"What must it have been like for the Buddha's wife to be abandoned the night after her first child was born? Surrey and Shem have a brilliant story to tell, one of a heart shattered by loss, a community that doesn't shy away from suffering, and a path to freedom that is radical yet ordinary, humble yet profound. The authors offer a healing vision, nurtured throughout their life together, that is just what our world needs."

—**Christopher Germer, PhD**,
author of *The Mindful Path to Self-Compassion*,
co-editor of *Mindfulness and Psychotherapy*,
clinical instructor at Harvard Medical School

"*The Buddha's Wife* is a riveting tale that will move your heart and shift your focus to the precious beings around you. In our world, where the social fabric is torn by violence, greed, and neglect, this visionary story offers us an alternative path beyond individualism and self-preoccupation. Drawing on the deep wisdom of relational and spiritual practices that Surrey and Shem have studied, created, and engaged in over decades, this timeless and beautiful narrative shows us what deep attunement to ourselves and to one another looks like, as well as the means by which we can work to manifest it."

—**Mary Watkins**, author of *Toward Psychologies of Liberation*

"*The Buddha's Wife* is a visionary work of profound insight, imagination, compassion, and scholarship. In telling the lost story of Yasodhara, Surrey and Shem give us a lamp for our troubled times, illuminating new paths and practices for all relationships."

—**Susan M. Pollak**, coauthor of *Sitting Together*

"Through a delightfully imaginative retelling of the Buddha's story from the perspective of his wife and others left behind, this innovative book brings alive relational Buddhism—the possibility of awakening through connection with others. Filled with practical insights and practices, it invites us to reflect on the origins of what we often take for granted in Buddhist teaching. This book is essential reading for anyone wishing to live a richer, happier, more connected life."

—**Ronald D. Siegel, PsyD**, author of *The Mindfulness Solution*

"Bless you Janet, Sam, and Yashodhara for pointing us in the feminist clarity that we serve best as an 'I' in the nest of 'we.' Being communal at home and in the world was the smartest decision of my life. Let's help midwife a loving world."

—**Dr. Hunter "Patch" Adams**, doctor, clown and activist for peace and justice

# The Buddha's Wife

# THE BUDDHA'S WIFE

HER STORY AND READER'S COMPANION

## The Path of Awakening Together

JANET SURREY, PHD
AND SAMUEL SHEM, MD

**ATRIA** BOOKS
New York London Toronto Sydney New Delhi

Hillsboro, Oregon

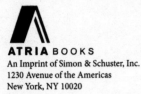

ATRIA BOOKS
An Imprint of Simon & Schuster, Inc.
1230 Avenue of the Americas
New York, NY 10020

BEYOND WORDS
20827 N.W. Cornell Road, Suite 500
Hillsboro, Oregon 97124-9808
503-531-8700 / 503-531-8773 fax
www.beyondword.com



Names of contributors in the "Ripe Moments" stories have sometimes been altered to protect identities.

Managing editor: Lindsay S. Brown
Editors: Henry Covey, Emily Han
Copyeditor: Jennifer Weaver-Neist
Proofreader: Mark Antonides
Design: Devon Smith
Composition: William H. Brunson Typography Services

First Atria Paperback/Beyond Words trade paperback edition June 2015



Manufactured in the United States of America

10 9 8 7 6 5 4 3 2 1

*Library of Congress Cataloging-in-Publication Data*

Surrey, Janet L.
The Buddha's wife : the path of awakening together : her story and reader's companion / Janet Surrey, PhD, and Samuel Shem, MD.
pages cm
Includes bibliographical references.
1. Yasodhara (Wife of Gautama Buddha). 2. Rahula (Son of Gautama Buddha), approximately 534 B.C.– 3. Religious life—Buddhism. 4. Women—Religious life. I. Shem, Samuel. II. Title.
BQ933.S87 2015
294.3'63—dc23

2014049912

ISBN 978-1-58270-418-0
ISBN 978-1-4767-1019-8 (eBook)

The corporate mission of Beyond Words Publishing, Inc.: *Inspire to Integrity*

For

Jean Baker Miller, Vimala Thakar, Rosalie Surrey,

and

Katie Chun Surrey-Bergman and her World

Dear One,
What might be of benefit, what teaching and practices offered, had two—or more—sat together under the Bodhi tree?

—**Yasodhara**, the Buddha's wife

# CONTENTS

Letter to the Reader....xiii
Introduction....xxvii
About the Book....xxxv

**BOOK ONE: YASODHARA'S STORY**

1....3
2....9
3....14
4....17
5....19
6....23
7....25
8....28
9....30
10....33
11....36
12....40
13....44
14....46
15....48
16....51
17....53
18....57
19....61
20....67
21....71
22....75
23....81
24....83
25....88
26....93
27....97
28....100
29....105
30....107

## BOOK TWO: READER'S COMPANION

Expanding the Circle: An Invitation ........................... 113

PART I: THE MEETING OF SUFFERING AND COMPASSION

1. The Gift of Desperation: Suffering and Compassion Co-Arise ........................................ 119
2. Creating the Circle of Compassion: Finding Power in the *Sangha* .................................. 139

PART II: THE PATH OF DEVOTION: ACCOMPANYING OTHERS THROUGH THE CIRCLE OF LIFE

3. Birthing and Nurturing the New ................................. 161
4. The Flowering of Mutuality: Spiritual Friendships, Couples Partnerships ................. 179
5. The Path of "Staying With" Through Illness, Old Age, and Death ......................... 207

PART III: WIDENING CIRCLES, RIPPLES OF CHANGE

6. Creating Circles of Peace, Diversity, Restorative Justice ...... 227
7. Going Forth Together: Communities of Awakening .......... 243
8. Conclusion: The Path of Awakening Together— Becoming Relational Activists .............................. 257

Acknowledgments ................................................ 265

Notes ........................................................... 270

Glossary ........................................................ 280

# Letter to the Reader

Dear Reader,

We invite you to join us—to sit with us—in the circle around Yasodhara, the Buddha's wife, as she tells her story. We hope you are as inspired in listening as we have been in the telling. We hope that this book will be of benefit to you and, through you, to others in your life.

You may be familiar with the widely accepted narrative of the Buddha's life: As "Siddhartha the Prince," he left his royal home to "go forth" alone to seek enlightenment and liberation from suffering. It is told that he left his wife, Yasodhara, on the night of the birth of his only child, Rahula, a boy, and that he left without saying goodbye. The rest of the story—about his journey to awakening—and the body of his astounding teachings have been a beacon for many for over 2,500 years.

Until a decade ago, we never fully absorbed the impact that his leaving must have had on his young wife, Princess Yasodhara, as well as on his stepmother, Queen Pajapati; his son; his father, King Suddhodana; and others in the palace community. The story of Yasodhara and these others began to captivate our imagination. What about Yasodhara? What about their son, Rahula? How did she survive her abandonment, grief, and desperation?

Siddhartha came home only once, as the Buddha, when his son was seven. He met with Yasodhara and Rahula, and his stepmother and father, among others. One of the frequently recounted stories from the early texts of the Pali Canon is that a few years after this one visit home, Yasodhara and Pajapati and many other women of the palace asked, through his attendant Ananda, to join his *sangha* (community) as nuns. The Buddha refused them two times; but then, when the women shaved their heads and walked from their home in the palace for several hundred miles to where his *sangha* was encamped, he finally agreed to accept them, under special conditions. It is also widely accepted that Pajapati, the Buddha's mother, became fully enlightened, and that Yasodhara (possibly under the name Bhadda-kaccana) was known for her wisdom and also achieved *arahantship*.

How did Yasodhara emerge from the pain and humiliation of the abandoned, grieving wife to become part of this strong, vital community of women who persisted after the Buddha's refusal to let them join his community? What spiritual conditions were present before they "went forth together" to "go homeless" into the holy life? How did this spiritual transformation occur for Yasodhara? How did her relationships help her to survive and nurture the healthy growth of her son, as well as to nourish her own spiritual growth and to cocreate a shared path of awakening?

We began to imagine the vivid scenes of Yasodhara waking up to Siddhartha being gone, of her grief and struggles to stay alive for her son, of her meeting with the Buddha again, and of the women deciding to shave their heads and risk everything to go forth together. We meticulously explored her story, looking for every mention of her in the early Buddhist texts.

The historical Buddha was thought to have lived around 450 BCE; and in the earliest texts of the Pali Canon, compiled a hundred years later, Yasodhara, the wife, is mentioned only in these ways: as "the mother of Rahulamata"; in her attempts to emulate the Buddha's austerity practices after he left home; in her refusal to go to meet the Buddha when he returned, so that he had to approach her; in her encouraging their son Rahula to "seek his inheritance from his father;" and finally, as one of the group of palace women who went forth together to become nuns and arahants in the Buddha's *sangha.*[1]

Though the early canonical texts provide almost no further information about Yasodhara, we have searched exhaustively for stories about the women in the Buddha's life, and read all we could find about the status and roles of women in his time.[2] We have given careful attention to the Therigatha, the early Buddhist texts that compiled the stories and poetry of the first Buddhist nuns, and the later Mahayana texts, which describe Yasodhara and Pajapati as goddesses with special powers. For our story, we have chosen to see these women simply as human beings.

From the little that has been written in the early texts, we have elaborated a story constructed both from a survey of these historic materials and through the lens of our own time and culture. It is important to emphasize that ours is an imagined re-creation of Yasodhara's life, not a factual biography (sadly, too little exists after 2,500 years to make such a book possible). Through Yasodhara's story, we want to offer the symbolic possibility of a complementary path that leads to a doorway of profound spiritual maturation and the awakening of wisdom and compassion, often through living deeply with others—beyond the solitary heroic journey.

For years we let her story ripen in us and deepen, as our imagination took over. Finally, several years ago, the narrative cohered, and the story began to "reveal itself." Both of us began to feel a growing connection to our fictional Yasodhara—even began to feel ourselves "speaking out for her."

We felt that telling her story as fictional narrative would be the best way to illuminate this relational path. Storytelling is a powerful vehicle for truth-telling and for building community; it is at the heart of the spiritual circles we describe in this book. The practice of deep listening to the honest, vibrating details of another's life story can open hearts into connection through profound recognition, and melt isolation and separation.

In Yasodhara's story, we found the seeds of a rich, "hidden" pathway of spiritual awakening with others—together, in community. Every spiritual path begins with the first step, and this first step of charting the way is crucial. The Buddha's first step was to go forth alone, to face the inner world of suffering with awareness. Yasodhara's first step was into relationship, to share the suffering with others.

## Our Personal Journey on the Path

We, too, have lived this story, for over four decades, first in our splitting apart onto separate paths, and then in coming back together, sharing a spiritual path. For us, the steps in the path of our relationship—our separate and then shared desperation—have turned out to be a gift, forging the spiritual enquiry that has carried us now for a long time. Our personal experience has been the stimulus for the work that we do, individually and together. Our shared passion and vision, and all of our work together and separately, has always been concerned with the perils of isolation, the healing power of good (mutual) connection, and the liberating power of right relation (we'll speak more about this shared Path of Right Relation later).

We met after our freshman year in college in Boston. In the three years that followed, we were joyfully loving and sharing our lives, and began planning our future together. Sam was planning for a career in medicine, at Harvard Medical School, and Jan was applying to local graduate schools in psychology. Sam decided unilaterally to apply for a Rhodes Scholarship to Oxford, England, which would delay medical school for two or three years. For months, he denied he would ever receive this scholarship, and refused to talk about what this would mean. Jan was left feeling alone, confused, and depressed.

"I felt I had no words—no effective way—to communicate what I was feeling, just tears. It wasn't that I didn't want him to go, but his inability to talk and walk through this together created the suffering." He did get the Rhodes scholarship, and the relationship suffered even further. In the fall of that year, he left for England. Janet stayed in Boston, and started a degree in psychology.

It was an abrupt, severe fracture in a loving, forward-looking relationship. We went our separate ways, on separate paths.

## Janet's Path

The path I took seems clear in hindsight but was full of confusion and doubt and pain along the way. After college, I started graduate school at Harvard but was still reeling from the rupture of the relationship. I left school after one semester and became involved in the politics of the women's liberation movement of the late sixties. I was thrilled by the excitement and sense of freedom growing between women; the sense of sisterhood and solidarity; the retelling and revisioning of our lives unfolding in consciousness-raising groups across the country. My own horizons expanded; and after a number of years working in the community mental-health movement in Boston, I reapplied to graduate school in clinical psychology at George Washington University in Washington, DC. There, I began my formal research into gender differences in depression, examining all contemporary theories of depression in women, and I found them all to be incomplete—biased in a negative way and not accounting for cultural roles or political realities of patriarchy and oppression. This left me with a pervasive sense that "something's missing here."

I returned to Boston for a predoctoral and postdoctoral internship at McLean Hospital, Harvard Medical School. By then, Sam was back in the United States, doing his internship in medicine at the Beth Israel Hospital. We were "trying on" *being with* each other again, but both of us were passionately involved in our own work and creative life. I was eager and restless to find answers to my search for a new psychology of women. In 1979, I began meeting regularly with my clinical psychology colleagues Dr. Judith Jordan and Dr. Irene Stiver, and Jean Baker Miller, MD, psychiatrist and founding director of the Stone Center for Developmental Services and Studies at Wellesley College. Thus began one of the most creative periods of my life, developing relational-cultural theory.

In working on the psychology of women with my close colleagues, I began to wonder if women were the "carriers" or practitioners of a more "Eastern" psychology in the West—a psychology of care, compassion, and relatedness. This led me to Buddhist meditation and the world of the 12-step spiritual community (there were still great wounds in my relationship with Sam and with my family of origin). In one 12-step meeting, as I began to open to the pain of these wounds and to the healing in deep connection, I experienced a moment of truth. An insight arose in the internal silence, and these words formed in my heart: "You are not alone." I understood what I had always longed for and had not yet been able to feel completely. This was a crucial moment of spiritual awakening in my life.

Something shifted in my way of being in the world. Surrounded by people my whole life, with family and many good friends, I had still felt alone with my pain, leaving me to struggle for release from a pervasive sense of isolation. But now, in this moment of clarity, I felt truly connected for the first time, and I knew it. Something profound opened for me, and I felt the tremendous power of coming into true community—both because it was there and because I could now open and let it in. This glimpse of the living truth of deep community is the vision that inspires the relational practices of my life.

## Sam's Path

I, like many men, didn't realize what I had lost until I had lost it. Never having been out of the United States before, I found myself in cold, rainy Oxford, feeling depressed and miserable. For the first time in my life, I had stepped off the conveyer belt of American educational achievement—and it was hellish. My grief, loneliness, and the feeling that I had made a big mistake by leaving Janet clouded every waking moment, and sleep was tormented.

I found solace through the other Rhodes scholars and from my Oxford PhD advisor, Denis Noble, Professor of Physiology. The community of scholars absorbed me and was absorbing—it was the late sixties and a tumultuous time, especially when America's actions in Vietnam and the flood of assassinations—John F. Kennedy, Martin Luther King, Robert Kennedy, Malcolm X—were viewed from the vantage point of other international students, from China to Australia, Cape Town to India to Moscow. Denis was a constant source of intellectual stimulation and company—his house and family were open to his students, with experiments in biophysics and neuroscience segueing into late-night dinners at his home.

I began to write. In a leaky thatched cottage named "Noah's Ark," ten miles from Oxford in the Cotswold Hills, I wrote journals, poems, short stories, and plays, mostly at night. One summer night at 3 AM, I found myself feeling desperate and terribly alone. Sitting on an ancient Costwold stone wall in the moonlight, watching horses graze and play across the fields, in my despair and isolation a phrase came to mind: "At least, I am." Something about that was comforting—a clear and deep relief. But it wasn't the words; it was what the words rode on: something beyond myself, something about existence itself.

In retrospect, it was a moment of the spirit. It was not the "I" of that phrase but rather the "am," an encounter with true and deep "being"—being without being anything "this" or "that," even myself. A moment when loneliness turned to solitude.

A few months later, on a road trip with a friend to Morocco and the Sahara, I decided that I didn't want to be a neuroscientist; I wanted to be a writer. Returning to Oxford, I went straight to Denis Noble's door—he had invested almost three years in me and had just gotten me a large government grant to buy a computer so I could finish my PhD—and blurted out: "Denis, I don't want to be a scientist. I want to be a writer!"

I waited, my heart in my throat.

"Well then, man," Denis replied, cheerily, "have a sherry!" It was a moment of communion—a sense that this teacher had no agenda other than understanding who and where his student actually *is*, and being *with* him there, affirming it.

I dropped out. For the rest of my time in England, I wrote; continued to build my community; and with others, protested the war. But at the end of the three-year scholarship in 1969, I faced a new choice: Vietnam or Harvard Med. I returned to the States to start medicine, which would be my "day job" to support my writing, and to see if there was still the possibility of a relationship with Janet.

In the 1970s, I was in medical school at Harvard—but writing every day nonetheless. Janet, though in graduate school in DC, kept in touch, and we saw each other periodically—and gingerly. We both finished graduate school, and we each were required to do an internship. We made the decision together to apply only to internships in Boston to see if, by being in the same city, we could make it work. She went to McLean Hospital; I, to Beth Israel. My experience there, combined with my Oxford/radical view of the world, led to the 1978 publication of my first "novel of resistance," *The House of God*, which, to my surprise, became remarkably popular. In the same year, two new plays of mine also opened—and closed quickly—in New York. "Samuel Shem" was now launched.

And so, twelve years after the severing of our "first" relationship and of our pursuing lives in separate cities and in separate ways, we slowly began the long, arduous journey back together, always supporting each other's separate creative lives.

## Our Shared Path

Through chance or luck or karma or fate, we began to find our common path.

By the early 1980s, we were in the process of slowly coming back together—of finding and trusting each other again. Even though we were committed to each other, we both had grown in new ways. Living together, we found ourselves struggling with the differences that proved difficult to bring together. Janet had become more connected to the community of women at the Wellesley Stone Center, to the peace movement, and to the 12-step and the Buddhist communities; Sam had developed a more solitary writer's life, supported by a community of writers. The tensions in the relationship grew. And on one freezing cold winter night in 1985, we found ourselves standing outside our door, in terrible conflict, at times screaming in rage at each other but mostly trapped in stony silence. We were at a total impasse.

Janet was about to leave for a two-week spiritual retreat in Holland with her Indian teacher, Vimala Thakar. Vimala was not only a spiritual teacher and poet in the tradition of J. Krishnamurti but also a social activist, having spent years with Venoba Bhave in the post-Ghandi "Land Gift Movement," walking across India arranging the transfer of ownership of land to the peasants. Sam had gone to a talk by Vimala a year before in Boston but had not been taken with her teaching.

That night, standing outside in the bitter cold, it seemed like things were falling apart—like a dead end. Sam had the sense that Janet could be leaving for good, which stirred up all the pain of their first separation—except now she was leaving him for something of vital importance to her. For months, after publishing his second novel, he had felt depressed and isolated—and desperate.

We were both paralyzed at the doorway; any movement seemed dangerous.

And then, at that moment, something else happened—something opened—and Sam said, "I'd like to come to the retreat with you."

This opened a new doorway between us, and led to our walking the spiritual path together. There was a sense of mutual surrender, of something new being born. Of walking through the doorway *together*.

We went to Holland and started on the path we have shared ever since. The fruits of this path include our coparenting of our daughter Katie, adopted from China, twenty-three years ago. We have also cowritten and been part of numerous productions of the play *Bill W. and Dr. Bob*, the story of the relationship between the two men who founded Alcoholics Anonymous and their wives, Lois and Anne, who founded Al-Anon Family Groups. We spent fifteen years leading gender dialogues all over the world, bringing together men and women, boys and girls in hundreds of workshops on bridging differences and conflicts to build authentic connection. Our book *We Have to Talk: Healing Dialogues between Women and Men* describes this work. The shared path has never been easy but always fruitful.

## The Great Turning, Today

Informed by Janet's years of immersion and creative work in the women's movement, in her therapy practice, and in the evolution of relational-cultural theory at the Jean Baker Miller Institute at the Stone Center at Wellesley College, Janet—and then Sam—had a deep understanding of the limitations of the psychological health model that emphasized the achievement of a separate, individuated "self," as well as a passionate appreciation of the power of mutual growth "through and toward connection." Janet and her women colleagues had written and practiced a fundamental hidden path of psychological development in connection. At that time, it was "hidden" or "invisible" because it was relegated mostly to the private domain of women and other subjugated or marginalized groups within Western culture, especially indigenous people; people of color; and those with diverse sexualities, health, and physical disabilities. The power of these hidden pathways to change the larger world are still not yet realized nor fully resourced.

Could this relational-cultural perspective reveal a path of spiritual freedom and awareness in relation with others? Our excitement of imagining this as the path of Princess Yasodhara, the Buddha's wife, was palpable.

Today, this relational path of development is understood as central to life and healing. Advances in psychological theory, neuroscience, and integrative social medicine emphasize the primacy of health and healing in connection. And yet, our culture at large promotes isolation and alienation from community. In a 2004 survey, 25 percent of Americans said they had "no trustable confiding relationships in their lives."[3] And the percent has been increasing since then.

The vision of the relational spiritual path is just beginning to emerge. We fell in love with this grand, untold story of Yasodhara; and then, using all of our experience with the re-emergence of relational thinking and practice in our Western culture today, we were delighted to find the rebirth of this lost path of wisdom now, anew. And so we tried to tell her lost story, and then show how it has been emerging as a new path of wisdom in our time.

The clues about Yasodhara's life were like the artifacts of an archeological dig, revealing to us the possible course of her liberation. How could Yasodhara and the other women have been ready to "go homeless" together unless they had already passed through moments of spiritual evolution in those crucial years? From our close attention as therapists in women's lives, through our own shared experiences, and in our encounters with current spiritual teachers, the pieces of the puzzle began to fit together. At some point, the familiar was right there, before our eyes.

*The Buddha's Wife* offers readers inspiration and resonance with our own contemporary lives. Suddenly, in many different arenas—from the therapeutic community and the 12-Step recovery program to the peace and social justice movement to the "green"/environmental movement—the idea that living into our connectedness is what heals and empowers is increasingly understood. Such a vision honors and articulates the power and perils of Yasodhara's path of freedom, aliveness, and spaciousness within relationship, and the way between the entrapment of isolation and the fear of being fettered by connections—between attachment and detachment. Especially in these auspicious times of great change and uncertainty, her path provides a way to move from suffering in isolation into building true community, healing, wisdom, and service. We believe that living together in such a way—in the fullest sense—is healing, even transformative. In *The Buddha's Wife*, we lay a new foundation for the work of our lives: relational practice, both close at hand and in the larger world.

There is the possibility of a fully realized meditative path to awareness in relationships. It is emerging today. The story we tell in Book One and the ideas we explore in Book Two are about the extraordinary potential of the ordinary. It is about honoring and uplifting what is already there but hidden and not yet fully realized, so that it can open wide the doorways to the wisdom and compassion of community.

Unfortunately, ours is not a culture which easily supports this way of being—of awakening together in relationship. In fact, it requires cultural resistance and a tenacious willingness to keep the faith and persist, to meet the challenge of all the dominant cultural forces and "isms" that divide and separate us. We all experience pain and suffering in our relationships—in families, work, politics, and even in our spiritual communities. We all get it wrong a lot, we all face challenging disconnects—relational ruptures, betrayals, and disappointments. What really matters is how we "hang in" through the disconnects, how we stay energized and faithful to our shared vision, how we persist and keep moving forward.

As we invite you into this circle, please keep in mind that we and so many others are *with* you. If sometimes you feel discouraged, or even despairing, you are not alone! Join with us in keeping faith in the possibility of another way—of leaning into the ripe moments we all have, glimpses of good connection and deep community, and being part of the evolution of relational awakening. We need this faith in ourselves and in each other to keep on keeping on. *If not together, how?*

We invite you to walk with Yasodhara on the shared Path of Right Relation and to become, together with us, relational and spiritual activists in our hurting world.

We wish you well,
Janet and Sam
September 2014

# INTRODUCTION

While little actual detail is recorded of the Buddha's life, it is written that at twenty-nine years of age, Prince Siddhartha Gautama, the son of the northern India king Suddhodana of the Sakyan clan in the foothills of the Himalayas (now Nepal), renounced household and family on the night of the birth of his son to seek spiritual liberation. Over and over it is told that he left his wife and child in the dead of night without saying good-bye.

This great renunciation is celebrated as the Path of He Who Goes Forth.

The story of the Buddha's wife, Princess Yasodhara, who remained behind to care for their newborn son with Siddhartha's large extended family, has rarely been told, however, and never from her own perspective.

Siddhartha's path to enlightenment has been chronicled in great detail over the ages, while Yasodhara's has been invisible. Our challenge has been to imagine her journey through loss, grief, and suffering to find her own way toward enlightenment as she lived immersed in community and participated in "ordinary" relationships.

*The Buddha's Wife* reconstructs Yasodhara's story of transformation through her realization of deep community and through her active participation in relationships with her mother-in-law, Pajapati; her father-in-law, Suddhodana; her son, Rahula; her own mother; a network of servants and friends within and beyond the palace community; and most importantly, the nuns who formed the women's *sangha* (community) within the Buddha's larger following. In comparison with the Buddha's path of leaving home and renunciation, Yasodhara's story illuminates the spiritual Path of She Who Stays.

We believe this path offers a timely and much-needed guide for contemporary living.

While traditional Buddhism emphasizes solitary meditation and spiritual seeking with community support, Yasodhara's experience speaks of the Path of Right Relation—of growing awareness not alone but together, fully engaged with others. The seeds of this relational path practiced two and a half millennia ago have been growing in the ordinary lives of people throughout human history, passed on from one generation to another. But it is a hidden path, often unnoticed.

In this path, the movement into relation—into community—opens the person to being part of something greater than oneself. The vehicle for awakening is in the relationship itself, and everyone who is part of it is changed.

## A Lineage of Wisdom in Relation

Yasodhara was left by her husband just hours after she became a mother, in the regal palace with their child and the extended royal family. We envision that from the moment of this loss of the love of her life, there was a lineage of wisdom that became available to her through the mothers and women and healers in the community. In her desperation, this gift allowed her to endure her grief, stay alive to mother her son, and ultimately, as "She Who Comes Forth in Relation," to enter into full awakening of compassion and wisdom, reflected in a life of accompanying others and being in service to them.

In our imagined story, both the Buddha and Yasodhara walk a spiritual path and become awakened. Each journey necessitates wrestling with solitude and communion, yet each entered through a different *dharma* doorway: he through solitude, and she through communion. Both are necessary for a fully realized path. And while the Buddha is a figure represented in solitary meditative repose, the fact is that, except for the very few days and nights spent under the Bodhi tree, he lived his first thirty years as a prince in a busy palace; and thereafter, lived in a huge community with other monastics. And after his enlightenment, he was always accompanied by hundreds—if not thousands—of followers. Yet, he was always the one teacher above all.

Historically, there has been a split in the Buddhist path between the householder and monastic traditions, and only monks have been the teachers. This split is being integrated today in the West with many "secular" teachers. The relational path has been practiced in ordinary, domestic, householder life but could well be practiced in relationship in monastic life as well.

Melvin McCleod, editor of *The Shambala Sun*, writes: "Some say that these truths were discovered by one man 2,500 years ago—the man we came to call the Buddha, the Awakened One. Others say these truths have been described and rediscovered since beginningless time and will continue to be discovered forever into the future."[1]

We believe this rediscovery to also be true of Yasodhara's path and suggest that *The Buddha's Wife* represents an illuminating interpretation of the Buddhist literature.

## Yasodhara's Hidden Path Made Visible Today

*The Buddha's Wife* begins by offering "Book One: Yasodhara's Story," re-creating the events of her life along with her attendant insights and transformations. Both in the community within the royal palace and then among the Buddha's followers, Yasodhara plays a central role: she is a figure who builds relational bridges and expands boundaries. The power of her relationship with Pajapati, forged in the time of extreme suffering after Siddhartha left, set in motion this relational path.

From the evocative scenes of Yasodhara's life, the book distills the wisdom of her path. It traces how her teachings are being made visible today and can be applied to all manner of contemporary suffering—from the stresses of relational losses and ruptures, the concerns of parenting and caregiving, and the pain of illness and grief over the betrayal and loss of loved ones, to domestic violence and substance abuse, social and cultural systemic violence, global inequalities, oppression, and environmental catastrophe. As we trace Yasodhara's path, the teachings of well-known contemporary Buddhists, many of whom we have studied with, will be woven throughout the book. We will also offer reflections and practices in the Buddhist tradition, to strengthen relational awareness and to lay out a way to optimize healing and spiritual health. While this path of Right Relation can be practiced by everyone, in all kinds of groups, we particularly envision groups within different spiritual or religious traditions working to integrate or align with these teachings and practices within their own community. The greatest power of this path is as a complement to all traditional spiritual practices, whether Buddhist or others.

About a thousand years after the first fully-ordained nuns entered the Buddha's *sangha*, this *Theravadin* tradition died out. Over the course of 2,500 years, Yasodhara's story was lost.

However, what is not lost is the everyday experience of those who "stay." It is often women who deal with their suffering—whether it be abandonment or abuse or loss of loved ones through disease and death—not alone, nor by going off on a solitary heroic journey as the Buddha did, leaving his loved ones behind, but by facing suffering together with others. Whether they know it or not, these sufferers and caregivers are walking Yasodhara's path. It is this path that can become the new doorway to the liberation from suffering offered by the Buddha.

This story, like the Buddha's, is a mythological one that can be understood as both a historical narrative as well as a spiritual one.

His story is one of He Who Goes Forth.

Her story is one of She Who Stays and then They Who Go Forth Together.

We have come to believe that both stories are paths to awakening; one begins alone and the other in the deepening of relationship. Together they form a complementary path.

Yasodhara's story represents an important life journey that resonates for many of us. Her story is familiar in the lives of the people—often women—that we encounter not only in history and literature but as the remarkable teachers in our current lives; and also (we have all had this experience, sometimes at the most unexpected moments) as that "ordinary" and "unheralded" person that we least expected to come forth to us—a person of humility, born of suffering, who shines with the compassion, grace, and wisdom of awakening.

## Relationships at the Heart

Relationships are the heart of our lives. However, as central as they are, often bringing great moments of joy and insight, they can also feel disappointing, burdensome, stale, and frustrating. They can bring profound suffering: abandonment, loss, violation, and betrayal. One way of responding is to retreat into isolation, self-protection, or retaliation, and then despair and bitterness. We may accept disconnections in our relationships without finding ways to revitalize and restore authentic and creative connection. We see and feel the close and personal yet miss the importance of the larger cultural web of relationships around us—how our physical, psychological, and spiritual health is threatened by disconnection and isolation, and thrives in Right Relationship.

Is it possible to stay—with family, friends, and communities—and walk the path wherever you are and with whomever is there with you, and to awaken together? How can we walk the ordinary path that many of us find ourselves already on—a "hidden" path that, without great notice, can lead through compassion to a new wisdom and a new happiness? Can we create freedom, aliveness, and spaciousness in our most intimate relationships? How can we find others with whom to walk a spiritual path and cultivate awareness?

Yasodhara's path demonstrates the potential transformative power of staying—and deepening—in relationship. Rather than "going forth" alone, it is "coming forth" together, into right, fully engaged, mutual connection. Yasodhara's story illuminates a path that has been hidden but is available and familiar to many: a path which grows into becoming part of something greater than oneself alone. This path has the potential to become a full compliment to the Buddha's path.

## Has This Always Been So?

One of our first teachers and colleagues, psychiatrist Jean Baker Miller, described in her groundbreaking book *Toward a New Psychology of Women* how women have been the unseen "carriers" of care, nurturance, and compassion in Western culture.[2] This domain of care and compassion has been relegated to the private domestic sphere, hidden—even "invisible"—and both trivialized and idealized by the dominant culture. Yasodhara, calling out in the pain of being left as so many others have done, was calling forth the immense power of compassion that flows in ordinary relationships. The depth of her suffering, her cry of pain, was a step toward the doorway opening to a well-worn, proven path. We believe this path has great, untapped potential—the path of awakening in relationship.

Siddhartha chose to leave and go forth alone on what, at his time, was recognized as the traditional spiritual path. He left home and "went homeless" to live the holy life and to find a way through the suffering he had *observed*, seeking liberation. And through his own awakening, he would then chart a path of awakening for all beings.

With Siddhartha's leaving, Yasodhara *experienced* immense suffering at her core for the first time and called out for help from her women, beginning the process of healing in relationship, until she herself began to show up and accompany others, including men, as a beneficial presence. We imagine that all of us who walk with her, in the process of communion with shared suffering, might find a way of liberation together too. This is not simply what is known by Buddhists as the "householder" path—distinguished from the "monastic" path of monks and nuns—but a path considered unlikely to lead to true awakening. Yasodhara's relational path has been hidden, unarticulated, within "domestic life" as well as within spiritual communities. Not simply for householders, and not only in domestic realms, the relational path has the potential to evolve into a revolutionary, shared awakening in all realms of life, as it is made visible and is explored in our time.

## The Split in the Path: Toward a Shared Path

With the Buddha's departure and Yasodhara's growth in spiritual community, "a split in the path was forged"—a split that has been furthered by the way the Buddha's teachings have flourished in the world. Patriarchal traditions seem to have fostered this prioritizing of the internal, individual opening to the spirit. This doorway can eventually open to a full engagement with all of life and humanity, but the possibility of the human-to-human relational opening, and the doorway to the spirit within particular relationships and communities, remains the more obscured, undeveloped, and uncharted path. *The Buddha's Wife* offers a possibility of healing the split, imagining into a shared inclusive path where all voices (male and female, monastic and householder, black and white, East and West) can be included and flourish. Many doorways, one path.

Some may argue that the Buddha's path is beyond all divisions and represents a universal path. We do believe that the Buddha saw the whole beyond the divisions—the "co-arising" of all things. However, the establishment and maintenance of the teachings have been transmitted over centuries, primarily through Asian, male, monastic communities. As the Buddha's teachings come to the West, the infusion of different voices—the sensitivity toward and the inclusion of women, people of color, different classes and sexualities, diverse ethnic and cultural groups—has begun. In this endeavor, careful and precise attention is called for. And so are boldness, courage, and creativity.

The Buddha's last words are said to be: "Be a light unto yourself; seek your own salvation with diligence."

Yasodhara's last words might have been: "Sometimes you need the light of others to see the way. Sometimes you need to be a light for others. And always, the light will shine more brightly when two or more are gathered in spirit."

And what about the shared path? We might say: "Every doorway opens to the path. All are necessary. There is no right door or right way. Sometimes in the dark night, we need to find our own way, or to lead the way alone; sometimes we need to rely on others. Always, we can share our light and find a new brightness in community, which will reveal to us what we are only beginning to see alone."

# About the Book

THE BUDDHA'S WIFE is divided into two parts: Book One is Yasodhara's story as we imagine it—a parable of a life of spiritual awakening and accompaniment. Book Two is a contemporary reader's companion, helping the reader make direct connection with the principles and practices underlying Yasodhara's story by offering ways to apply and live the wisdom of her path in our modern-day lives.

We suggest that you read Book One completely before you look at Book Two.

You might find a spiritual friend or friends, or a partner, or spiritual circles, or a reading group to work through the reader's companion together. Each chapter of Book Two will offer reflection questions that will help illuminate our relational life. Where are the healthy relationships and communities? Which are not healthy? What is missing? What can be built on and what needs to be left behind? How can particular relationships become a doorway opening to the larger human and greater human community? What relationships and communities are spiritually enlivening? How can we participate in building these?

Each chapter offers particular relational practices to support your walking this path toward becoming a "relational activist" in your life. Commitment to ongoing practice is the most important way to live this path. And practicing together accelerates and expands the possibilities.

# Book One

# Yasodhara's Story

Stay together, friends.
Don't scatter and sleep.
Our friendship is made
Of Being awake.

The water wheel accepts water,
And gives it away weeping.
That way it stays in the garden,
Whereas another roundness
Rolls through a dry riverbed,
Looking for what it thinks it wants.

Stay here, quivering with each moment,
Like a drop of mercury.

—**Rumi**, "The Water Wheel"

# 1

"Hear it, remember it, and pass it on." Thus I have heard.

On this occasion, I, Kisa Gotami, and the four other novice nuns of the Buddha's *sangha* were gathered at the Bamboo Grove, in the Squirrel's Sanctuary. The Buddha, accompanied by many monks, was teaching far away.

We were with Yasodhara, who, many years ago, had been married to Siddhartha, now the Buddha, the Awakened One. This was before he left home, on the night of their son's birth, to seek liberation.

Pajapati, the Buddha's stepmother, was gravely ill.

Yasodhara was with her in the inner chamber of the small almshouse.

We nuns had visited Pajapati the evening before, when she was still lucid; but after sitting up to speak with us, she fell back on her bed, exhausted, and we were sent out. We spent the rest of the day and evening in meditation on the nearness of death. We called up loving-kindness and joy for her liberation, and performed the other devotions. In the hush of the evening, we spoke about the ordinary sadness of a mother, dying far away from her beloved adopted son, the Blessed One. We knew that Pajapati was remembering her much loved sister Maya, who died suddenly a few days after the birth of her child, Siddhartha. In that time of desperate grief for her sister, Pajapati had received the infant Siddhartha and raised him as her own son.

I know the sorrow of a mother losing a son. It was the death of my son that led me to the Buddha.

I am the mother described in the Buddha's teaching of the Mustard Seed. The sudden death of my young son, and then my grief driving me to madness, led me to the Buddha. I could not accept my son's death and carried my dead child in my arms, looking for medicine to "cure" him. Someone sent me to the Buddha for help. In his great compassion, the Buddha sent me on a journey to find a mustard seed from every household where death had not visited. I was to bring back the mustard seeds to him so that he could prepare the medicine. As I went from house to house, pleading for help, I experienced great compassion from the villagers. Of course they were unable to provide me with a single seed since they, too, had known death. It was their sorrow and their stories that touched my heart and brought alive our shared human suffering. I became ready to let go and finally buried my son. Then I was ready to hear the Buddha's teaching, and I came here to be in this community of women, of nuns.

Yes, I know what it is like to lose everything and then to be offered freedom.

We sat waiting in the shelter of the outer chamber of the Sanctuary. It was the rainy season, but from time to time that night, we could see the moon through gaps in the clouds resting above the bamboo. Yasodhara came out of the room and stood before us.

"Pajapati is dying," she said to us. "Come."

The moon's light lay aslant on the dirt floor. In the amber candlelight, Yasodhara's face was the color of burnished gold. The scent of jasmine filled the room. On the bed lay Pajapati, thin and pale, her shaved head wet with sweat. Her thin face made her eyes full. Here was a great Queen, the mother of the Buddha, dying in this small dirt-floored room on a bamboo bed and tended by a princess. Both of them were dressed in the modest brown robes of the nuns. Yasodhara took her seat beside Pajapati and took her hand. Pajapati turned her head to her, and we sensed the power of the love between them.

We bowed to them.

"Last night, when you were here," Yasodhara said to me, "you told us that you had spoken to a new monk—a young man who had joined the order less than a month ago. You, of course, bowed to him, as is the rule. He said that he had come from hearing the Buddha tell the story of the Mustard Seed. He had heard that before your awakening, you were Gotami, the Mustard Seed Mother. And then you told him of the awakening power of your insight into impermanence at the core of this human life."

"Yes, that is right."

Yasodhara looked to Pajapati. We could feel the radiance of the communion between these two women who had shared deep suffering in their lives together. When Yasodhara spoke again, it was clear to us that she was speaking of the understanding between them.

"It is about impermanence, yes," Yasodhara said, "but it is about more—much more—than that. And last night when you left, Pajapati and I sat in silence, meditating together. From what you said, we sensed that our experience as nuns is in danger of being subdued, that our authentic experience of the path of awakening in community is being lost. Your life story and all our stories of coming to awareness are now being subsumed in the powerful and healing *dharma* of the Buddha's teachings. But that is not enough; it is not *our* whole experience, not exactly the path we walked. Are there not *many* doorways to the *dharma*? Could it be that we have entered through another door? Could it be that there is another way—a companion and sister to his—of entering and walking *together* on a path that leads to the same place? Could we not bring forth his and ours interwoven, a shared path? Would that not be grand?!" Her eyes were shining with excitement. "Dear ones, listen."

And then Pajapati nodded as Yasodhara continued.

"Your experience with your son and the Mustard Seed is not *only* about your insight into the impermanence of life but a teaching for us all. What allowed you to let go and bury your son was sharing your story of suffering with the villagers and hearing their stories. Your desperation—and your being on a mission from the Buddha—opened their hearts to you. The healing moment, the movement out of grief and isolation into community, came in your *being with*. In 'right relation,' true communion can take place. This is our practice: not alone but with others. It is compassion and insight co-arising between us."

She paused, with care, as if to find the right words.

"This insight into impermanence vibrates between us. What can never be held in the single human heart may be held in the great ocean of shared human compassion."

A gentle smile came to her lips.

"In the Buddha's teaching of the Eightfold Path, we find right view, right speech, right action, and right meditation; we don't find right relation. Is this not also worth its own place on the path?"

Yasodhara's voice was passionate now. She was looking directly into Pajapati's eyes. We all sensed that this was an auspicious moment, illuminating before us the creative power of right relation. And then she turned to us again and said, "Through this, we understood 'right community.' The *sangha* is born in the release of the self, and the embrace of the we."

"Please help us to understand this fully," I said.

"We will tell you," said Yasodhara. "This is why we called you in. There is great urgency here. We joined the Buddha's *sangha* and embraced the teachings, yes. But for those seven years before we joined, our own path to awakening grew out of our shared suffering—our loss and our grief—and then our finding our way together.

The Buddha was on his own path of awakening, far away, ardently seeking enlightenment. Now, after the few years we have spent in this *sangha*, we have come to understand and benefit greatly from his teachings. But in our experience, our path, and our practice—we sense something else, which is still unseen by the monks. Perhaps, from the Buddha's fully awakened perspective, he understands this. But it is not clearly spoken in his teachings; it is not being transmitted as we must transmit it."

Yasodhara paused. She and Pajapati looked at us closely, to see how we were taking this remarkable statement.

"Do not worry," Pajapati said, with effort, the shadow of concern on her brow. "We are offering our own experience, not renouncing . . . any of the Buddha's teachings. It is urgent . . ." Her head fell back on the pillow.

"The experience we gathered from the years of being together on our own journey of awakening may be lost," Yasodhara said, smiling. "Now, with Pajapati near death, we must tell our whole story to you."

Pajapati looked intently at Yasodhara. "Dear one, you must tell your story. . . . It must not be lost!"

"Yes," Yasodhara said, nodding her head, and then spoke again to us.

"Maha Pajapati, the Awakened One, has told me that she is aware that I still wait and have not achieved full awakening. Tonight, she spoke to me about her realization that I alone have known the *full* journey of Siddhartha—as my first love, as my husband, as the father of my child, and as the Buddha, . . . my . . . ," she hesitated, "teacher. I am still finding my way to be in 'right relation' to *all* of these manifestations of this man. Pajapati said to me, 'Because of this, you are a true *bodhisattva*, one who holds back, goes forth with others, and *helps all find their way along the path*. Remembering our path may help to free us fully. It is your last gift to me, to us, to the world.'"

She paused and looked around at each of us in turn.

"And so Pajapati has asked me to tell our story first, in full detail. Then we will make clear the path—our teachings and our *moments of awakening* on the path leading to our practices. This belongs to all of us and especially to you, our new members. In the telling itself, in our telling and in your open listening—our *being with*—let the truth arise, vibrating between us—a living being, a great web of awakening. If we do not bring this forth, many may suffer. They may not have this doorway open to them."

Pajapati raised her head higher. Her eyes widened. Suddenly, this frail pale body seemed to grow in power and strength, reaching out as if she were being held still by each of us and also holding each of us, like sometimes when you see a small flock of birds held, still, in a pocket of the wind. She spoke, and for the first time that night her voice was not agitated, but calm.

"Let it never be forgotten."

And then she smiled—a smile broken up by a harsh cough, and another, on and on, wracking her body. Yasodhara supported Pajapati in her arms, then lay her back down on the bed. Her breath was rapid and shallow, her shoulders straining to bring in air. Her lips were paling. Sweat was beading on her brow.

Yasodhara gestured for some water and a cloth to wipe her face. When Pajapati seemed more comfortable, Yasodhara went on. "The Buddha achieved freedom by leaving—by going forth alone and then bringing others along. Our path was in staying—in learning to be with each other more and more deeply, and then going forth *together*. It is the Path of She Who Stays, the Path in Right Relation. It portends *learning to live together*. You must hear it, remember it, and pass it on."

She paused and then looked deeply into each of us. The silence was full, cradling.

"First, our story. Then the moments of awakening on the path, and the wisdom of the teachings."

Pajapati smiled.

# 2

Yasodhara awakened before dawn to the cries of their newborn baby. Siddhartha was gone. It was not unusual for him to leave before she awoke, but he always touched her cheek and murmured a goodbye, and this time he did not.

As the newborn nursed in her arms, Yasodhara tried to piece together the past weeks between Siddhartha and her—how he'd been restless and distracted. Last week, traveling out into the kingdom with his servant, Channa, he had come back deeply agitated from witnessing the sickness, old age, and death that permeated life outside the palace. As if it were a sign, he saw a homeless monk and noticed that while the man had neither rich clothes nor worldly wealth, he had an air of serenity and joy. Siddhartha spoke to her of how he saw that those with wealth and comfort inside the palace were tormented by greed, jealousy, and discontent. He talked about his father's futile efforts to protect him from the suffering of the world. He spoke the unspoken—the prophecy of his birth, that he would either become a great king or a great spiritual teacher—and how he could no longer stand feeling "trapped" in the role of a prince, especially with the birth of their child. He had begged his father the king for permission to leave and to follow the path of the monk. His father had refused.

A chill passed through her body.

*Was he gone for good?*

*Wait. Think.*

She heard, again, his words from a few nights before: "Gopa, listen to me: I can't learn about suffering, in us and in the world, if I stay. This life, this place—the palace will destroy me. I feel myself drawn to go out into the world, into the peace of the forests, the life in the rivers and sky. But how can I leave you and our baby, who is about to be born?"

Now, trying to calm herself, Yasodara thought of the depth and passion of their love and friendship. She was a princess raised in another kingdom, and she was his cousin: her mother was his father's sister. When she was fourteen and he sixteen, she was told that Siddhartha was coming to a festival at her palace, preparing to pick a bride. Young women were coming from long distances to present themselves.

He thought that he had won Yasodhara's heart by triumphing in several feats—archery, swordsmanship, horse racing, weightlifting—but afterward, in a quiet time together in the shade of a mango grove, something else had happened between them: a *shared moment* that would become their touchstone forever, their heart bond. It was when he told her about the bird.

"Your brother, Devadatta," he said, "had put an arrow through the wing of a great swan in flight. We ran to where the bird had fallen, one wing pierced, blood on the lily-white feathers. It was flapping around, terrified. Deva wanted to kill it, but I stopped him. I put my arms around it and held it tight, saved it. 'It's mine, now,' I said to him. 'I'll heal it, release it, and set it free.' He protested, wanting to serve the swan for dinner that night—to show his merit to all. And I said, 'The creature belongs to the one who saves his life, not the one who takes it.'"

"You stood up not only against my brother but the whole law of the land!"

"I never thought of it that way," he said. "I just . . . ," he stopped and carefully considered what to say. Silence. When he spoke again, it was in a voice of what? Yes, the word is reverence: "I saw myself in the swan and the swan in me, and I could not watch him be killed, nor could I walk away."

"You were courageous."

"I never thought of courage. Once, a year ago when my servant, Channa, risked his life to rescue a boy from certain death in a skirmish, sweeping him up and running through a gauntlet of men to safety, I said to him, 'Channa, you were courageous to do that—to risk your life for someone you didn't know.' And he said, 'I never thought of courage. It was just the right thing to do.'"

How could she not love him? She had seen to his core—his honesty, intensity, kindness, and boldness—and how he was not afraid to speak up and take action against something he saw as unkind, whatever the consequence. He was a questioner and an enthusiast. His nature was that of an *enquirer* (a word that was special to them)—someone who pierced the surface of things—and his gentleness belied a great inner strength and an unwillingness to compromise, which sometimes led him into trouble.

They were as close as two can be; and their son, Rahula, had just been born the day before Siddhartha left—the baby that they had wished for thirteen years to have. Surely he would not leave all this—leave her and his newborn son. Even Siddhartha, whose name meant "one who accomplishes his aim," could not do such a thing. A wave of terror passed through her.

Her hands, clasped over the baby at her breast, tightened.

She realized suddenly that this was the moment she'd been dreading for a long time. He really was trapped between two choices—one, to become king, which involved military power, violence, and compromise; and the second, to leave and go homeless, to seek the only path toward spiritual freedom. She feared how her pregnancy may have set the wheel in motion, and the birth had propelled him to leave.

No. He would not do this to her and to their son. He would not disappear, no matter what.

*Or would he?*

Her mind raced back to that first shared moment and how they had gone on from there to marry, sharing enquiry into the meaning of their life—of life itself. His mind, and her mind with his, was like a flower in spring: opening, exciting, and even fragrant. They shared and explored everything—*everything*! From the ancient Hindu Vedas and the questions the texts brought to their minds almost every day (like the sun brings light); to the *yoga* practices of meditation; to the differences between themselves and their servants, and the suffering in the world.

Together, in the palace library, they once came upon shards of bamboo bound up in wire with a *mantra* of thin white words—"I am not that"—scratched into the ancient brown stalks by an unnamed Hindu yogic teacher from hundreds of years ago. The writing was mostly decipherable but clearly unread for centuries, and they pieced together some of what this *mantra* might mean. *Together*. It was their shared enquiry.

Despite the king's prohibition of their study of these things, they already knew some of the yogic practices of repeating a *mantra* over and over until its meaning unfolded. They came to understand that this *mantra*, "I am not that," could lead a person to become aware that I am not "this or that": not "prince" or "princess," or even "man" or "woman," or "angry" or "kind"—not anything specific; that at the core of "I am" is pure awareness—that all else is illusion and, therefore, suffering. Their practice was to repeat the *mantra* over and over, and hope that this would cause the specific, worldly names and qualities to drop away, leaving a mere enlightened being, the simple, I am.[1]

How excited they were—how hard they tried this ancient mantra practice. Despite their effort, it did not bring awareness. But it did change them. Another *mantra* they deciphered in the bamboo shard book became theirs, through difficulties they would later have together: *The mind creates the abyss, and the heart crosses it.* Yes, there were difficulties, even for all of their wealth and ease of living—fierce difficulties, like not being able to conceive a child for thirteen years.[2]

Now Yasodhara recited it over and over—"*The mind creates the abyss, and the heart crosses it*"—and as usual, it opened up her love to the great love that had blossomed in their shared enquiry; opened like a door to the *dharma*, the truth. Was this abyss too great? As deep and dark as the hell realms?

"He would never leave us," she said out loud. Never.

*But he has.*

# 3

Unannounced, Siddhartha's servant, Channa, came into Yasodhara's chambers. He had been injured several years ago in a fall from a horse, and ever since then, he walked with a limp. As he always put it with a smile, "I walk like a flickering flame."

As soon as she saw his face, she knew. Never had she seen this confident, kind face so twisted, so pale. In his hand, he held Siddhartha's sword.

Shocked—and yet not shocked—she clutched the baby closer and looked at Channa for a long moment.

He was a short muscular man about Siddhartha's age, the son of Siddhartha's servant. Channa had grown up, step by step, with Siddhartha until he was of age to replace his father as the prince's manservant. His love for Siddhartha was total, and he had delayed marrying for many years, until Siddhartha had married, to be sure that his devotion would not be divided. His two children—two girls—were the wished-for children that Siddhartha and Yasodhara had dreamed of; and when Channa and his wife learned of Yasodhara's pregnancy and Rahula's birth, they were overjoyed.

Channa, seeing the shock in her eyes, could not speak, for the torment of the words, once heard, would never be forgotten. He tried to talk, but nothing broke through his tears. Instead, he walked closer and handed her a lock of Siddhartha's hair and a golden necklace.

"Is he dead?!"

"No."

"Thank the gods! What, then?"

How could he give her news that would hurt her so deeply? He felt himself wobble on his feet.

"Pardon me, Princess, but I cannot stand up. . . ." He felt her hand leading him to a cushion, and sat.

"Tell me."

Channa said that Siddhartha and he had ridden out beyond the bounds of the kingdom, where his master then dismounted and told him to take his horse back, sending along the lock of his hair and the golden bejeweled necklace for her, and his sword for his father, King Suddhodana. At that very moment, a monk chanced to walk out of the forest. Siddhartha offered him his princely robes in exchange for the monk's simple garment. And then Siddhartha walked off into the woods.

"The last thing he said was, 'Do not follow me. Have faith. I am going forth on behalf of you and all beings.'"

There was a look of amazement on Channa's face, as he told this. "I thought he had gone mad or had been struck by a god—and not a good god either."

All at once Yasodhara grasped it—*all* of it.

*He is gone.*

All the blood seemed to drain from her. She looked down at the baby boy, who gazed innocently into her eyes. Had the baby caused this? Is this why Siddhartha had named him Rahula, which meant "fetter"? Had Siddhartha mistaken her understanding of his suffering—her sadness at seeing him distracted and raw—for permission to leave?

*He's gone!*

The shock made her feel that everything she knew had broken apart, fallen out from under her feet, been taken away, become thin as air, was unreal. A doorway to all that she loved had been slammed shut. She couldn't breathe. She screamed.

# 4

The other nuns and I had never heard the details of Yasodhara's dark time. We sat in the stillness, listening to every word and nuance.

"Now, looking back," Yasodhara went on, "I realized that I could not leave and try to follow him; I could never leave our child. It was unimaginable! The most painful part, and the most terrifying, was that he had closed the door on our deeply shared enquiry into the spiritual meaning of our lives—of our shared life, our shared spirit. No more. Now I was alone."

In the sanctuary's candlelight, her face showed the depth of that loneliness—that abyss into which she had plunged so many years before. She breathed in and out, came back up from that death. She went on.

"The chasm between this savage grief, this plunge into darkness and the effort of staying present for my child, the joy of holding this new life—these are the conditions of ordinary human life and suffering. There is suffering in all lives, but there comes at least one moment in every life when extreme suffering knocks on the door—a ripe moment."

She paused and pushed aside a lock of her dark hair, so that it again framed her face.

"And so, dear ones, we must ask, what are the ripe conditions?" Her eyes were both steady and in movement, holding each of us sitting around her and Pajapati, and moving on so that we all felt the touch of them like a lingering caress. "Under ripe conditions, this ordinary path has extraordinary power to sustain our lives and can lead us toward enlightenment."

# 5

When Yasodhara cried out, everyone heard it.

Her wail of grief was echoed by the animals in the palace, animal to animal, from the royal dogs to the peacocks in the garden—even to the rock-solid white elephant that Siddhartha had been given when he had won her hand in marriage. Her cries brought the women rushing into her chamber—first her servant, Rohini, and then the others. They found her sitting on the floor, arms tightly clasped around herself, rocking. The baby was on the bed, fitful. Two servants went to her, another to the baby. They tried to comfort Yasodhara, but she pushed them away. Someone went to find Queen Pajapati.

When Pajapati appeared, Yashodhara screamed, "Gone! Your son's gone! Forever!"

Pajapati saw a wild terror in Yasodhara's eyes as they desperately raced here and there to every face, searching the faces and the chamber itself for some answer. Pajapati understood at once, and it hit her in the belly—a blow of sorrow, rocking her on her feet. But she understood from her past losses and sufferings that her focus now had to be on Yasodhara. Without a word, Pajapati walked slowly toward Yasodhara, who was still huddled on the floor. The queen stood before her and opened her arms to hold her.

As Pajapati came toward her, Yasodhara felt as if a great kindness was approaching, even—yes—as if a goddess had appeared. Pajapati was standing so tall and alert but so very calm. Yasodhara was drawn to her eyes, so wide, and reflecting her own shock. Yasodhara realized, then, that in Pajapati's eyes was more, something else beyond shock—something powerful, pure and *powerful*; it was compassion. Their eyes met and held. Yasodhara rose. Pajapati took her in her arms, and asked Yasodhara to tell her what had happened. She did.

"Is he really gone?" Pajapati asked.

"Yes, I'm sure."

Later, Yasodhara would come to understand that the depth of her grief and the presence of the newborn baby had called up in Pajapati memories of her own experience thirty years before, when Maya, her beloved sister, died after giving birth to Siddhartha. Pajapati had taken the infant into her arms and had raised him as her son. She recalled simultaneously feeling devastated by the grief of death and the call to life—to care for the child. Finding Yasodhara in such distress had brought it all back vividly; and she was overwhelmed by what this would mean to her—to lose her own son, Siddhartha—now.

But holding Yasodhara in her arms, feeling her whole body shuddering uncontrollably against the embrace, all at once she realized that she was more experienced in grief than Yasodhara, who had not suffered in love before—had never lost anything that she held so close to her heart. Pajapati knew she had to rise again, to "mother" and strengthen Yasodhara. In that moment, she surprised herself with the strength and clarity that arose in her tight embrace of this dear child's suffering; and then what this would mean to Yasodhara's newborn baby, echoing down and up through all generations.

All of this spread out before her as a story being told, from mother to mother, child to child, from time past to time future. She had a moment of clarity, strong as stone: *What has been, is. What is, will be. What matters is now.*

"Come, dearest," she said, pulling away so that Yasodhara could look into her eyes. "Look at me, dear."

Yasodhara blinked, and their eyes met and held for just an instant. Pajapati sent the others away. The two women went to the newborn baby, and all lay down together on the bed.

After a while, Yasodhara began to weep again. Sobs tore at her body.

"I have no idea how long we lay there together," Yasodhara said, glancing at the frail body of Pajapati, who was lying quite still, with her eyes closed. Yasodhara looked at each of us circled around her, and continued. "But when my sobs stopped, I raised my head from Pajapati's breast and sat up, looking again into her eyes. Her gaze was penetrating and steady, holding me there as her arms had. And then, with care, she spoke to me, these powerful words:

'He has left to find his way through suffering. You must do that here, now. We are with you in this. All of us are with you. I know that in this moment it is impossible to believe, but you must listen: *I* found a way, *we* will find a way, and *you* will find your way. Your child needs you, as Siddhartha needed me. A new door has opened for you, and you will walk through it with us. This is the path of the ones who stay, who endure, who come forth with each other in love. Like Siddhartha, this is your first taste of what everyone must feel—of suffering.'"

"In this deeply shared moment with Pajapati," Yasodhara said, "I heard Siddhartha's voice in my head telling me how he had come to profoundly feel the suffering that each human and each person they love must go through—sickness, old age, loss, death, bearing the suffering of those we love. For the first time, I felt his presence and joined with him for an instant in facing this truth."

"That's when Pajapati turned to my servant, Rohini, and said: 'Tell the other women that she must never be alone.'"

# 6

As Yasodhara paused, I looked up at her face, and for a second, her eyes caught mine. In our listening circle in the sanctuary, the other nuns and I felt the emotion that Yasodhara was once again experiencing from so many years ago. Pajapati's presence rippled through us and the words.

"In Pajapati's act of coming to me in my desperation," she went on, "I had a first glimpse of how suffering and compassion co-arise. 'When the student is ready, the teacher will appear.' When the sufferer is deeply heard, compassion and insight arise. Everything the listener has learned, all the wisdom, comes to bear on this moment, and a 'right' creative response arises—sometimes going beyond what the listener ever knew she had in her. The energy of love and compassion generates a 'right action' for that moment—it was not there before—it actually is an arising in the momentum of the relation. Wisdom co-arising to meet suffering, in the act of relating."

Yasodhara smiled at us and spoke the words of the familiar chant:

*Compassion follows suffering as the cart follows the ox.*
*In suffering, she who comes, who offers love and hope,*

*And the truth of the path,*
*She who has seen everything and is still smiling,*
*Opens the door to the end of suffering.*
*This is the law, ancient and inexhaustible.*[3]

She turned to Pajapati and stroked her sallow cheek. Pajapati's eyes opened and showed her gratitude. Perhaps she nodded, perhaps not. Yasodhara turned back to us and sat with us in silence for a while. In the Bamboo Grove, as our silence deepened, the night sounds grew in the fertile, still air—an owl, a peacock, perhaps a deer or a tiger. Out of the stillness came a voice, Yasodhara's voice:

"Unless we agree to *be with* suffering—to *be with* ourselves and each other in suffering," she said, so softly that the words themselves seemed just another sound of the night, "we cannot be free of suffering."

# 7

For the first time in her life, Yasodhara was torn between life and death—between joining the living or joining the dead. Pajapati worried that Yasodhara might take her life and had arranged for someone to be with her, in waking and sleeping, helping her to care for her newborn baby. Firmly giving Yasodhara the infant to nurse seemed to rouse her out of her grief momentarily. But her dark feelings—shock, shame, fear, suspicion, rage, and disorientation—replaced all the sweet and gentle moments of her former life. And she felt a raw humiliation—her pride had been deeply wounded.

In all the faces around her, Yasodhara could see the question: How could this happen? Over and over the demons circled. *How could he? How dare he do this to me, to his son? Was I too understanding? Not strong enough?*

Each day, over and over, she questioned Channa: "Had this been planned? Had he ever said anything to you about leaving?"

"No."

"Did he know the monk who came out of the woods, or was it by chance?"

"It seemed by chance."

"But you're not sure?"

"No, I'm not."

"So he could have planned it!"

Strange, alien thoughts came to her, erupting in slashes of more questions: "When? Why? Could he not bear to stay and become a father? Or bear me as a mother? Now that he has fulfilled his duty to provide a male heir, is he free to leave? Had he been waiting—planning—for this chance? Was everything . . . *everything* he said to me false, a lie? Did I ever really know the real Siddhartha?"

Channa stood there before her, his solid body seeming to wither under these questions, but said nothing.

"Answer me!"

Silence.

"He has shut the door on me, and I have to understand! Tell me!"

Channa said angrily, "He shut the door on me too!" Then he turned and left.

*What do I care about him?* she said to herself. *Channa's grief is nothing compared to mine.* And the next day, it would be the same questions, over and over again, and no answers. Channa never refused to come back. He stayed close to her, but he had no answers that helped.

Siddhartha's horse, Kanthaka, refused to eat or drink, lay down in his stall of gold-rimmed hitching posts and troughs, and died a few days later.

Watching this majestic and beloved animal sicken and die, Yasodhara knew that this could be her. The feelings of grief terrified her—the grief seemed larger than her body or mind could ever hold. Rumination overwhelmed her, like voices whispering. She could not eat or sleep. Often, in the heat, she shivered and could not get warm. Putting on a robe, she was drenched in sweat and flung it off, away.

Yasodhara could not stop telling the story over and over to everyone—to *anyone* who would listen—not imagining that anyone had ever lived through such vast grief as hers.

The king, Siddhartha's father, finally came. He told her that he sensed that his son would be gone for a long time—possibly never to return—and that she must start being the mother of his grandson.

"Stop crying for him," he told her, as if issuing a royal command, "and start caring for your child."

"Get out of my chamber!" she shouted.

"If you won't take care of your baby," he shouted back, "the queen will."

Soon after that, Yasodhara fell into silence. She withdrew from those closest to her and even from her baby, who was being nursed by a servant. She would not leave her chamber.

"I can't live without Siddhartha," she said to Pajapati one day, when she had been coaxed out to her private garden. "I am going to die."

"You will get through this time of grief, dear one," Pajapati replied. "And your determination will benefit others."

"No, I don't have the spirit in me anymore. I feel dead. I don't know what's real."

"Stay close, with *us*," Pajapati said again—something she said to Yasodhara often. "Let us be with you. In time, your spirit will return in a new way."

"I'm tired, leave me alone. Everything before my eyes is black."

"Then look to your baby. He needs you to live."

Yasodhara turned away from her and walked back inside.

# 8

Together with Pajapati, the women who had been keeping watch over Yasodhara and her baby soon understood that it was too consuming for each of them to care for her alone. She was angry and bitter, withdrawn and lethargic—there was no respite from her bitterness and guilt. To be alone with her was too painful for any one of them, for any length of time.

And so, Pajapati arranged for Yasodhara and all the other women of the palace to gather together at dawn in a grove of pines, shaded by the deep green of the ancient trees.

Beside a pool there, a small Hindu temple had served as a sacred site for millennia—a doorway for their prayers to the panoply of gods. It had become known as a temple of the goddesses of fertility, where Yasodhara and Siddhartha had made many offerings and prayers before she became pregnant.

One morning, the women of the palace and their servants waited in the cool, misty air. They listened as the birds began their day. Pajapati entered with Yasodhara, supporting her by the arm. Yasodhara, head downcast, sat down in the grove. Her body seemed to have caved in; her face was flat and her eyes puffy, mere slits.

The others sat in a close circle around her. One woman lit incense.

Pajapati began to chant the Hindu prayers.

It was as if the energy that existed on the ground in that grove, beneath those ancient trees and beside that pool and temple, was being called forth to meet the desperate Yasodhara and the circle around her. The dawn prayers and shared chants—the moments of silence—seemed to gather the old, deep energies of the earth and nature to focus it amongst the circle of women.

Yasodhara's tears seemed unending. She wept in silence.

The gathering that morning didn't last long—there was work to do—but it had a calming effect.

The women decided to meet again at dusk, and this simple ritual practice seemed to take hold and then take shape. The morning prayers were chanted to ask for help for the day from the goddesses and gods. The evening gathering was to give thanks to all the gods for their daily care.

Asking for help. Giving thanks.

Every morning.

Every evening.

They called it, this gathering at the grove, their *Circle of Compassion.*

# 9

*Asking for help.*
*Giving thanks.*
*Asking.*
*Giving.*
*Help.*
*Thanks.*

Day after day, without exception, no matter what.

And finally a day came when Yasodhara began to speak—to talk about her pain.

And she wouldn't stop. She would tell her story repeatedly, and at first was listened to intently, by everyone. But after a while it started to become a burden for the other women, hearing the same thing, again and again.

Pajapati realized that Yasodhara needed not only to speak but to listen—and listen deeply. She tried to help Yasodhara to understand.

"Dear one," she said, "the only thing in your mind is your grief, circling and circling without end; you are obsessed with it. Any obsession is a turning away from the act of living—from life itself. The only way out is through being in relationship with others."

"I don't know how to do that now. What else can I say to them? They haven't suffered like me—so publicly, shamed in the sight of the whole world!"

"That's how you see it, and that's all you see. You would be surprised at what all the rest of us have lived through, especially we older ones. Shame? Yes. And worse."

"But I don't know what to say to them, what to do."

"Do you want to help them?"

"Yes."

"Then do nothing, but . . ."

"Nothing?! I'm doing nothing, and it's destroying me!"

"Let me finish."

They stared at each other.

Yasodhara felt herself about to go down the usual path of words, carried by bitterness and resentment, but this time she stopped herself.

"Go on."

"Do nothing except what you are doing for me right now."

"What's that?"

"Listening. Just *listen*. You don't need to lift a finger. Just listen, and take in what the other person is saying and feeling and being—and you don't need to do or say a thing. Can you do that? Silence your own mind to receive theirs?"

"I don't know."

"Just try?"

Yasodhara felt a hit of anger at this condescension—this treating her like a child. But she agreed, "I will."

In the following days in the circle, each of the women began to share her own life stories and daily learnings. Periods of speaking and listening in silence became the rhythm of the circle; they became part of the daily ritual. Wisdom and compassion grew.

"I remember," said Yasodhara to us, smiling, "how I came to see our circle as sacred—holding all of us, with love and compassion arising like a fire in the forest, burning away the undergrowth in our minds. It not only warmed us but surrounded and held us all, infusing each of us with a certain clarity. Each became part of the whole, no longer separate but illuminated by the fire's light. And after a while—I have no idea how long it was—I no longer sat in the center of the circle; I moved to be *part of the circle*. Instead of everyone turning in to me, each turned to each other in the circle, and I joined in that turning to the others. It was at that moment that, looking back, I can say I began to heal."

Yasodhara looked to Pajapati again and went on.

"Pajapati told me how she came to understand that something had been created of great value, beyond what she had even imagined. She saw the circle as a vessel containing earth and water; a well of compassion able to create and nurture new energy, new life, new understanding and wisdom. The heart of each person opening, becoming a channel of that compassion—and the whole circle infused with it, available to all."

# 10

Weeks later, a young child in the palace became ill and died suddenly.

The mother, Nayla, was a servant of another of the palace royalty. The women and men gathered at the cremation grounds.

The cremation of an adult often took half a day and part of a night. At the shore of a river, a distant, small source of the great Ganges, the cremation grounds in the kingdom of Kapila was, in miniature, a copy of the ancient sacred City of the Dead in Benares. There, dozens of cremation grounds were tended by the Untouchables, who were experts in knowing how much wood, fire, air, earth, and water needed to come together to do their solemn work.

The small pile of wood, the tiny wrapped bundle—all seemed *too* small, *too* fragile for death and burning; *too* brutal and unjust.

The flames finished their part too soon, much too soon—in a few hours. After the cremation, the mother of the child refused to leave the cremation grounds. She sat, watching as the smoke died; as the child-size pile of ashes cooled, settled into dust.

Eventually, the men left, but for her husband.

The women could not leave the grieving mother—neither the royal women nor their servants. Their hearts, as mothers and daughters, had been torn open to see this child, whom they had all known, gay and energetic, playing in the gardens of the palace just a few days ago, now turned to dust.

For Yasodhara, the pain was severe. Rahula was healthy and happy, but death was so near—a tap on a baby's shoulder that could come at any time. As his father had gone: at any time. Here. Gone. Staring at this young mother, only a little younger than she herself, Yasodhara found herself sobbing, not only for her but for all mothers, all sons and daughters, all who are born and must die, clenched in the metal hand of death.

Channa, who had taken upon himself the supervision of cremations, also stayed, at some distance away. He and Yasodhara had become much closer through their shared betrayal, their sensing the doors closing on their hope to see Siddhartha again.

Night came, and with it, the first night rain. Many of the women wanted to leave and tried to get the mother to come back to the palace with them. She refused.

"Come," said Yasodhara to them, "let's form our circle."

They began to move, and, as if on its own—a live thing—the circle began to form, starting on either side of the mother. There were so many women who had stayed, the circle was large enough to move all the way around and include, at its center, where the fire had been and where the ashes now were. The women all sat. Yasodhara noticed that Channa and the woman's husband were still there, sitting apart, and she gestured to them to join the circle. They hesitated, shook their heads no.

"Please come in," said Pajapati. "We invite you in. Be with your wife, as we are."

The husband looked to Channa, to follow his lead. Channa looked at Yasodhara.

She stretched out her hand to him and said, "Come with."

With his usual difficulty in rising from a sitting posture, Channa stood, and he and the husband walked to the circle. Pajapati gestured for the husband to sit with his wife; Channa sat beside Yasodhara.

The rain came harder. Soon, their bright-colored funeral saris were sticking to their bodies, their scarves hanging down and molding to their heads so that they might have seemed, to an ignorant observer, to be a shadowy group of poor monks with no shelter to go to, or who were praying to the Rain Gods in the dark night—a sect of lost and tired ascetics, even flagellants.

But afterward, many of them would remember it in the same way: not as a chilling rain of rebuke and despair but as a spring rain, soft and promising.

# 11

"That broke my heart open," Yasodhara said to us novices.

The cool night air was driving through the grove and into Pajapati's inner chamber, and we were gathered closer together around Yasodhara. She closed her eyes and breathed deeply for a time. Pajapati's eyes were closed as well, though she breathed softly, as if in a gentle slumber.

Yasodhara continued in a hushed tone: "The next day, as usual, Channa came to sit with me and the baby. I said to him, 'My heart went out to that mother, Nayla, and to her husband; and it tore me apart to imagine my baby dying with his father, Siddhartha, nowhere to be found. I hated him, Channa, right then!'"

'Sometimes I do too,' Channa said. 'It's like a poison in me. I hate myself because I'm treating my wife and daughters badly. I can't seem to help it.'"

Yasodhara paused and took a few breaths.

"Dear ones, I remember his words shocking me. In that moment, I realized that my hatred was poisoning me as well—was separating me from my own child—and I said to him, 'Yes, I feel that too.' And at that moment, we saw things so clearly! Our hatred was no longer mine nor his but merely human. Temporary, a dark cloud. And it just then blew past, leaving light."

She smiled. A ripe moment.

"Listening to him, and after that long day and night and dawn on the cremation grounds, I learned something. Despite myself, in relation to Channa and those women, something else had begun to take hold. I began to see that . . . well . . . that perhaps my enduring could help another person to endure. Now I can see that, one by one, the linking of each to each other was opening a way to . . . I'm not sure how to say it . . . to feeling the power of love working at the heart of the universe. A law of love, as sure as the law of gravity, that keeps us on solid ground—like a mango falling *down* to the earth and not *up*." She laughed, as did we.

"I reached out to Nayla, the grieving mother, trying to talk to her. She had no words, no desire. I suggested that we just sit side by side in the circle. We did so. It became our shared 'place' in the circle. After a while, we began to talk a little, lingering in the sunlight after the circle had ended for the morning or staying after the evening sitting. Just the two of us; sitting side by side, we would talk. After a few more weeks, we made the decision that we would meet at other times during the day. We shared the intention of the two of us helping each other on a regular basis. We realized, without saying it, that we two were being held by the strength of the many, as the many were being held by the strength of we two.

"This became the model—for all of us—of what we called a 'spiritual friendship'; Nayla and I named it. We referred to each other as 'spiritual friend.' Many of the other women, seeing this, developed individual friendships of this nature. As did Channa and I, as well.

"Something began to change in me," she went on, her tone lighter. "At first, I had hope for nothing more than that the pain would cease. Now I understood that my suffering might not come to an end but to a new beginning, a glimpse of something else, something greater than myself and my grief alone, something not yet seen or understood. I had the image of joining Siddhartha on his journey out into the world—but that was impossible. I wondered whether I could survive by trying to stay with him, or whether I should try to erase his presence inside of my heart. I vacillated and wondered if I actually had any real choice in this enquiry—or if it was merely *occurring*, like when you're swimming in a cold stream and a new, warm current is first noticed.

"In the moment of wanting to die," she said to us, "I chose to live."

She nodded, not to Pajapati or us, but to something else, in what I sensed was a wave of remembrance. "We chose to live. I set out on this journey."

She fell silent. I knew all of us were touching not just her journey, but all of our own journeys, bringing us together here, to this sacred night.

"I've come to understand," she went on, "that when we came together in the Pine Grove at the palace all those years ago, we were discovering a new teaching, a new practice—coming together in the circle with a clear intention, finding a way of being and speaking together, what I have come to call a 'practice *with* others,' or 'relational practice.'

"When you step into a sacred circle, you practice a new way of *being with* others in your life, in deep listening, and a new way of speaking that vibrates with the ring of shared truth. You bathe in the well of compassion. I remember the beautiful words of Pajapati: *We are our temples.*

"All of us who were there began to feel stronger, more fully alive, being held in that circle of care and concern—a circle for each and for all—more balanced and grateful for each other. Participating in this *mindful* relationship with others was at the center of our lives, and, we came to understand, at the center of each and every precious and whole human life. Not standing alone but *with* others—

with the trees, the grove, the stones and the dirt and the minerals and the animals and birds and plants—with *all* living things! With all those who have passed on, who have been born, and those still to be born. Without knowing it, we had lived through another ripe condition, and began to sense an immense power entering this Circle of Compassion."

# 12

Accompanied by the circle of women—mothers, grandmothers, sisters, and friends—Yasodhara began to turn fully toward her baby and to come forth as a mother.

From the first awareness of their child growing within her, Yasodhara had always had a powerful sense of responsibility to this baby, as well as an aura of fear about his birth.

"In light of Siddhartha's loss of his own mother at birth," Yasodhara said to us, "I was especially aware of the importance of this fragile and tender time."

However, her grief was so overwhelming after Siddhartha's leaving that she could not be truly present with the baby in those early weeks—another deep wound that added to her guilt and shame. In those quiet and lonely moments when she turned to Rahula and saw him try to "find" her and could not, a shocking look of fear would come into his eyes. It could not help but bring her back into presence with him, at least for a while.

"Everything in the world was in that look on my baby's face!"

She perceived her impact on this little being, which aroused her commitment to continue to learn to be fully alive and present with him. More and more, hour by hour, then day by day and month by month, she began to know him. He no longer represented to her the absence of Siddhartha but the presence of himself: Rahula.

"I began to see in the expressions of his eyes and face—his joy, his first smiles, his curiosity, and above all, his clear interest in the world, and particularly in me, and his yearning for connection with me. I saw that at those times when, in the fog of grief and rage, I was not able to be with him, he panicked and struggled to bring me back. *He* brought me back."

At times, he was able to bring her to life, as she had given birth to him. This became her sacred work—struggling to not let her own grief and anger get in the way of mothering this precious being. Yasodhara made a vow to stay alive, vitally alive and present and responsible, for her son and to her son—*no matter what*. And to be honest, there were times when, still overwhelmed with waves of despair, she was unable to do this.

"In our circle of women, I spoke that promise."

Pajapati had noticed that Yasodhara was more and more able to take part in feeding, bathing, and even playing with her baby, and she understood the power of the circle they had created to support her doing this—the power of Yasodhara's emerging relationship with Rahula to "call her forth" into life. Pajapati reflected back to Yasodhara her joy and wonder in seeing this.

The women began to talk about the suffering that Siddhartha had caused them by leaving without saying good-bye, and wondered if he knew what his action had done, spreading so much suffering through all who loved him in the palace and throughout their whole world.

When Rahula became old enough to ask the whereabouts of his father, no one knew exactly what to tell him about whether he would ever return. They tried to answer each question with openness, kindness, and compassion, leaving room for the boy to ask more questions.

As the years passed, the shared suffering of Rahula, Yasodhara, and Pajapati was named and addressed, and became clear in their questions to each other—the enquiry—and in their answers, the truth of their mindful dialogues. The stories that they then told him about his father were always about how Siddhartha the Prince, seeing the suffering that comes with illness, old age, and death, decided to do his best to try to fully understand this human journey through life, and find a way to end this suffering for all beings. It was a choice of great sacrifice and generosity. He had gone forth alone across the kingdoms and spent each day in rough-spun robes as a humble monk renouncing the world in an effort to achieve understanding through living the holy life—a quest that had always been honored in the traditions of the land. Yasodhara and Pajapati did not share their anger over Siddhartha's leaving.

The little boy seemed to accept this explanation, though he often asked, "When will my father return?"

Yasodhara had no answer, except to say, "When he is ready, dear one. We are confident that when he is ready, he will return. And perhaps when you are ready too."

"But you don't know for sure, right?"

"No, I don't."

"Does Grandma or Grandpa?"

"No."

"Who does, then?"

"No one."

"Not even my daddy?" His eyes were wide with astonishment at this, and he kept on looking into his mother's eyes, steadily.

Like, she thought, Siddhartha himself always looked into her eyes when they, together—yes, almost always then, *together*—would make a remarkable discovery about their lives, about the world—all the freshness of their enquiry, together. The little boy looked so much like his father that tears would come to her own eyes, then, and before she could answer him, his astonishment at her torment changed to pain, and tears came to the boy too.

"Doesn't he know *anything*?! He is *stupid*!"

"Rahula!"

"Stupid!"

She reached out to hold him, but he turned and walked away, his little shoulders slumped and shaking for the first time, carrying the burden of his father's seeming indifference to and abandonment of them all.

A shock went through her. She had tried to protect him, but she realized now how deep his pain went. She sat there, stunned, but knew that that was all she could do right then—to stay, waiting for him.

Soon he came back to her, and they talked some more; and she was filled with gratitude that, even at his tender age, he seemed to understand that the most important solace and refuge was in staying close and *being with*.

Smiling lovingly at our strong, close circle of nuns—all of us gathered in the same way that we had begun all those years before—Yasodhara leaned back and sighed.

"I felt an enormous sense of gratitude for how my beloved little one had understood. In the honest and caring environment of our circle of women, this little boy, at the first arc of the circle of his life—my dear Rahula—in his own way was becoming an enquirer on the path with us.

# 13

Yasodhara's mother, Queen Pamitha, became very ill and was brought to the palace. Yasodhara's father, King Suppabuddha, had died many years earlier in a freak elephant accident, on a December night thick with fog. King Suddhodana had invited Pamitha, his close cousin, to come and live in the palace to be attended to by Yasodhara and Pajapati, and the other women.

Yasodhara began to sit in silence with her mother every day, as she grew closer and closer to death. Her mother was joyful to be reunited with her daughter, and it was a deep nostalgic joy to talk together about their lives.

Yasodhara began to understand that her devotional practice to her son and with the others in her circle could expand to encompass the arising of life to the vanishing of life, the letting in and the letting go, the *being with* birth and the *being with* death, the first in-breath to the last out-breath—the whole universal circle of life. In sitting with and *being with* her mother, she committed herself to being mindful, present, and earnestly awake through each moment of the dying process. She felt herself stretching, expanding, to hold this great arc of life—privileged to be held in her own circle, glad to be called forth, and able to *be with* both her son and her mother, ardently.

"In the position of caring for both my child and my mother," Yasodhara said, "I made a vow to be a beneficial presence for these particular others on this shared life journey. And I understood how this vow resonated with the lives of the other women in our circle—this journey that is the core and span of each and every life. The unique yet ordinary stories of the women *accompanying* parents, children, husbands, and friends through life had a universal resonance: the life journey of accompaniment—*walking with* as a relational practice, from birth to death—became a spiritual path, the ordinary devotional path held in the larger circle." She nodded to emphasize this teaching.

"Under these ripe conditions, the particular opens to the universal, in the ordinary blossoms the extraordinary—the ordinary can open the door to the extraordinary."

As a rush of rain swept down on the sanctuary's bamboo roof, Yasodhara took several easy breaths, until it passed. "I understood that what we were touching every day in the sacred circle was the practice of accompanying—staying with, *being with*, and walking with, no matter what, as a shared *intention*. Even when it is difficult, this practice cultivates the soil and creates the ripe conditions for awakening."

# 14

These devotional practices, over time, helped Yasodhara to understand and accept how deeply she still loved Siddhartha. She made a decision to try to find out as much as she could about him.

One day, she called Channa to her chambers and, binding him to secrecy, asked him to leave the palace from time to time to keep an eye on what Siddhartha was doing, and report back to her. He told me that he had been wishing he could do just that, and, after telling his family, left at once.

She soon heard back from him of Siddhartha's extreme asceticism. He was starving himself and baring himself to the elements, living like a wild man in the forest—walking barefoot and wearing only a yellow robe, eating only once a day from his wooden begging bowl or from what he found in the forest, and sleeping on the ground. So she, too, began to wear yellow, to eat out of wooden bowls only once a day, and to sleep on the bare floor.

"For a number of weeks, I tried these practices, to make a spiritual link with Siddhartha," she told us. "They never seemed to help me, or help the few other women who joined me. The practices felt foreign. Rather than helping me 'be with' Siddhartha, they left me more distant.

"And then, one day, my failures at this illuminated a remarkable truth: what we women had been doing, together in our circle, here and now, were our practices. Perhaps these very practices offered possibilities of liberation through our shared relational creation. It was a moment of . . ." She paused, looking around at all of us and at Pajapati, and in a voice as clear as a bell, she said, "Of light! I took my discovery back to the circle, and the others understood at once!"

And yet, Yasodhara knew that she was still deeply in love—and in close dialogue and enquiry—with Siddhartha. He was always *there* with her, especially when she sat in the women's circle in the Pine Grove. She tried to accept this, and with mindfulness she described it to the others, and tried to bring him more fully into their circle.

He was always there, yes, but still painfully absent.

# 15

King Suddhodana sent messages three times to meet alone with Yasodhara. He said it was time for her to marry again, to replace Siddhartha and provide a father to his grandson. Yasodhara knew that she was still in love, and now in spiritual partnership, with Siddhartha. The first two times, she did not answer the king. The third time, she refused him. The king was now angry at Siddhartha *and* her. He was not used to disobedience. But Yasodhara was intent on her own survival and her devotional practice as a mother.

"Looking back now, after all these years," Yasodhara said, "I have come to be aware that the devotional practices must be made as a conscious choice and an expression of service. Not slavery to household life, but a choice and a commitment. Not simply out of necessity or obligation. It is like the devotional practice we learned as Hindus, but it is not the giving all and doing all for a guru. This is a different way, an ordinary practice—not to a guru but to the ordinary people we live with, day after day, year after year. To do this without the circle of care would be isolating and dangerous. To be truly present with others, you must have others present with you. And to practice without a clear path of growth, a wisdom path, would be limiting.

"In our circle, I had other mothers and grandmothers and aunts and servants, and this *sangha* held me, and I them, on our path *together.* Walking a compassionate wisdom path together. This is what makes the ordinary extraordinary. This allows what, for all our lives and for many centuries before has been named merely 'householding' or 'caretaking,' to become *a true devotional practice.*"

"I found this first with my son and my mother, holding birth and death so close to me at that time, and now, holding it not only with this great queen lying here by my side but also with you, dharma sisters. We all must learn to be midwives of the new, bringing forth the creative spirit, and also caregivers of the dying, helping those who are leaving to do so with grace and wisdom. Life arising and life falling away. Is this not the most fundamental teaching of impermanence there is?"

She stroked the back of Pajapati's slender and still hand. "This is our fundamental practice—to be called forth into life, not called away alone. Learning to be with the suffering of those we love, and with our own suffering, right here, right now—at home." She smiled, as if remembering. "And with the joy."

We novice nuns were struggling to understand these familiar words being spoken in this new way. Several spoke up:

"I came here to live the holy life and leave behind the superficial meaninglessness. Can it be that leaving is not necessary? But this is not possible alone. . . . No."

"And I came when everything was lost—my husband gone, my children and my parents dead of an illness that left only me behind. I am dead to the past. The only life for me is here. It is all that is left of who I was . . . all else is dead. You are my only refuge now."

Even I, Gotami of the Mustard Seed, spoke up: "The Buddha saved my life. I myself understood, then, his teaching. And now you are saying that there's something else and that it is here in this circle?"

Yasodhara nodded, considering our questions. "I hear you all, deeply. It is my experience too, and that of our beloved Pajapati. Each of us has our own path—and yet, because of our already having walked our lives in relation with others, caring for others, *being with* others, and learning from that *being with*—we have something else to offer."

She looked at me directly, kindly. "The healing of your heart, Gotami, was in the mutual sharing of your story with that of others, in dialogue. And I cannot forget how a young monk told you that it was all about impermanence, and how you had to bow to him, when he had just arrived at the *sangha* and understood *nothing* yet, really!" There was anger in her voice, and it took her a moment to calm. Excitedly she went on, "But see for yourself! Let us keep on, in loving connection, *on the same level.* Let us each help each other find *our* True Way."

"Yes," I answered, "let us continue." I looked from one to the other of the three nuns. "Let us listen together and then speak what we each hear in Yasodhara's story."

# 16

Rahula was now a slight and agile child of five years. His hair was a silky black with, in the light, a russet shine. He had dark eyes and a magical laugh. At times, he was withdrawn, caught up in his own thoughts and feelings—dreamy. Yasodhara was becoming more respected and honored in the palace community: a leader in the circle of women, who continued their practice of sitting together.

Since Siddhartha had left, sickness, sorrow, aging, and death had come openly to the palace. The king was more silent and would allow no mention of Siddhartha in his presence. No longer trying to protect his household from the natural sufferings of life, he became more and more intent on his grandson, Rahula. He was reconciled with Yasodhara and relied on her calming presence. He stopped speaking of her remarrying. Yasodhara and Pajapati were becoming known as healers in the palace community, comforting those who came to them in need, regardless of caste or class.

"I was often called on by those in distress," Yasodhara said, "with every kind of suffering. Over time, Pajapati and I found that our practice, growing out of our circle experience, could work with even just two people—as long as the principles were still followed: sitting on the ground, eye to eye, on the same level with the person in the grove of the ancient shade trees; touching the earth, open to the world of the animals and birds and plants and minerals, being present and attuned to each other. We offered our presence, listening deeply and *being with* the person in a mindful way that seemed to allow the creative energies of communion and Right Relation to arise. We enquired together into the nature of the suffering we each and all knew—how it arises, how it can be held in compassion and awareness, and how we could find the way through, together.

In the sitting, we offered our faith in the possibility of *being with* the suffering, helping others to meet it as well—opening the mind and the heart. I came to understand that this experience was of benefit to the other, and it drew out of me words and counsel that I did not know I had. Often, more often than I would have thought, the sufferer and I deeply touched the moment together; and then something else—something new—seemed to happen within us, around us, and between us. I came to realize that what happened grew out of the intermingling of each person's experience. Pajapati and I called this our 'sitting with' practice. This was the part of my life that I came to see had rooted and budded—if not yet flowered—in the soil of my suffering and become my greatest gift to others."

# 17

By Rahula's sixth birthday, the king determined that the boy would train to become a warrior. After witnessing Siddhartha's path, Suddhodana was clear that the boy needed to begin early to prepare to become his successor. He became more and more invested in making Siddhartha's son into what he had wished Siddhartha had become, and preventing Rahula from entering the same path of "going forth" that his own son had taken.

Yasodhara and Pajapati became quite sure that the path of the hero—of the warrior—was not in the gentle child's nature, and that the king was blinded by his own smoldering grief and the fire of his anger. He tried to send the boy away, to wrest him away from the women, not realizing that this was the same way he had tried to control Siddhartha, leading to the outcome contrary to what he desired. Yasodhara and Pajapati did their best to help him see this, pleading with him not to repeat this same course; and the king finally relented—temporarily—saying that he would wait one more year before issuing the final command.

Rahula was confused by this. When he came to Yasodhara in distress, she would listen carefully and reassure him that his father would return someday to guide him to the right path. Somehow, against all signs, she hoped and believed that he would return, though doubt and confusion still visited her heart.

She had ceased trying to stay connected with Siddhartha through the austerity practices that mimicked his: not eating after midday, sleeping on the raw earth, wearing yellow robes. Although she was comfortable in the palace, none of the former pleasures of her life, nor the austerities she had tried, provided lasting peace. She began to feel restless and ready to step again into the unknown—ready for something new to happen, for some moment of clarity and transition in her life, for *something else*. For quite some time, she had had no news of Siddhartha. He had disappeared, far away, into mountains and deserts, and perhaps even cities. Channa had not been able to find him, or even to get news of him from anyone. So she waited.

"But then one day, finally," Yasodhara said, "Channa brought news of a buddha's awakening. And the Buddha was Siddhartha." She blinked her eyes, telling us this. "Imagine my surprise! Pajapati and I were shocked, overwhelmed. For some reason, despite this profound event, when we looked at each other, we both burst out laughing! Imagine?! After all, he was her son, my husband, Rahula's father!" She laughed at the memory. We joined her—and we all laughed hard, together. The moment, recalled from so long ago now, came so alive!

Pajapati stirred at the sound but didn't awaken.

"Channa told me that it took place in Bodhgaya, near the holy city of Benares. He had sat in meditation under a Bodhi tree for thirty-nine days and was transformed into the Buddha, the Awakened One. Shortly thereafter, he gave his first dharma talk to a small gathering of holy men, where he spoke of what he called the Four

Noble Truths and the Eightfold Path, which offered any true seeker a path to the end of suffering. Since then, he had been traveling about, teaching this path. His teachings were attracting great attention. Hundreds were following him as he walked the Ganges Plain, giving *dharma* talks to large gatherings from all walks of life, including the caste of Untouchables.

"*Untouchables?* At first I was surprised. But then I understood how in tune this was with the young man I knew him to be, in tune with his true nature. In fact, yes, his Buddha nature. I was very pleased."

The news awakened deep happiness within Yasodhara, happiness for Siddhartha. She was curious and hopeful to learn more. But now, having attained his goal, would he come home? She wondered if his teaching echoed her own dawning understanding of suffering and the end of suffering. There was a sense of knowing that his journey must in some way parallel hers.

With these new thoughts, the searing loss, betrayal, anger, and hurt rose up again. Their relationship was still painful and still profoundly confusing. *Who was he now? What was their marriage now? Now that his enquiry was complete, would he return?*

And always, like the bite of a snake: *How could he ever come home again—expect to be welcomed back—after what he set in motion when he left?*

But then Yasodhara realized that, for her own enquiry, she had to go deeper into the truth of what was happening in this widening crisis between grandfather, grandson, and absent father. In the crucible of the relationships between herself, her son, and the king, and with an awareness of Siddhartha strongly in her heart and sensing that he was somehow coming closer, she began to prepare the soil for Siddhartha's return.

One day, sitting alone in the royal orchard, watching the peacocks strut and bob for insects and worms and seeds, it came to her that not only was she evolving spiritually in her practice of *being with*, but she was bringing something new to it—to struggle against her son becoming a warrior king meant that she might be embracing the spiritual life for him.

Something new was called for in her spiritual practice: the power to resist.

# 18

In this fertile time, new ideas seemed to sprout like spring shoots after the monsoon. Rahula was too young and too restless to sit in silence with Yasodhara or talk with her in a deep way. She kept searching for ways to listen to him. Once, as she watched him play with other children in the sand in the courtyard, a strange idea came to her: she would play with him in the sand, watch him play with his toys, and listen to the stories he would tell of what he was creating.

To her surprise, when she brought this same quality of deep listening to their play, the boy loved doing this with her. Suddenly, in the sand, there would be warriors and a king and a queen and a father; and monsters and dragons and eagles and gods from the Vedas; and even then, over and over, a missing father returning home wearing simple clothing, looking for his son!

First, the son would turn away in anger: "You are not my real father!" he'd cry. Then he'd fight with his father, pushing him away and saying, "I hate you!"

Finally, Yasodhara would play the father; "I have come to be with you—to make amends and to bring you the treasure!" she'd say. "And to bring you the gift of what I have learned. Now that you are ready, I am here."

Yasodhara was sad but also flushed with delight—to have found a way to watch with her son the crucial people in his life as they moved around under his hands, the boy creating stories full of adventure and honor and anger and the cutting off of heads; him flying through the air like his hero Lord Rama, The Blue-Skinned God, who ruled over the whole wide world! She had found a shared language between mother and child; and in it, she could listen and be with his suffering. It was being created between mother and son, a "Right Dialogue" for the two of them together that she could use to prepare him for Siddhartha's return.

"And then I began to bring the same practice with others to my relationship with Siddhartha."

Yasodhara explained: "Up until that time, Pajapati and I had been sitting with actual persons in the external world. But what I am telling you, dear ones, is that I now brought the relationship with him inside myself; it became internal. I imagined him sitting with me, and I entered this new practice in this way. My challenge was to see the truth of my relationship with him, both the early ecstasy and the ongoing joy, and the anger and sorrow as well. I wanted to be clear about that—in order to be ready to help my son.

"I tried to use the same circle practice internally—attuning to what was between us, to where he was with me, to where our relationship truly was, in this present moment. I had great swings of feeling—the old demons of devastation and grief, bursts of insane rage, wanting to retaliate; I even thought of bowing to the king's wish by agreeing to send off my son to become a warrior. But I also had moments of great forgiveness. I realized that Siddhartha, like any of us, had no choice but to follow his own spiritual path, wherever it might take him—to open to whatever might come. This is what I saw in *being with* him in my practice.

"A new world of possibilities arose, and I felt released, free, no longer bound by blame. And I was no longer demonizing, nor idolizing him. I found myself *holding* him, my first love, in loving-kindness. Even more than that—it was astonishing to me at first—I understood that we might still be in the enquiry together. I began to sense a profound source of connection with him and was ready to hear, directly from him, what he had come to understand, practice, and teach."

Her face was radiant, excited.

"Nuns, do you see? It was amazing—a kind of miracle—*being with* him in this way! Experiencing the relationship with him—*all* the different parts of it—coming alive in my meditation! I felt more clear and sure in challenging the king. And in my practice, I often had the vision of my son encountering his father for the first time, even hearing what I might say to my son: 'Here is your father. Claim your inheritance. Not from the king, not from the palace, but from your father.'

"I tried to ready myself for Siddhartha's return, or perhaps I should say the arrival of the Buddha, yet I could not come to peace. Nothing but seeing him again would bring that peace—if that were ever possible! I needed to *see* for myself, with these eyes and this heart, who Siddhartha had become, and hear from him, face to face."

She fell silent for a few moments. The moon had moved on, and the two candles gave different light. The night birds called, and the animals of the dark rustled like leaves in the still black.

"Now that I, for several years, have been touched by the *dharma* of the Buddha's teaching, I realize that at that time before he returned, our devotional practice became meditative, a meditational practice for us. We women, together, were establishing a way of sitting with, breathing with, listening and responding with, entering deeply into connection on a fundamental level. Letting go of old ideas and images, truly entering the new dimension of relationship, releasing ideas of separation, and being embraced in the field of compassion.

"Breaking through, piercing the heart of each to each other so that there was nothing else but compassion, becoming one with the Law of Love at the heart of the universe. Here was the wisdom and insight and practice that arose along the Path of Right Relation. We became aware that every wise relationship creates a *sangha*, and helps to turn love toward ourselves too. Love and care arising for each other and for ourselves, keeping oneself in the circle of care no more and no less than others. This was our deep relational practice."

She looked slowly at each of us, to see if we understood.

"I was not at all sure," she went on, "but I wondered . . . trying . . ."

She paused, glancing at the sleeping Pajapati, and then closed her eyes for a moment, as if to make sure she said it right.

"I realized that as I was with others, so was I *being with* myself—no difference."

She smiled, a little shyly, it seemed, and nodded to herself and to us all. And then she turned her eyes toward me. I was surprised, and trembled.

"Gotami," she said, "what I learned is what you learned as well. In searching for the mustard seed to bring your child back to life, you came to appreciate each person you met as a unique expression of the shared human experience. Through each particular connection, compassion arose in you for *all*—so deeply that it touched the ground of all beings everywhere, through all time. Your compassion flowered *forever*. Our path, our truths, our teachings and practices, all grow through these *particular* connections to each other. And now I realize that it joins the Buddha's path, the Noble Truths, and the Eightfold teachings and practices, moving toward a deep awareness of this human suffering *as a whole*, and its release."

# 19

Toward the end of that year when Rahula was six, the king had said it was almost time to send the boy away. Yasodhara had secretly sent Channa with a message for the Buddha: "For the sake of your son, you need to come."

After a month, Channa returned with news.

"I have seen . . . ," he hesitated. "Yes, with my own eyes I have seen Siddhar . . . the Buddha. I never had a chance to speak to him; I could only stand far back in a clearing, in the forest before the foothills of the Himalayas. The gathering was of many hundreds—perhaps more. I could not get near his inner circle, even to his cousin, Ananda, who, I learned, is his closest spiritual friend now. You know him well."

Yasodhara nodded, focusing on every word, every sound.

"I sent the request that he come home and made sure that it was passed to Ananda."

"Are you sure he got it?"

"Yes. I did not leave until Ananda sent back a response through a messenger—it took two days. Others are always trying to get Ananda to arrange for personal audiences with the Buddha."

"How did he reply?"

"He said he would give the Buddha the message."

"So he may come?! When?"

"All I know is that he is not walking west—toward us—directly but farther south, on the Ganges plain."

Yasodhara, unsettled by this news, asked Channa to come sit in the circle and tell them about the Buddha.

Channa came and sat with all the women. Pajapati and Rahula were also there.

With awe in his voice, Channa said that the Buddha was traveling from one refuge to another, often to the estates and houses of rich followers, teaching the *dharma*. Siddhartha now spoke with the presence of an Enlightened One, and his words flowed out in deep, coherent wisdom. Certain monks were assigned to memorize each talk exactly—three monks for every talk—to make sure each word was remembered and to pass it on. The gatherings were growing in number. Many had left their homes to become members of the *sangha* traveling with him. The gatherings were growing to *enormous* size—over five hundred—and all castes were welcome, even the Untouchables.

"Women too?" Yasodhara asked.

"No. I mean, I saw no women."

"Does he sit on the ground, speaking as one in a circle?"

"No," Channa said, "he speaks to the others from a platform, raised up above. They are sitting on the ground, in many semicircles, listening deeply. If he were on the ground, he would be invisible to almost all of them. The crowd, despite its size, is orderly and silent—so that the sounds of the breeze and the birds and the insects are loud. He is . . . he is *lofty*, yes. I, too, felt uplifted and changed in his presence. It was hard to leave, to come home."

"He has succeeded in his quest!" said Pajapati, rejoicing. "He has become The Enlightened One! We must now put aside the past and

prepare a royal welcome! Rahula, your father is now the Buddha! He will be coming home to us!"

Pajapati looked at Yasodhara.

Yasodhara said nothing.

Pajapati was startled but waited for her to speak.

The silence grew and the space began to vibrate with unease, as if a wall began to arise between Yasodhara and Pajapati, whose profound relationship had held the circle intact, without encumbrance, for so long.

Rahula hid his face, thrown into confusion.

Yasodhara watched him, then she put her arm around the boy.

"We all have to think of Rahula now."

When the circle had ended, Pajapati came to Yasodhara, who remained silent.

That night, Yasodhara spoke to Rahula, who, quiet and overwhelmed, said little. She then spoke to Channa. They sat opposite one another on cushions in her private antechamber. Eye to eye, she continued their dialogue far into the night.

"How does he look?"

"Beautiful. So beautiful. Glowing."

"Does he eat and drink only what he is offered, begging as other monks do?"

"Yes. He carried a simple wooden begging bowl, the same as all of them."

"Who are they? Who is with him?"

"A small inner circle of four monks, who have been there from the first talk at Sarnath, and then several hundred who have come to learn and take their vows, and then, perhaps, thousands—of all ages and castes, short and tall, crippled and whole—the faces graced with serenity, joy, and peace—and I must say, not just admiration, but awe. All of that is immediately evident."

"Did *you* feel all that?"

"Yes. I was tempted to stay—to join in fully."

"Why didn't you?"

"My vow, now, is to you. And I believe in our wisdom teachings, our circle."

She smiled and touched his hand in gratitude. But as she started to ask the next question, a sob broke through and she had to stop. Channa waited. She composed herself and went on, "I know, from what you said and the look in your eyes, that he has changed."

Channa nodded.

"But is there anything left of our Siddhartha?"

Channa, confused by the depth of the question and how crucial it was to her, held her gaze for a few moments. Then, with his hand, he moved his withered leg to a more comfortable position.

"For me, the echoes in his voice, yes. Perhaps, in his passion and heart, and in his confidence in what he is saying, yes. It's a radical new way, very different from what we were all taught about the *Devas*." He let this, an invocation of their Gods, settle. "He has been transformed. I'm not sure how much, or what of Siddhartha, is truly left."

"Will he be on this path now for his whole life?"

"I believe so."

"Never mind me, but Rahula? His son?!"

Channa had no answer to this.

An owl called. A nightingale, irritated, responded.

"You have not asked me about his teachings."

"No."

"Shall I show you?"

"Please."

He explained the basic teaching of the *Anapanasati Sutra*, sitting in silence with eyes closed, following the movement of the breath and noticing where it is felt—the length, the warmth, the rhythm, the irregularity. Just letting it be exactly as it is.

"When your attention drifts away from the breath, note what it clings to in your mind, and then bring it gently back to the breath. This is the mindfulness of breathing. Remembering and cultivating this, noticing the turmoil of the mind, which goes on and on incessantly, until the turmoil becomes so familiar that it drops away, leaving some peace. I found—once or twice—that I had a new awareness of the burden of the suffering in the mind—and of its release."

"Let us try this together," Yasodhara said.

They sat this way for a long time, and she found her mind grasping and snatching at different things—thoughts, feelings, memories, and expectations. She wished, in a way that they could just sit with their eyes open and speak from the posture of silence—a shared meditation—as she was used to.

After this, they talked, and she realized that Channa had changed too. No longer was he merely the humble servant of a prince, he seemed earnest, ardent about what he had experienced. He had an aura of new learning, purpose, even a touch of wisdom. Sensing all this, she was excited, and deeply moved. And he was not only a resource for what Siddhartha—the Buddha—was teaching, but seemed suddenly an equal partner with her. She saw that this was the culmination of what they had endured together, all these years.

"You have become a *kalyana mitra*, a spiritual friend," she said.

He seemed somewhat surprised but knew this to be true. He bowed his head for a moment, moved by her words, and then spoke. "The Buddha said, several times while I was there: 'There is no greater thing than a spiritual friend. This is the whole of the holy life.'"

Tears came to her eyes. The first part of what he had said—"There is no greater thing than a spiritual friend"—was what Siddhartha and she had always said to each other as lovers, and as husband and wife. What did this mean, his use of these words in this new way—"the holy life?" Was he returning or never returning? Was the marriage over? Fatherhood erased? She closed her eyes and breathed mindfully a few times, and the confusion and sadness eased a bit.

She told Channa about the spiritual friendship that had blossomed among the women—how the devotional practice had become a meditation itself, and how it had established and strengthened the community of women in the palace. Connecting and honoring the circle had become the central practice of their daily life. She invited him to join them.

"I want to," he said, "but fear the king's displeasure. I would be breaking an unspoken law that men and women should not sit together in this way. And if he found out that I have been on journeys to observe Siddhartha and have seen him as the Awakened One? I and my family would be thrown out of the palace." He grinned, "I'd be selling beans on the streets."

"I understand."

"And," he went on, "even the Buddha forbids this."

"This?"

"A man and a woman sitting together in meditation—not to mention in a circle, facing each other in dialogue."

"And you told me that there are no women in the *sangha*?"

"There is a small group following along, on the outskirts, but they are not allowed at the talks or included in the *sangha*."

"Yes to Untouchables, no to women! Then how can he claim to be fully enlightened—the Enlightened One?!"

Channa nodded, and shook his head to show his agreement with her surprise and her disappointment.

Their eyes met and held.

He sensed her fear of what this would portend for the future of her relationship with Siddhartha.

# 20

Pajapati and Yasodhara went to Suddhodana. Pajapati told him that, indeed, Siddhartha had become the Buddha, the Jewel, the Awakened One—perhaps the most honored holy man in the world. She hoped for his return in a few months and was ready to give him a royal welcome, although Yasodhara was still hesitant about this.

The king erupted in rage, angry and scornful.

"I have heard this also, but it does not touch me. The damage Siddhartha has done, the renunciation of his birthright, his name, is unforgiveable. I'm not convinced of the truth or depth of what he has discovered and is teaching. Every enlightened being I have ever met was fraudulent. Knowing my son, I see no reason why he should be different." His bitterness filled the air. "Siddhartha the Buddha? If he is, he has nothing to do with this real world—not with me, or us, here. To me, my son is dead. He has no right to come back here uninvited."

Pajapati knew that the king did not allow any disagreement or disobedience, but she would no longer hold back. There was no other way to resist. She began to express her long-unspoken anger at him, with as much care as possible, saying that he had never let go of the expectation that he could have his way with Siddhartha nor acknowledged his wounded pride at his son's leaving. His efforts to erase the memory of Siddhartha and to influence Rahula in a different direction had made it worse for the whole community.

Yasodhara, silent throughout, left the chamber. Pajapati was speaking for the whole community, and she appreciated that. But she was the queen, and could try. Yasodhara knew this resistance was dangerous for all of them—for Rahula and even for Pajapati herself.

That night, from the royal chambers, angry voices were heard between the king and queen, startling to all. This lasted for a long time.

The king had the final word, and unleashed his rage: "He tore us all apart when he left, and now he's tearing us apart by coming back!"

In the morning, he issued an edict: "Siddhartha is dead. He will not be welcome here."

Pajapati came to Yasodhara, who listened deeply to what she was saying but refused to give a verbal response. The queen spoke with passion and joy about Siddhartha returning home. Then Pajapati asked why she was silent.

Yasodhara said, only, "Rahula needs him. We need to get Suddhodana to allow Siddhartha to come. You and I need to hold together. All of us need to, and to be open to Siddhartha, for Rahula's sake. And if he travels back here and chooses to talk with me when he arrives, I will do so. But I will not initiate the meeting or the conversation. I'm asking you to help me with this."

At this, Pajapati grew angry with Yasodhara, and walked away from her. Yasodhara understood that Pajapati was unprepared for the reality of Siddhartha's return—or his nonreturn. She knew that as the Buddha, he had no particular "home."

The conflict continued between the king and the queen. Yasodhara refused to enter in words, though she watched it all carefully. She felt sad that she could not help Pajapati with the king. For these weeks, the palace was in turmoil, sometimes cloaked in sullen and accusing silence, sometimes unraveling in anger. The smallest event could bring a great outburst from Suddhodana or Pajapati. The wall growing between them forced both of them to speak unskillfully, creating great suffering. Yasodhara watched the suffering spread, so that soon, others were taking sides, divided in harmful gossip and ill will. The women, especially, split into different and contentious groups; it was as if the palace were caught up in an internal war. Only Yasodhara and a few other women came to the circle now. Their shared life of enquiry and harmony was being tested to the core. Yasodhara asked Pajapati to attend, saying that the only way to get through this would be to allow everyone to speak in the circle—to accept and receive the differences, and to allow the space to hold them all together, now more than ever!

Pajapati said that while she wished she could do this, she could not. There was now too much unrestrained anger in her and in so many of the others.

The break between the king and queen became even more painful and divisive. The harmony within the palace community was gone. The king issued an edict that he would send Rahula away to become a warrior before Siddhartha arrived: "I won't allow him to be influenced by his miserable father. I will send him away as soon as I can arrange it."

Finally, Yasodhara went to the king and said she wanted to listen to his grief.

"Grief? I told you, my son is dead to me."

Yasodhara heard this deeply and sat with her eyes closed, mindfully breathing for a long time. With tears in her eyes, but her voice strong, she said, "And yet you have never wept over him."

The king fell silent. Still angry, he said, "Leave now! And say good-bye to your son. He will be gone tomorrow!"

"Tomorrow I will stop speaking and eating and drinking, and you will have my death on your hands."

The king sent her away. That night was torment for him. Pajapati was sleeping by herself and refusing to talk to him; and Yasodhara's words had pierced him. There was no relief. In the morning, he was told that all the other women, including Pajapati, had decided to join Yasodhara's fast, withdrawal, and silence. The servant delivered the message to him: "They will stop speaking, eating, and drinking. And you will have their deaths on your hands."

Another lonely night passed. At dawn, he called Yasodhara to him.

"I cannot bear this. What is to be done?"

"Come and sit with us in our circle."

"A king joining the women? Sitting with servants?"

"Women who care for you and respect you, and will listen deeply to anything you say, for as long as you want."

"How can that help?"

"It has helped me and Pajapati, and your grandson, and many others."

She rose to leave."I cannot talk with you about this again, unless it's in the circle. And we won't eat or drink from this moment forth unless you allow your son to return, and let my son meet his father. Suffering *alone, in isolation*, spreads more suffering around; suffering with others—with caring others who have been through their own suffering and will listen—offers peace. *Being with* suffering brings peace to all."

She stood there until he met her gaze.

"Please, I beg you: join us. At least respect the suffering spreading like ripples around you."

# 21

The first day after the king threatened to send Rahula away passed with the boy still there.

The women resumed taking water and juices.

The second day, Rahula announced in the circle that the king had called for him and asked if he wanted to become a warrior or stay to meet his father.

"Grandpa, I'll do my duty to you."

The women listened but said nothing.

And the next day, Rahula was still there.

They began to eat again.

Finally, after a week, the king asked Yasodhara to meet with him alone in the circle grove. They sat quietly. Staring at the empty cushions, the king felt even more alone. And then he began to feel strangely in touch with the absent ones. Sitting next to Yasodhara, remembering how devastated by anger and grief she had been, and how those around—in what she and Pajapati had called a "sacred" circle—had saved her, touched his grief and his own deep sorrow. In his aloneness, he felt a depth of shared communion here.

To his surprise, it was as if the silence had a life of itself, and within it, there was room for a shared sorrow with her—she whom he had always loved as his precious son's wife and then his grandson's mother. He was startled, when he spoke, at how close to tears he was.

"I . . . ," the king stopped. He choked on the words—so unlike him.

"I will not impose my will on my grandson. He must find his own way. I release him from his duty."

The king paused, struggled to gain control, and, failing, finally he lashed out, saying, "But I can never forgive my son!"

Yasodhara called the others into the circle with him, and called Channa too. Pajapati still refused.

As the women sat down on the cushions and the circle resumed, Yasodhara wondered whether the king would leave. He sat there until the circle was filled, but for one empty seat. This was the seat that they had been leaving for Pajapati. When the king realized that the empty seat was hers, he left.

Yasodhara told the women what he had said. Silence. The shifting and the flow of feeling were palpable. The women began to speak, showing their respect for the king's words.

Pajapati emerged out of the woods, silently entered the circle, and took her seat. Yasodhara bowed, but no one knew how to begin to heal the break in the circle. Searching for a path, Yasodhara suggested that they create a ritual of restoration, of facing the conflict and suffering in a new way.

First she asked everyone, including Pajapati, to meditate and hold the intention to heal. Then she offered to have two of the women—the elders—sit close to them, one next to Yasodhara and the other next to Pajapati, and speak their understanding and perspective of this rupture between them.

When both Yasodhara and Pajapati felt heard and understood, each of the other women around the circle spoke their wish to find a way to reconcile, offering suggestions and speaking to the necessity of healing in the circle. The broken threads of the circle were carefully and wisely rewoven, giving birth to surprising new patterns.

Finally, Yasodhara and Pajapati spoke to each other, offering understanding and apology, and forgiveness, not only of each other but of themselves.

There emerged, then, a long and magnificent silence. One seat, where the king had sat, was still empty.

All of them could not help but think of Siddhartha.

This was to become the practice: to leave an empty seat open, to leave room for other voices not yet spoken or heard.

Now that the threat to the circle had been honestly met, the fracture of the community mended, and the circle felt rich and joyful again, somehow containing an even stronger commitment to peace—healing stronger for the break. The whole palace community felt the power of the peace of reconciliation. Built out of encompassing and acceptance, it was a remarkable shift: from the fierce division of difference and disconnection, to finding the way to move through the differences to create new connection.

"One night, perhaps a week later," Yasodhara went on to us novices in the Squirrel Sanctuary, "I found myself wondering whether the peace and happiness we touched in the circle that day was what Siddhartha was describing as he walked the land: the deep peace and cessation of suffering of the Third Noble Truth." Her eyes brightened with excitement.

"And . . . and listen to this!" She shook her head in amazement at what she was about to tell us. "It was no more than a few days later that marvelous news came from Channa—the Buddha and his multitude of *sangha* were coming close—coming to us—and could arrive within a few weeks. It was as if, somehow, when our peace-making was completed, he would come."

# 22

However, it took more time than that, for wherever the Buddha went, others would ask him to come to their nearby town or village, and he was generous with his acceptances.

Finally, a few months later, the Buddha sent word to his father, the king, that he wished to come to the palace to meet with him.

King Suddhodana granted his wish in a formal message, saying that he would meet him in the receiving room of the grand hall of the palace. Pajapati asked that it be less formal, that they meet in the family rooms where he had grown up.

"He is the 'Enlightened One' now," Suddhodana replied, with some sarcasm. "And so we will welcome him as befits his *status*—with you and I sitting together on our royal thrones." Pajapati tried to reply, but he would not listen to her.

The king and queen, in royal robes, sat on their high-backed, gilded chairs at one end of the long receiving chamber.

The Buddha entered, far down the vast chamber, followed by four monks. The bright sunlight of the afternoon was at their backs, so the king and queen saw only the five shapes in shadow, each barefoot, clothed in a saffron robe, and carrying a wooden begging bowl.

Suddhodana again felt a surge of shame, seeing his son, the prince, reduced to a life of poverty and begging. The resentment of Siddhartha's renunciation rose inside him once again. Each step closer was like a jolt to the king, who sat upright as if to brace himself against any recognition. But as they drew closer, something else began to happen. Even before he could see Siddhartha's face, he saw, through the harsh light behind, his walk. It was different from any he had ever seen in his child—in anyone else, really—in that it was . . . what? The word that came was "gentle." It was deliberate, yet there was a lightness to it; calm yet purposeful, without the nervous thudding step of the many supplicants who wanted something from their king.

Just *walking*. Strange.

And then the Buddha stood, below him.

Suddhodana found himself greeting him begrudgingly.

The Buddha looked into his eyes for a moment.

Holding his gaze, Suddhodana again sensed something else—but what?

The Buddha, with a slight smile, clasped his palms together and bowed to his father. Then, looking into his mother's eyes, he bowed to her. He then again turned his gaze on his father.

Sensing the depth of the Buddha's respect and caring, Suddhodana searched with his eyes for the young man he had loved more than his own life—and could not find him. He was confused, even shocked at the change in Siddhartha, the blood of his blood. Speechless, he stood in awe. It seemed to him that it was not his son standing there before him—not really anyone's son—but a *presence*. He looked radiant, happy, healthy, and *beautiful*. Full of life.

As if his son had understood all that Suddhodana had felt and thought in that brief connection, he smiled and nodded, saying as clearly as if he had spoken it: *All is understood—all suffering, all release. I am here for you. Join me.* And then Siddhartha turned toward all those who had come, and smiled and bowed to each, with as much respect and honor and caring as he had shown the king, his father, and the queen, his mother.

The grand hall fell still. The silence was so strong, as if it were a great hand, caressing.

Siddhartha spoke a few words of gratitude for *being with* them again.

King Suddhodana sent for Yasodhara and Rahula to come to greet the Buddha.

Yasodhara sent a message back that she would not come. If Siddhartha wished, he could come to her. She asked Channa to stay with Rahula in his chamber and waited, alone.

The king now felt deeply moved, as he saw that his son had indeed become the Awakened One—a "king" in his own realm. He was unsure of how to address Siddhartha but invited him to come sit with him and his mother at the royal table, to partake in a celebration of his return.

The Buddha said, "We have eaten today."

The king glanced at the begging bowl in his hand and said, "Our clan, the Sakyans, do not beg."

"I am now one of those who beg."

At that, the king understood that he was no longer one of them; he would not be returning to stay. He had a flash of sorrow and fell silent, his head down.

All fell silent.

"You do not need to suffer about this, Father," said the Buddha. Suddhodana lifted his head to look into his enlightened son's eyes. "I am here with you now. And with my dear mother." He turned to her.

For a long time their eyes held, as if time had stopped.

Pajapati felt a rush of yearning to touch him, take his hands, and take him in her arms as she had when he was a baby, a boy, and a young man. She took a step toward him to do so—she thought she saw a flicker of yearning from him, even sorrow—but suddenly she stopped still, an instant away. The astonishing thing to her, she realized only later, was that she was stopped not by his distance but by his closeness, not by his reserve or stature but by his kindness. His *kindness. Kindness itself!*

The Buddha noticed all of this, how old she seemed in body, but not in spirit or in love for whom he had been. He sensed her question of whether he now could be loved in the same way and her realizing not. He felt her settle into *being with* him now. He saw something fresh in this woman, his aunt and true mother: a new awareness in her way of *being with* him—in her acceptance, her peacefulness, and her dignity. He smiled and bowed to her and the mother in her; and then he bowed to the king, and the father in him.

"We are sorry that Yasodhara has not come to meet you," the king apologized. "She has refused, and has asked us to tell you that she is keeping Rahula away until she herself meets with you first."

The Buddha took this in and said, "Then I will go to her."

As he walked away with the monks, he said to them: "If she touches me, though it is forbidden in our *sangha* for a woman to touch a monk, let her. Respect her grief and great suffering from my abandonment of her and our son."

As Yasodhara saw Siddhartha walking toward her, she was overwhelmed with feeling and fell to the ground, sobbing.

The Buddha felt the depth of her suffering. Flashes of feeling her own and then the compassion for all suffering. He waited.

Finally, Yasodhara stood up and looked directly at him, searching to find who he was, there before her now. Images of the past, of all the years with Siddhartha—the restless, tormented, sensual lover and husband—clashed with the now, this calm, open-eyed, and fully Awakened One—the Buddha.

*Then.*

*Now.*

*Siddhartha.*

*Buddha.*

Images flashed back and forth before her eyes like light and shadow through leaves in a sunlit forest, restless in a wind.

The monks were astounded as the Buddha stood there meeting her gaze, both of them in silence for what seemed a fracture in time—an endless and timeless moment.

As the monks watched, to their amazement, a single tear flowed slowly down the Buddha's cheek.

Yasodhara was unsure what it meant; the tear was her only glimpse into his sorrow. He showed nothing more but stood calmly as the tear dried, leaving the slightest trace. His eyes had never wavered, a constant serenity and compassion in them. All at once, she understood that he was no longer to be her husband, Siddhartha, and she saw that he understood that moment in her. She was profoundly touched by his *immensity*, his abiding presence. She felt like a strong wind entered her body and lifted her up. Compassion. Ardent. Fiercely *human*.

She had a sense of him seeing deeply into her *own* transformation. As if he, too, in that wordless moment, was seeing both the old and the new at once, and understood that she was no longer the young woman he had loved and left behind. She felt he was seeing into the depth of her struggle and the light of her spiritual attainment. And she saw so clearly that they were sharing a moment suddenly lightened with awareness itself, in and from them both. A moment of profound meeting and *mutual* recognition. It was recognizable to her, resonating with the moments of mutual understanding she had shared with the women in the circle: *I seeing him; he seeing me; each of us seeing the other being seen. Infinitely resonating between us, time before and beyond time.*

In that instant she felt liberation from the past, breaking free and willing to let go. *At last!*

And then, in the most subtle movement of his eyes away from hers, the past stormed back in, and she saw, again, the boy she had fallen in love with, and the young man who had been her gentle, passionate lover and the father of their child.

Thinking of Rahula, she flushed at her son's loss and her own desperation and lonely rage at the abandonment, the betrayal. She glanced down again, afraid. When she looked back up at him, she seemed to see in his face and eyes a slight shiver of feeling her pain.

And then it was gone.

It was time for Rahula to meet his father.

# 23

Yasodhara called for Rahula. The boy, now seven years old, came with Channa but was shy, and hid behind his mother. She said to him, with quiet power and equanimity:

"Your father is here."

The boy kept his eyes cast down.

Eventually, his mother's loving encouragement and the Buddha's gentleness and grace helped Rahula to approach his father.

"Receive him as your father," she said to Rahula. "Claim your inheritance."

"What does that mean, Mother?"

She explained it to him.

As she spoke, the Buddha was moved, understanding that she had protected and nurtured his son to be ready to receive his father—to neither hate him nor reject him. The Buddha held out his begging bowl and smiled.

Rahula hesitantly smiled back and wondered what to do.

The Buddha offered him the bowl.

He took it, shyly.

The Buddha smiled again and nodded, then turned to leave.

Yasodhara could not believe that he was leaving again—not so much leaving her as leaving Rahula—without acknowledging what he had done or what had happened to her and their son.

"I must have another meeting with you," she said. He turned back to her. "It will be best if we are alone. Tomorrow. In our Pine Grove."

He nodded; and then, for the first time, he spoke. "Yes, I will meet with you alone there tomorrow, at dusk."

He and the monks walked away.

Yasodhara's heart rose up into her throat, and a flush went through her whole body.

*It is the same voice as my beloved Siddhartha! In the midst of all that has changed and is new, his voice still is as it was.*

Her love for him ignited and filled the world, the solid ground under her.

She felt her child's hand in hers, squeezing. Rahula was looking up at her in puzzlement, the wooden bowl in his other hand.

Solid ground once again.

# 24

Siddhartha did come alone.

Yasodhara had regained her strength and clarity since the previous day, and invited him to sit with her in the Pine Grove that had been their special place, always. They walked to where the cushions were arranged in a circle. He took a seat a few cushions away from her.

They sat together alone, in silence, each of them feeling the new power of the place that had been sanctified with their love, their youth and marriage, and the birth of Rahula. Her eyes were upon him; his eyes closed in meditation.

When he finally opened his eyes, she said, "I have heard from Channa about your teachings. With Channa's instructions, we have tried to practice them here."

"I am happy about that," he said, smiling.

This voice had only a hint of her Siddhartha.

There was a long pause as they looked at each other. She yearned to break the barrier between this Buddha and her own Siddhartha but somehow dared not. There was a majesty about him now—not a kingly majesty, but a holy one. At last she spoke, choosing her words as if they were fragile and needed to be placed in the air carefully, lest they break the familiar sacred power of the silence.

"After you left, . . . Siddhartha . . ."

She stopped, wondering if he would have a reaction to using his name.

He smiled a broad expansive smile, and nodded for her go on.

"My desperation, my desperate suffering, brought out from Pajapati and all the women an astonishing compassion, what Channa says you have taught as the force of 'loving-kindness.' It saved my life and the life of my . . . of our child. It began a shared journey we have walked together for these seven years since. We have called it the Path of Right Relation. Can I tell you about it?"

His eyes brightened at this, and he said, "Yes, tell me what you have found."

And so she told him about it, the sacred practice of the circle, and of their journey in relation, including the king, Channa, and the other servants, both women and men. She made amends, asked for forgiveness for her suspicion and doubt of him after he left, and for how her suffering had ignited that of all of those who loved him in the palace community.

He listened and said, "I, too, am making amends now—to you and through you, to the others. Dear one, I am profoundly sorry."

She was astonished at his words. Fresh tears came to her eyes—tears of relief and gratitude.

They seemed to see deeply together, the *suchness*, the way that life had moved them both to this exquisite moment . . . just this.

"You, the Buddha! I . . . I . . ." Words failed her, and she blushed. He smiled, in a way that seemed to carry their love timelessly, a blanket. "And you are," she went on, "despite my best 'Right Intention,' you are the person who will always be my beloved . . ."

He laughed gently and nodded.

"You have described the truths that will end suffering. The path is the one you yourself took alone, leaving the worldly things behind—the Path of He Who Goes Forth. Sitting in meditation until the end of suffering became clear, and then offering this to all beings—it is a blessing to all!"

She paused, suddenly nervous about asking this great man to hear what she had come to feel as a sacred learning for her and of all the women enquirers.

"And," she said, "it is not just the women who have followed the Path of Right Relation. I have sat here in the circle with Channa, your mother and father, and Rahula—all of us on the same level. And they have all benefitted from the circle. None of them had to leave their lives here to become more awakened and alive. Channa and I have shared what we call a spiritual friendship—and you know how rare that is between a woman and a man. You and I had the beginning of it, I think, in our love, when we declared ourselves spiritual friends."

She worried that she had offended him, but there was no sign of that.

"My question to you, dear one, is this. Is there another path, the Path of She Who Stays, the Path of Right Relation? Is it necessary to go forth alone and leave all you love behind in order to be holy and whole?"

His face showed a shimmer like the mirror of a pond, disturbed not by a stone thrown in or a wind, but by a surface breeze.

"Or is it also possible to live in the world," she went on, "to live deeply and truly in the everyday suffering of the world, to stay with others and to walk through that *together* into awakening? The path that we women have walked, perhaps always, but which has not yet been illuminated as a holy path? Can there not be a . . . a practical path, walked hand in hand with ordinary, *particular* others—one by one, family by family, community by community *with* others—to the end of suffering?" She took a deep breath in and let it out slowly. "This path . . . perhaps this 'hidden' path—hidden from the eyes of the great world? Is this not a true sacred path and holy life, as much as the monastic?"

He sat absolutely still. She waited. Finally, he spoke.

"Your journey, Yasodhara, is deep and strong. You and the others have discovered this for yourselves, as I have for myself and all beings. I offer you my teachings. I have taught the Three Jewels, the Three Refuges of this path: the Buddha, the *dharma*, and the *sangha*. And you have begun with the *sangha*—with the wisdom and compassion arising within community. It is one path with many doorways. And I also teach . . ." he paused, then said, "that Spiritual friendship is the whole of the holy life."

She realized that he was reminding her of what she had always been to him and would always be—that "spiritual friend." Both smiled.

She went on, "Dear One, what might be of benefit, what teaching and practices offered, had two—or more—sat together under the Bodhi tree? Can these paths be woven together?"

He was silent for a long moment.

She sensed the depth of his considering this. And then she spoke to him from the most tender place in her heart, "Can we go forth *together* now?"

It was a moment as charged as that between life and death.

Finally, he said, "We will see what will be seen. This is only to be understood in the unfolding. Yasodhara, She Who Stays, follow your teaching and live your understanding, with all your heart."

They looked into each other's eyes. Then he closed his, in meditation. She looked at him sitting there at peace, took this dear being in with all her heart. And then she closed her eyes too.

Now, telling us the story at Pajapati's deathbed, Yasodhara paused, at peace. Tears pooled in her eyes, eased down her cheeks.

"He and I sat together in that empty circle for a long time in the stillness," she went on. "The silence was filled with all things. A depth of care and gratitude, an awareness of shared grief, of immense loss . . . of the *suchness* of this worldly life." She glanced at Pajapati.

"When I opened my eyes again, he was gone."

She paused, nodding.

"Again, there was no good-bye. In his presence in the circle, I had entered a timeless state—it might have been minutes or hours. I heard Rahula call me, and I called out 'I'm here!' As I waited for him to come to me, I felt this incredible mixture of joy and sorrow."

She sat before us, radiant, then her face dropped in sadness. She said, softly, "I knew that would be the last time I would ever see him or speak with him alone. I felt happiness, but tears came too."

Tears were in her eyes as she spoke to us again.

"And then, sisters, I heard the voice: 'Mamma?'

"My treasured son was standing at the edge of the circle, trying to find me, the begging bowl still grasped in his hand.

"He saw my tears, and he ran across the circle to me as fast as he could. And I lifted him up into my arms."

# 25

Early the next morning, Channa reported that the Buddha and his four monks had left during the night to join the larger *sangha*, which had been encamped in a vast mango grove owned by a wealthy landowner who had embraced the *dharma*. It was a week's journey at least, and the *sangha* would probably continue to move north toward the mountains of the Himalayas.

All those in the palace who had seen him had been awed. The royal family was astonished at the transformation—and sad too.

Rahula was especially excited that the Buddha was his father and began to talk about wanting to follow him, live in the *sangha* of monks with him, learning the *dharma*. He was told that there were no boys his age—even near his age—in the *sangha*, and that he would have plenty of time to decide.

Soon thereafter, war broke out in a neighboring state. Two women, a mother and a grandmother of a family of bakers, arrived at the palace distraught, telling of a desperate situation in their community. All the healthy men and older boys, including the leaders of the village, were gone to war. There were shortages of food, water, and medicines. Two of the children had died, and one was deathly ill. It seemed that some terrible disease was spreading in the community. Could they help?

Yasodhara had shared the story of her meeting with the Buddha with the other women of the palace, and her new vitality had energized them all. She seemed to have grown, not only in the sureness of her speech and action but in her physical presence. A strong, kind leader. She and the others became more and more aware of the suffering outside the palace—drought, disease, violence, chaos, death—and they were moved to take action. Yasodhara and Pajapati went to the king and asked if he could do something. He said he would at least provide some medicines.

Then they dared to ask for something new, something they had never done before. They told him that they felt called to go out of the palace and stay together in the village. They asked for his blessing to go forth, to see what could be done to help these women and their families, and the larger community. The king had truly changed in his respect for them and granted their wish. Some of the royal women thought it beneath them to do this and stayed back, but all of them supported the mission.

The women went out from the palace to the countryside village, bringing herbs and medicines and food. The situation was much worse than they expected. There were shortages of food and clean water, which bred rats and insects. A terrible illness had spread to the babies and small children. This led to panic. Conflict and chaos were turning families against each other in the competition for scarce supplies. The community was splintering apart along family, caste, and class lines, creating fierce enmity, hoarding, and violence. The community fabric was torn and unraveling.

In the jasmine-scented night in the Bamboo Grove, Yasodhara went on: "There was a war between the women, which, sadly, reflected that of the men far away. We asked the women of the village to come together to create a listening circle; we called it 'a peace circle.' Here, conflicts could be spoken and held in the circle, then sifted like flour through the inner workings of the circle so that something new could emerge, unseen as yet for the good of their larger community. At first, the women were skeptical, but they were desperate enough to try.

"Over many days, there were great difficulties and setbacks, but we held the vision that their differences could lead to reconciliation and healing in the circle. Keeping the faith in our practices and a vision of creating harmony, we gradually helped small groups sit together in huts and courtyards. It started one by one, small circle by small circle; and after a time, these circles rippled out to others until there was finally one large circle including almost all, coming together in the shade of bare mango trees in the village square. Order began to prevail; the women began to be kind again to each other. The glimmer of Right Relation and ripe moments on the path began to appear to many, and then most members of the community.

"It was remarkable to see our vision work!" Yasodhara smiled broadly. "Decisions were made about setting up leadership councils, allocating resources, treating the ill ones. Things settled. Order came. The power of giving voice to all in the circle in a time of harsh conflict and critical emergency surprised even us.

"Eventually, a new peace and wellness prevailed. We had indeed built a peace circle within which conflicts could be resolved for the good of the larger community. Over time, the fabric was rebuilt, and people started to work together again. The able men were still gone, off to war. This was, strangely, a blessing—a rare chance to see the power of the women's circle expanding beyond our own power. It was an opportunity for the women to explore this new way of making peace and solving problems. In this, our circle was challenged. We also had to work on the conflicts around what we were doing and find new ways together, sometimes blindly. Pajapati and I realized that enlarging the circle and growing new ones could benefit others, while guiding and strengthening our own path as well.

"And so we were given a vision of peace," Yasodhara went on, speaking slowly; remembering the gift of peace now so palpable in the room as we gathered around Pajapati. "Now we can see that our path began with our own *sangha*, our circle, which held and illuminated us all, and was something greater than all of us. And please do see! We learned that we can create and hold ever-widening circles, rippling out. What power there could be in that!"

Her excitement lit up the small chamber.

"After great conflict in community, there can be great release, liberation from suffering. Is this not the same liberation the Buddha teaches?"

The question lay in the humid, deep night air.

"Our circle began in severance and grief, then opened into deeper levels of *sangha* and became, as I have described to you tonight, the Path of Right Relation. We began to see that expanding the circle in this way was our doorway to *dharma*, the Truth, and to the great peace, and the moments . . ." She paused, seeking the right words, ". . . the moments of truth are not *already there* in you or me, but are *arising* in the moments of our *connecting*, and in our *being with*, in true community. These moments arise as a living field—energies of pure being—vibrating, alive, and connected. Not simply within us but between us, among us, holding us." She blinked several times, as if focusing on something.

"We could call these *ripe moments* of awakening on our path."

She looked around and saw that we understood.

"It's so difficult for truth to be seen fully by any one of us. To see the flashes and depth of the extraordinary truth the Buddha saw so clearly, we must learn to see with *sangha* eyes; listen with *sangha* ears; breathe, laugh, and weep with *sangha* lungs; love with *sangha* heart. . . ."

With a glow in her eyes, she went on: "Now, we must continue to cultivate the practices, and walk the path of awareness and awakening in our *sangha*. This, my sisters, is what we must never forget. Relation and *sangha* first. All else follows. Like the cart follows the horse."

# 26

After many months, news arrived that the Buddha was walking back south and would pass nearby the palace.

"I'm proclaiming my son to be a buddha," King Suddhodana announced, hearing this news. "I will give him my majestic forest of teak for his *sangha*—he can stay here forever if he wants. I myself will attend *dharma* talks and encourage all men to join him. I've decided to become a follower. In my judgment, my son is an enlightened spiritual teacher—the best that anyone has ever seen. I will receive his teachings, but I will not be giving up my throne. My goal is not only to become enlightened but to bring this enlightenment to my kingdom."

This proclamation was made in the king's usual royal manner, calling all the members of the palace and the people of his city to hear it.

To Yasodhara, this seemed a strange path. The Buddha suggested that wholehearted effort was necessary on the path to awakening and that the greatest step to end suffering was to let go of attachments, such as this vast kingdom. But at least there would be no more conflict in the palace about Siddhartha being dead to the king.

No more suffering about that. Clearly the king basked in the fame of his son. The king was still very much a king.

Pajapati said to Yasodhara, "There is much suffering as king and much suffering created by a king. This proclamation can't hurt—and might help."

But then Yasodhara's worst fear came true.

"Mother," said Rahula, with strength in his voice, "now that the Buddha is coming back again, I have decided to become a monk, joining my father's *sangha*—the *sangha* of the Buddha. I will join when he gets here. He will take me with him."

Yasodhara could not conceal her shock. "You're so young! There are no boys."

"I shall be the first boy!" Imitating the tone of the Buddha, he said, "It is my path too. And I even have my special bowl—*his* bowl!"

"And I'm your mother, and I say no—not yet, not now. Seven is too young. Maybe when you are older."

"It has to be right now because he will be leaving soon, and I want to walk with him, learn from him—learn *everything* from him."

"I will not allow it. And I doubt that Siddhartha will allow it."

"I already asked the Buddha—with my bowl in my hand. I asked. He said yes."

"Are you lying to me?" She looked at him sternly.

Rahula stared at her.

"You need to stay until you are of age. And when he comes back again, if you still want to, you can join him."

The boy turned and walked away.

And did not give up. Sullen and withdrawn, he ate little and went out less.

Suddhodana and Pajapati began to relent. Both spoke to Yasodhara about this question, strangely encouraging her to let him go.

"You didn't want him to become a warrior," the king said, "and I agreed. The path of the spirit is what you wanted for him, did you not?"

Channa was in agreement with Yasodhara and tried to convince Rahula to delay this decision, but the boy would not be denied. Yasodhara sent Channa to talk with Ananda. Channa explained Yasodhara's concern, and returned saying that there were no restrictions on how young an aspiring monk can be. Ananda had reassured them that if he joined, as the youngest monk, the boy would be carefully attended to, but other than that he would be given no special treatment. He would walk and beg, listen, and practice mindful breathing and the other practices.

Yasodhara and Channa suffered; but on the day of Rahula's departure, they each tried to be kind and hopeful. Two monks arrived to take him away. They handed him a simple robe, and he slipped it over his head. Yasodhara moved to kiss him good-bye. Rahula moved toward her. The monks protested the touch. She stopped, stunned.

Rahula then took off his robe, and moved into her arms. He held her very hard.

Feeling this little body that was of her body, Yasodhara's sobbed. She felt him shake too, and cry out. And then finally, they both let go. He put the robe back on, and she drank him in—all of him—to always remember him this way.

"Good-bye, Mother."

He turned and walked away.

To see her little boy, now dressed in a simple robe and carrying his bowl, walk off with two strangers was wrenching: *He is going off with his father?! Even to go off with the Buddha, after such close contact with me for so many years, growing up with me and the other women, learning to sit in our circle and speak up in our circle and share his child's wisdom there, freshening all of us like spring rain.*

Even though she knew she had encouraged it, it was a tremendous loss: *He is breaking the connection I have held in my deepest spirit, the connection that is the lifeblood of all I have come to value in body and in spirit. I must do everything to stay close to him—to follow him as the sangha travels—and why not? There is nothing left now, here.*

Her anger at Siddhartha rose again.

Yasodhara missed Rahula insanely, which brought her back to the desperate time after she was abandoned by Siddhartha—and how, at first, the only reason for her to try to live was Rahula. She went to the Buddha's forest gathering to meet with Rahula, but he could only sit with her outside the *sangha*. Despite all their past, a wall began to be built between them. On that first journey to see her son, Yasodhara only saw the Buddha from a great distance away, through the trees, as he sat on his seat above the large crowd of his admirers, teaching. Women were not allowed to come any closer into the *sangha*. She continued to visit, but less and less. Sometimes she would simply stand there alone, hoping for a glimpse of the boy as he passed by in the line of monks, going out to beg for food. As he passed, she would give him some rice and a fresh mango. The first time, his eyes lit up and he laughed. Then he bowed to her, and she to him. The next time, he seemed to be suppressing a laugh but giggled and smiled.

On the day that he and the other *arahats* were leaving the Teak Forest, his face showed no emotion. He made a slight bow.

Back home, Yasodhara became more and more reluctant to practice any of the Buddha's teachings.

# 27

Pajapati began to embrace the Buddha's teachings wholeheartedly, and could not fully accept Yasodhara's reluctance. Over the next year, Pajapati sought out her son, the Buddha, on two occasions, sending messages to Ananda requesting permission for her and other women of her *sangha* to enter the spiritual community as nuns. Twice the Buddha refused, saying, "This is not the place for women."

Pajapati understood that to include women was in the spirit of his teaching. After all, he had welcomed men of all castes, ages, and conditions of bodily health to join him. She persisted, though she understood his reluctance, as there would be great danger to women who had left their homes or were living together without men. Yet the Buddha had already declared that women were capable of full awakening! Pajapati knew that bold actions were called for.

She gathered the women of her *sangha* together. They sat together in the circle to discern what next action to take. After examining all the risks and dangers, they decided to stop waiting and take their leave. In a ritual ceremony, each woman shaved the head of another, and they left home with none of their possessions—none of their beautiful saris, sandals, and shawls. They walked together serenely, with begging bowls, to where the Buddha was teaching. Yasodhara had hesitated before agreeing to go with them, but sensed that, even if she could not fully commit to the Buddha's teaching, she would choose to be with Pajapati and the others. And it might be the way to stay closer to her son, whose loss lay now like a cold stone in her heart, next to the loss of her husband.

There was great joy in their decision to go, a sense of great adventure and freedom. They were frightened but hopeful. Still not knowing what would happen, they walked the path together into the unknown joyfully and courageously, touching the strength of their shared enquiry. On the narrow dusty roads, they walked two by two, sometimes talking, sometimes chanting, sometimes in silence—and the circle held all. Channa followed, to help.

News of the women's leaving home and walking toward the Buddha preceded them, and crowds started to form to watch them pass. They walked hundreds of miles and arrived exhausted, hungry, and worn. When they finally arrived at the entrance to the Jetavana monastery, Pajapati asked to have a meeting in person with the Buddha. The venerable Ananda saw and understood that they were a dedicated group of practitioners, already well on their way to crossing over to join part of the spiritual community. He spoke with the Buddha on their behalf, but the Buddha refused.

"They've shaved their heads, donned their robes, carried their begging bowls; and they've walked together many miles, to get here. They're at the door."

The Buddha knew how difficult it would be to have women join the *sangha*. Women alone, unprotected, were subject to great danger; and the presence of women would be a difficult temptation for the monks. But finally his heart opened and he relented, giving his permission to the women as long as they followed some special rules of the order made to protect them, and the monks too.

A new monastic community of women was formed alongside the men's *sangha*. Word spread like the monsoon rains that the queen and the princess, and many other noble women and their servants, had joined the Buddha's *sangha*—something, as yet, unheard of!

Sooner than one might imagine, and not without many challenges—from concerns about dress to "right" manners, to serving the monks meals, to cleaning, and to what to do when several women arrived with their children—they created a refuge for women, who came for many different reasons; from the richest landowner's wife to the impoverished and abandoned wife. A great number of those who came were seeking refuge from lives of brutality, servitude in their families, homelessness, or terrible loss of children and family. The stories they told in the circle brought tears to all.

Often, women would compose poems that were recited in the circle:

*My children both are gone, and in that bush,*
*Dead lies my husband; on one funeral bier,*
*My mother, father, and my brother burn.*
*And then, at last, I saw him as he went*
*Within that blessed city, Mithila,*
*Great tamer of untamed hearts—yea, Him,*
*The very Buddha, Banisher of fear.*[4]

In the circle, this immense grief, held by all together without "even lifting a finger to make it go away"—often softened to sorrow. And like alchemy, the shared sorrow often eased into shared understanding, kind acceptance, and actions to help others.

# 28

Pajapati flourished under her devoted practice of the Buddha's teachings, embracing them thoroughly. She and Yasodhara and the other nuns of the Buddha's *sangha* lived apart from the monks, in their own camp. There was little contact, and the nuns sat in a separate group when the Buddha offered teachings. Channa had left them, and returned to the palace to be with his wife and children.

Through Pajapati's growing reputation as a revered elder, her compassionate nature, and her wise *dharma* talks in public gatherings, other women were attracted to become nuns in the Buddha's *sangha* and were supported there. Many of these women entered the community in a state of desperation, with nowhere else to go. Yasodhara saw in them her own story and remembered how Pajapati had come to her, nurturing her through as they developed the sacred Circle of Compassion and the Path of Right Relation. Other women were drawn to the community upon hearing the Buddha, and tried through every means to obtain permission from husbands and family "to go forth" and live the holy life.

Still, Yasodhara held back from fully embracing the Buddha's teachings. She felt uncomfortable with his sitting on a raised platform, high above all, as the Awakened One. This was how he offered his teachings, rather than sitting on the ground, as one among others, in the Awakened We, as the women had.

In addition to the teachings of the Buddha, both Yasodhara and Pajapati, along with the other women, still sat in their circle. This was the heart of their own *sangha* practice and a way of including the new women. The women of the palace had been saved by—and had nurtured—the ripe moments arising on and illuminating this path, and the practices that helped. They were now continuing what had healed them, offering teachings and wisdom to the women as they entered. The circle expanded to include these new ones. Yasodhara and the others continued to go forth together to those in the villages and towns close by. Yasodhara was intent on offering these women freedom from the suffering of daily life and from the oppressive burden of their householder existence, as well as refuge for those in the most extreme circumstances.

Pajapati became more focused on the monastic *sangha* of the Buddha's nuns. The nuns lived quite separately from the monks, except for the monks' oversight of the women's community as per the *vinaya*—the laws of the order. Sometimes they traveled with the Buddha *sangha* and sometimes they remained behind, bringing new women into the fold.

For a while, Yasodhara was able to continue seeing her son—at least seeing him pass as the monks walked out of their encampment to the village for alms, and to pass by on the way back. Sensing his growing adulation for the Buddha his father, and the other older monks, she saw him becoming more and more distant from her. Each time she saw him, the wrenching sadness was evoked anew.

Pajapati felt Yasodhara's suffering in the estrangement from Rahula and in her continued reluctance to fully embrace the Buddha's teachings.

Finally, troubled by the fractures in their friendship, Pajapati suggested that the two of them sit in the circle alone together and try to come to an understanding. After sitting in silence, they spoke.

"Why is it not possible for you to commit fully to the Awakened One's path and practices?" Pajapati asked.

"Dear one," Yasodhara said, "you and I had different relations with him, when he was Siddhartha. You, as his mother, can still see him as your son, beloved no matter what. And I, as his wife, who fell in love with him and made love with him, and gave birth to and raised his son, had a very different relationship. In a way, he is still Siddhartha to me, and despite trying for all these years, I can never totally forgive Siddhartha for what he did and all that has occurred." Yasodhara could sense Pajapati's stiffening. "*Please do see this—please! I will never again be able to sit alone with my son!*"

Pajapati was startled by the fire in these words. "I know," she said, "but the Buddha has spoken about this—this clinging—and has shown a way through it."

"'*Clinging*'? Is that what you call this bond between mother and child? It is as deep a love as anyone can know. It's not about letting go, or about renouncing the bond with him, it is about all of us together as one *sangha*, and *never* losing this special bond. I'm not sure I can remain here."

She paused.

"Pajapati, dear one, I know you are disappointed in me. I may have to leave, as painful as that will be, but it may be the only way I can survive. Like the grace of your compassion when you first came toward me, when I wanted to die, I chose life. I have the strange sense that when I walk out of this *sangha* and fully commit to the shared path, I will feel a rush of life, as alive as when he left me and our baby so suddenly that I wanted to die. How strange . . ."

She paused again.

"As alive as when I wanted to die."

Stillness. The break between them, the chasm, loomed large.

And then Pajapati reached out and took her hand, saying kindly, "He caused us great suffering, yes, but that suffering birthed our path and our awakening together; and we can be grateful for that."

"I am," Yasodhara nodded. "The Buddha himself cannot walk this path—I sense that deeply. But he pointed the way for me and I will never abandon it. I will take from his teachings and help to create a shared path. I will stay, for now."

"Can both these teachings coexist together, as they belong?"

"I'm not sure." And then, with a hint of mischief, she said, "But, to use the Buddha's own word, they do *co-arise*, yes?"

Pajapati chuckled, and nodded. "Yes." She took Yasodhara's hand, and gently stroked it. "Dear one, I understand."

The first russet of dawn crept into the Sanctuary.

"Both Pajapati and I knew that I was holding back in a way that she was not," Yasodhara continued, "and at first, this created a distance between us. But still we lived on and worked together, until our traveling *sangha* of women, traveling with the Buddha, was thriving. Together, we tried to join our own wisdom and practices with the monastic rites and practices of the Buddha, expanding both paths so that there was something of a joining of the best practices and teachings of each.

"Pajapati embraced the Buddha's teaching with an earnestness and devotion as tenacious as anyone, and soon became recognized as an Enlightened One—an *arahat*—known as *Mahapajapati*. She was reknowned for her compassion and wisdom, and offered *dharma* talks wherever the Buddha went, bringing more women into the *sangha*—women like you. This was a radical turn toward affirming the great Buddha-nature of all sentient beings, including women.

Women have become more valued, and their great potential for spiritual attainment has begun to be recognized—although they still must follow all the special rules of the order."

She paused, then said, "But we still have our spiritual freedom, the vows and practices that illuminate the power of our own *sangha*."

Pajapati stirred. Yasodhara's face was caught in the day's first light.

"Let us chant our morning vows together, so Mahapajapati can hear."

*May we be a guard for those who need protection,*
*A guide for those on the path,*
*A boat, a raft, a bridge for those who wish to cross the flood.*
*May we be a lamp in the darkness,*
*A resting place for the weary,*
*A healing medicine for all who are sick,*
*A vase of plenty, a tree of miracles.*
*And for the boundless multitudes of living beings,*
*May we bring sustenance and awakening,*
*Enduring like the earth and sky,*
*Until all beings are freed from sorrow*
*And all are awakened together.*[5]

# 29

"Years passed," Yasodhara went on as the sunlight crept more boldly in. A mourning dove cooed and was answered by its mate. "Our women's *sangha* grew and matured within the rules and practices of the Buddha's monastic community. The power of his *sangha* was great, and more and more of the teaching centered on individual attainment. Mahapajapati and one or two other *bikkhunis* became full *arahats* and were recognized for this, as was I. But I still could not embrace his path fully."

A whimsical smile was on her face. "I kept wondering: *What if, in that second meeting I had with the Buddha in the Pine Grove, he had said to me, 'Dear one, let us go out and teach a true shared path—where the two paths meet—together?'*"

All of us listening looked at each other—was she serious? Seeing the look on our faces, she smiled, and we all smiled back.

With joy, she said, "What a time that might have been! What a path that might have become!"

We noticed that Pajapati was resting more peacefully, her breaths rare but unlabored. Yasodhara stroked her forehead, her cheek, and cradled her hand. Pajapati's eyes fluttered open for a moment, and met Yasodhara's sad and loving gaze.

"I was continuing my work in the *sangha* with the new arrivals—with some of you. Then, a week ago, Pajapati became very ill. It was determined that nothing more could be done to help her. As she had come to me so many years before, I went to her bedside to attend to her and be with her through her death. The Buddha was far away, and I knew she would never ask him to come to her. I put all else aside to be with her. Our deep love and gratitude began to flow as we remembered and talked about our lives together. The sacred circle of her life and our lives together was holding us close again, with the depth of silence and the clarity of right speech and right listening. We were, again, in Right Relation. Our beloved Pajapati seemed to see deeply into my heart, and even with her diminishing strength, poured all her mental energy toward me. She spoke of my separation from the Buddha and how I had never been fully released from my suffering. She called me a *bodhisattva*, one who holds back from attaining *nirvana*—full enlightenment—to help others along the path. Seeing deeply into the whole of our lives, she seemed to come to a great insight. This is what she said."

Tears pooled in Yasodhara's eyes, and through them, she spoke Pajapati's words: "You have tried hard to keep alive our path of *awakening with*, of going forth together on the Path of Right Relation. But the truth of this doorway is already being lost. We must keep it alive. Yasodhara, dear one, you must tell your story and all must listen deeply and remember. You must be heard."

# 30

Yasodhara sat quietly, watching Pajapati's eyes open and then close for the last time. As Pajapati entered the realm of the deathless, Yasodhara, once again in sorrow, felt herself born into the unknown.

Following Pajapati's death, Yasodhara and we novices accompanied her body back to the palace, to the cremation grounds, where King Suddhodana received her, and made the ritual passage of her body and spirit to the air, wind, earth, fire, and water.

We all grieved the passing of this great *arahat*, the first woman ordained by the Buddha.

When it was over, we novices were to return to the nuns' *sangha*. With great love, Yasodhara told us that she would no longer stay in the community of nuns following the teachings of the Buddha. She would no longer "subdue" her story. She had to be true to her understanding, and find a new way to live and teach in the light of her own wisdom. Yasodhara felt profoundly sad, seeing that she was irrevocably choosing to live the split in the path, yet her words both saddened and, as always, inspired us.

Two of the other novices left and returned to the Buddha's community. I, Kisa Gotami, stayed, along with Nayla, Yasodhara's oldest friend.

Suddhodana invited Yasodhara to stay at the palace. She could tell that he was not well. He was sorrowed by his queen's death, and by the loss of his son and grandson. Yasodhara agreed to stay with him, but not in the palace itself. She would stay in a dwelling that he would construct adjacent to the Pine Grove that had been the site and source of so much grieving, and, beyond all hope, the birth of the Path of Right Relation.

He immediately agreed: "I shall build you a grand temple."

Yasodhara refused the scale of it and asked for a simple hut, much like the Squirrel Sanctuary.

"There, I will receive all who wish to learn about our path of awakening. I will teach those who stay, who do not ordain in the holy life, but instead take their vows within their devotional relationships. This path is theirs too."

The king smiled, happy to have her home again.

The event of Pajapati's death strengthened Yasodhara, and her clarity burned brightly. She knew that she no longer wanted anything from Siddhartha. There would be no more "clinging" to a teacher—even to the Buddha, the Awakened One. For Yasodhara, it seemed that he had forever shut the door on their shared, mutual enquiry. She would choose to keep the possibility alive, the door remaining open.

Nayla and I stayed with Yasodhara. Others came—men and women—and sat with Channa and us in the Pine Grove, in a circle on the solid, level ground. They came seeking refuge, spiritual wisdom, and peace. Yasodhara grew in presence and awareness, as she, listening deeply to all, realized and taught more and more clearly the

wisdom of the moments of relational awakening on the path that had come to life here.

Channa, his wife, and their grown children joined the enquiry.

Yasodhara always spoke of him as "my most constant and great spiritual friend."

Her teachings became more and more simple and strong.

She and Channa stayed with Suddhodana through his death.

I, Kisa Gotami, traveled back to rejoin the nun's *sangha* of the Buddha. Nayla remained with Yasodhara.

Many years passed.

When I heard that Yasodhara had died, I traveled back to the palace and spoke to Channa. He was aged in body, more twisted than ever, but his spirit was strong. His eyes, which had seen everything, were still as expectant and joyous as a child's.

Channa said, "Yasodhara lived quietly here with Nayla. She offered her teaching to those who came to enquire with her. She also responded when asked to visit other communities, often in strife, to share her wisdom of compassion, nonviolence, and peace-keeping circles."

He thought carefully.

"What was so beautiful about Yasodhara in these later years was the depth of her *listening*, as deep as the ocean and as wide as the expanse of sky on the great plains of the Ganges. The listening of one who has known great suffering, one who has lived through great love and loss, and has come to peace. *She listened deeply to everyone.* 'Right Listening' or 'Wise Listening,' she called this, her final spiritual practice. She felt that her silent meditation practice with the Buddha had come to fruition. 'Opening,' 'listening,' coming again and again to the wholeness of each moment, each relation. Hearing

the unspoken, the silence behind the speech, the space that births the words and the reality that lies beyond the words, arising out of and vanishing back into the deep well of compassion—within us, around us, and between us—the *dharma* of love at the heart of the universe."

He nodded his head, slowly, several times, in gratitude. "She said, 'We, together, weave the invisible thread at the heart of the universe that connects us . . . *all*.'"

A sigh, carrying a depth of satisfaction with life itself.

"She had a deep well of faith in what had been seen and felt on the Path of Awakening With, and she shared that with all."

A sense of stillness.

"As she grew old, she was cared for by me and my family—especially by my grandchildren—she loved being with the children!—here at home, when no one else who had known her as a princess was still alive. We cared for her as we had cared for the king. She died in the heart of our love. We were all at peace."

He paused and, with tears in his eyes, said quietly, "She never saw her son, Rahula, or Siddhartha again."

"Before she died, Yasodhara seemed to see the future. She made a prophecy." Channa was transfixed, his eyes shining as if he, too, was seeing the future. "Her prophecy was this: 'While the conditions are not ripe today for the full flowering of this shared path, the seeds have been planted. I do not know when, but sometime they will sprout, bud, and blossom. *There will come a time*.'"

As for me, Kisa Gotami, my own life will be ending soon. Now, but for you, Yasodhara's story and her teachings will be lost to the world.

"Hear it, remember it, and pass it on!" Thus I have heard.

# Book Two

# Reader's Companion

The next Buddha may be a *sangha*.

—Thich Nhat Hanh

# Expanding the Circle: An Invitation

"Hear it, remember it, and pass it on." Thus I have heard.
—**Kisa Gotami**, in Chapter 1 of "Yosadhara's Story"

The time is now! Our lives, our suffering, the global challenges we face—along with the terrible fractures and divisions we encounter—are leading many of us into a spiral of despair and alienation. Climate change, continual war, the growing inequality of wealth, unceasing racism, and our "screen-centered" and consumerist lives all portend the coming of danger and global catastrophe. We desperately need to find sources of hope, action, and possibility. We have to learn to live together—finding new ways to heal and take action together.

The only way through must stretch us beyond our individual, self-centered "selves," opening us to each other and into communities, starting with friends, couples, neighborhoods, or spiritual communities and expanding the circles until we know ourselves and our actions as part of the whole global community. We can see how close the global community is becoming each day—news of suffering spreads through the World Wide Web like wildfire. And yet, so can words of hope and change.

Social activist and meditation teacher, Vimala Thakar, has reflected that, "While our massive institutions are collapsing under the weight of their own contradictions, new healing energies are also arising. Keep your eyes on what is arising."[1] This is a rare moment in time when the creative forces of change—the alternatives of community and connection and spiritual health—are beginning to flower. The long-dormant seeds of Yasodhara's hidden Path of Right Relation are growing, pushing up through the charred earth. Her path is coming alive now, when we most need it.

Buddhist teacher Joanna Macy describes this as a time for a "Great Turning" toward a new way of living together, joined in our care for each other and our natural connection with all forms of life that are threatened.[2] The energy of spiritual awakening is being called forth in the searing grief and fierce love at the heart of this interconnected web of life.

We hear many voices calling for a spiritual awakening to our true nature—our interconnectedness and our collective human capacity for wisdom and compassion. Yasodhara's story offers such a way, where our relational potential can be the foundation for connection, energy, and action for change. She offers a courageous path of awakening together—the Path of Right Relation, a way of accompanying others through the circle of life. This relational dynamic organizes many aspects of our lives. Learning to tap in to the spiritual and communal power of relational practice, Yasodhara and her Circle of Compassion offer an illuminating path for others to join.

We offer this reader's companion to Yasodhara's story as a direct application to our lives and challenges today. This is an invitation to join with a contemporary movement of spiritual teachers and leaders who are pointing the way. We offer simple, direct practices to walk this path in our own personal lives, our relationships, and our communities, with an abiding appreciation for our shared power to change the world through the widening ripples of relationship and community.

Book Two is divided into eight chapters, each drawing from the path that Yasodhara walked in relationship with the others in her life (as told in Book One) while reflecting on the *ripe moments* of awakening within and toward community. These ripe moments instruct and serve as teaching and turning points that we can all make in life today and every day. Also woven throughout are profiles of people we have met in our many years of practice—people who have experienced for themselves the healing, restorative, and transformative power of circles of compassion and awakening. Each chapter ends with suggested reflections and useful practices relevant to contemporary times. It may be helpful to keep a journal and write down your thoughts and responses.

You can practice privately and/or with a friend, partner, or group, though we invite you to create your own *sangha* or join one of the already established, modern-day *sanghas* or spiritual communities in the world. There are a variety of communities that continue the legacy and spirit of Yasodhara's path of awakening through relational practice. You may want to create a "Yasodhara book group" to read and experience the reflections and practices together.

The Path of Right Relation is a lifelong one that invites everyone who is seeking to walk this path and experience the strength and support of compassion, connection, and community. The circle is ever breathing and expanding.

This reader's companion is an invitation for you to be part of a movement of awakening together, to become a relational activist in your own life.

# Part I

# The Meeting of Suffering and Compassion

*The possibility of paradise hovers on the cusp of coming into being—so much so that it takes powerful forces to keep such a paradise at bay. If paradise now arises in hell, it's because in the suspension of the usual order and the failure of most systems, we are free to live and act another way.*

—**Rebecca Solnit**, *A Paradise Built in Hell*

*If not now, when?*
*If not here, where?*
*If not together, how?*

—**Yasodhara**, the Buddha's wife

# 1

# The Gift of Desperation: Suffering and Compassion Co-Arise

Yasodhara awakened before dawn to the cries of their newborn baby. Siddhartha was gone.

—Chapter 2, "Yasodhara's Story"

The mythical story of the Buddha's leaving home, of He Who Goes Forth to seek freedom from suffering, is well known. But how did his leaving impact others in his world—especially his wife, stepmother, father, and son? What was the path of She Who Stays? Of "those who stay"? Of the "one who hears the cries"?

The woman staying and the man leaving is so common as to be mythic. Once the man faces great danger and emerges a "hero," he's ready to return home and become head of the family. This is the myth of the patriarch, as in the ancient Greek epic, *The Odyssey*. In some sense, the Buddha fits this myth: he goes forth alone and ultimately becomes the great teacher with many followers.

Historically, in Western psychology, the normal developmental journey of the boy to the man emphasized the fashioning of a strong, independent, and self-sufficient self, at some point ready for a "mature" relationship. Women, characteristically, were seen as making a more continuous journey of *self-in-relationship*, not so much having to leave or separate, but rather to grow within relationship as a way to grow to maturity. Each of these pathways has its particular power as well as peril. In our contemporary times, of course, the classic gender pathways are no longer so clear or differentiated; there is far more diversity.

The journeys of the "one who leaves" and the "one who stays" are ultimately larger than male or female. At best, both of these journeys can become not simply about survival, but about awakening. And at best, both can become vital strands of a greater, inclusive path of many voices and colors.

What choice did Yasodhara have? In her world and culture, it would have been impossible for a woman to choose to leave and go homeless. And even if she had been the kind of woman who fought tradition and culture, and contemplated leaving, she probably would not choose to leave with her baby; but neither would she leave her baby behind. In some sense, as for so many women in history (and still today) who chose marriage—and especially motherhood—there was no right way out of that dilemma. And in our modern world, there are many single mothers for whom the centrality of mothering is the crucial organizing factor of their lives, and becomes their source of inspiration and spiritual connection.

There are many ways and types of staying. Staying can mean stasis, without choice, feeling oppressed or trapped in the only role that seems to make sense in your life at the time. Yet staying can also mean "staying power": gutting it out and going about your life with nothing changing except the fact that you have, for the moment, actually chosen to survive. You may become "a rock" in the relationship, perhaps for the good of the family, child, or children—a caretaker for others—or perhaps for economic or other reasons.

Staying can also mean "staying alive," in psychological terms—not giving in to senseless deadening that may persist for decades.

In Yasodhara's life, we see her emerging choice to stay alive as a mother—to stay aware, open, empathic, and responsive for the sake of her child.

At best, staying can be active and powerful. It can mean going beyond the psychological limits to become an opening to a spiritual practice and path—even leading toward self and others' liberation from suffering. This way of staying involves finding a way to be with others in vital, authentic, life-sustaining relationships and communities, grounded in something beyond the individual separate self, grounded in spiritual awakening.

Leaving also can take many forms. Not all leavings are physical, with someone walking out the door or dying. Leavings are, of course, psychological and emotional—being there physically but not being truly present, being withdrawn or distracted.

We all move between choices to stay or to leave. The Buddha's leaving his family and old life behind to become homeless can be understood as a metaphor for casting off attachments or fetters—his son's name, Rahula, in fact means "fetter." This is especially relevant, as the Buddha's teaching places attachment as the root cause of suffering. Yasodhara's story raises the compelling questions: Can there be freedom within relationships—a middle way between attachment and detachment? Can we learn to grow within particular relationships while loosening our attachments? Is there a way to go forth to liberation from suffering together? Her story illustrates that we can.

It is suffering itself in the form of abandonment and loss that is Yasodhara's first ripe moment toward opening the doorway to a well-worn path—a path that has great untapped potential for awakening in relationship. Her internal world resonates with many of us. We know her suffering in relationship—in our own losses, separations, divorces, loved ones' deaths. Horrific loss is traumatic, and the persistence and helplessness of loss over time is draining and deadening. The spiraling fracture of being left is all too human. Yasodhara's life story leads her to the end of life as she knows it; she simply cannot return to the old way—that way is a dead end. But she doesn't yet know where she can go. Her desperation could lead to isolation, depression, suicide, or insanity. She could, like so many of us, crash and burn, sometimes quickly, sometimes slowly. But her desperation and the response she encounters could generate potential for something else, something new, to happen. It's almost a law of life that, if we're lucky, we all learn: suffering at our core can lead us to connection and understanding.

> When Yasodhara cried out, everyone heard it. (Chapter 5, page 19)

In the Mahayana tradition of Buddhism, goddess Kwan Yin is known as the *Bodhisattva of Compassion*, "the One who Hears the Cries," who appears wherever and whenever there are cries of suffering. She is the symbol of compassion arising in the face of desperation. Represented as having a thousand hands, with an "eye" in each palm, she is ready to serve, and to meet and respond to the needs of anyone who cries out.

> Pajapati saw a wild terror in Yasodhara's eyes as they desperately raced here and there to every face, searching the faces and the chamber itself for some answer. Pajapati understood at once, and it hit her in the belly—a blow of sorrow, rocking her on her feet. But she understood from her past losses and sufferings that her focus now had to be on Yasodhara. Without a word, Pajapati walked slowly toward Yasodhara, who was still huddled on the floor. The queen stood before her and opened her arms to hold her. (Chapter 5, pages 19–20)

In Yasodhara's story, it is Pajapati who comes forth. She is not a totally liberated being, nor a goddess or a *bodhisattva*, but a human being who herself has known suffering—especially after her beloved sister, Maya, Siddhartha's biological mother, died seven days after giving birth. She, too, had to "stay alive" to become the adopted mother of the baby Siddhartha. The repetition of this constellation of overwhelming grief and passionate commitment to "stay with" allows Pajapati to use her life experience, her wisdom, to benefit Yasodhara.

Yasodhara has received the "gift of desperation" and a willingness born of necessity—as a mother—to choose life. She thus turns toward and opens her whole being to being lifted up in love and to receiving the wisdom of Pajapati, who is "called forth." Pajapati's compassion moves her beyond the strength she has known before in herself, to meet Yasodhara, with wisdom grown through a life of meeting and being met in suffering, as a fellow human being, a woman, and a mother. Pajapati is not a goddess, fully formed and ready to serve, but her compassion and wisdom emerge in meeting the suffering of one that she loves.

In situations of extreme shock, pain, and suffering, the words and actions of a "first responder" are of immense importance—and can have a profound positive (or negative) effect on what follows. How a doctor delivers bad news has a tremendous impact on the whole course of treatment and recovery. Pajapati's compassionate words and strong relational presence echo this. As she says to Yasodhara:

> We are with you in this. All of us are with you. I know that in this moment it is impossible to believe, but you must listen: *I* found a way, *we* will find a way, and *you* will find your way. Your child needs you, as Siddhartha needed me. A new door has opened for you, and you will walk through it with us. (Chapter 5, page 21)

Having been abandoned, Yasodhara is, at first, left alone with her pain and suffering. But the community is called forth and responds.

They embrace her with the great human gift of *being with*, which grows into what psychiatrist Dr. Jean Baker Miller called "the great unsung gift of mutual empathy."[1] The cries of the suffering awaken Pajapati, and she attunes and moves toward Yasodhara—who feels, and is moved by, that sense of being attended to. This generates a process, simultaneously arising, so that both feel joined in right—or wise—relation. This is not a static process of "putting yourself in another person's shoes," but rather a movement in which each joins and feels joined, sees and feels seen, moves and is moved by the other. Each senses the other "being seen" and being moved. This is the *movement of mutuality*. Each feels that the other is *present*, knows this immediately—some would say, each one "gets it." Through this, movement, wisdom, and insight co-arise. True meeting, as Martin Buber has written, is beyond words and of the whole person, including all mind and body states. Judith Jordan emphasizes this true meeting as "creating the actual experience of joining"—of being with, touched and touching, co-creating the unfolding moment. This could be described as "mutual relational presence."[2]

Pajapati connects to Yasodhara's actual experience of the moment through her empathic attunement. She also brings to bear on the moment all her *past* experience—all that has been passed on to her—and her understanding of Yasodhara's life and her past history. She brings the universal spirit of compassion, which goes through and beyond the particulars.

Empathy is to compassion as the particular is to the whole. Empathy is the doorway into—and the doorway arising from—compassion.

## The Five Good Things about Connecting

Described by Dr. Jean Baker Miller as "The Five Good Things," every growth relationship of mutual connection leads to an enhanced experience of five characteristics for each participant. Each feels more:

1. Zest
2. Empowerment
3. Knowledge of self, other, and the relationship
4. An increased sense of worth
5. A desire for more connection[3]

These five things are felt by participants as arising in the *movement of connecting*. This is an example of the movement of mutual empathy—an example of the one who calls out and the one who comes. It feels like it's happening almost simultaneously, as if co-arising. Certainly, it is mutually arising.

Contemporary neuroscience offers a window into the biological underpinning of this phenomenon. The first studies of "mirror neurons" in the brain show how completely we're wired to share each other's experience. Originally, there were studies of monkeys with electrodes implanted in their motor cortices. Monkeys were known to mimic each other, and these studies showed that when one monkey did some action, the same brain region or neurons in the other monkey began to fire, as if this monkey were doing it too.[4] This can be seen in humans as well. When one human yawns, the other person's neurons get triggered in the same brain area, as if this person is yawning also—although they are still aware that they're not. Then sometimes, each has the experience of the "contagion" of yawning, actually yawning in response.

In humans this is true for sensory, motor, emotional, and higher cognitive functions—the whole human body-mind or brain-mind is aligned, programmed for the "sharing" of experience. Studies of mother-baby interaction show that a mother's following and mirroring the facial expressions of her child (smiling with a smile, grimacing with a grimace) takes place at the limits of measurement—a matter of milliseconds. And if the mother's face ceases to follow the baby's expression—or if, in a few experiments, the mother was told to have a "still face" and not respond at all to the baby—the baby shows extreme distress and attempts to re-engage.[5] Thus, we come into the world "wired" for mutual responsivity and programmed to take action to reconnect. The challenge to "stay" and engage in finding pathways to repair and restore "attunement" is fundamental to all relational human development.[6]

Research was designed by John Decety at the University of Chicago to study the neurological correlates of empathic relationships. He studied the activity of two human brains in relationship: one an observer and the other a person in pain. When one person experienced pain—for example, a pinprick on the finger—the same areas of sensory-motor and limbic systems became activated in both brains. In the observer, there was greater activation of the brain in other cortical areas and less in the sensory-motor, suggesting that in addition to "feeling with" the pain, the observer can bring to bear higher cortical functions—perhaps past experience, compassion, understanding, wisdom, responsiveness, and an appreciation of what might be useful or helpful to the sufferer.[7] Tibetan Buddhist monks whose practice had been centered on developing compassion for suffering showed enormous responsiveness to pain and suffering in a laboratory setting, as well as a readiness to respond in action. This research suggests that the fruits of experience, the mental training or cultivated mental states in one person can be shared with another when they meet in the moment of suffering.[8]

Thus, mutual empathy is not just "feeling with" another or "putting yourself in their shoes." It is the process of actually offering understanding and compassion *to the other*, and finding a way to help the other "receive" it. Both people adapting and aligning in the offering and receiving. It also shows a basis for joining in another person's pain, but it also shows that practice—both in life and in meditation—shapes and enlarges the capacity, intensity, and competence of each person in this exquisite interactive process.

## Steps on the Path of Right Relation

The teachings of Vietnamese Buddhist monk Thich Nhat Hanh reflect his deep attunement to the isolation and alienation from community endemic in Western society. This awareness led him to focus on building retreats and communities—both monastic and secular—emphasizing the primary importance of people practicing together. This group practice is one of the traditional "Three Jewels of the Buddha," the *sangha*, the community. (The other two jewels are the *Buddha* and the *dharma*).

At one of his first American retreats for psychotherapists, he was asked a question: "How do you understand the importance of the self in Western psychology?" With a wise and impish smile, he responded, "The self is made up entirely of non-self elements."[9]

In an elegant way, this clarified the Mahayana Buddha's classic teaching on "dependent co-arising," and also what he would come to call in his own teaching "interbeing" or "co-being." He elaborated on this, saying that: "Happiness is not an individual matter."[10] That is, we suffer, and become free of suffering, together. And this led to his remarkable prophecy: "The next Buddha may be a *sangha*," the community.[11]

"Interbeing" is his way of describing relatedness, or relational being. Thich Nhat Hanh takes relational being to the fullest dimension of interbeing. It's the teaching and the wisdom that Dr. Martin Luther King, Jr. described: "We are caught in an inescapable network of mutuality, tied to a single garment of destiny. Whatever affects one directly, affects all indirectly."[12] We are caught in a net of suffering we create together, but we also can create pathways to wake up and end the suffering, together.

Buddhist teacher Joanna Macy echoes this in her elaborating on the planetary dimension of the Path of Right Relation, in what she calls "the *sangha* of all Beings."[13]

Thich Nhat Hanh deeply appreciates that the rooting of spiritual practice is within *particular* relationships—within couples, families, and communities—and describes practices, which can be a doorway to the larger dimension of interbeing.

"Happiness is not an individual matter."[14] And we would say, *suffering is not an individual matter.*

Focusing on practical steps to apply this teaching in close relationships, Thich Nhat Hanh offers his "Four Love *Mantras*." *Mantras* are simple phrases that bring calm concentration to the mind. These are offered as relational concentrations, and they give clear intention and attention to being in right relation:

1. "Dear one, I am really here for you."
2. "Dear one, I know that you are here, and it makes me very happy."[15]

These two *mantras*, taken together, are an example of mutuality. They clarify the primary intention to be "present with," and to recognize the presence of the particular other with joy. When both people are practicing together, the power of mutuality is tapped. The practice strengthens depth and stability of being present together, of *being with*:

3. "Dear one, I see your suffering, and that is why I am here for you."
4. "Dear one, I am suffering; please help me."[16]

These third and fourth mantras, also taken together, are a mutual commitment to turn toward suffering with another. To share, to join, to know, and to respond to suffering. This is of particular import in our culture, where we often turn away in order to maintain the familiar, more superficial level of relationship. They also help us to be mindful when we are *not* present—to recognize that one is not *there*, and then to come back to *being with*. (In our work with couples, we often say, "It's not just what you say or do—no one gets it right all the time; it's what you say or do next.") Being there for and with the other, with care, interest, respect, equanimity, and acceptance of shared human suffering—this is the practice of remembering and cultivating these qualities of presence. Thich Nhat Hanh calls it the path of true love.[17]

Thich Nhat Hanh's *mantras* and practices emphasize the particular relationship (couple or family) and also emphasize mutuality; not simply the offering of presence and care but also the necessity of receptivity—standing in the truth of one's suffering and asking for help. There is an emphasis on the necessity of mutuality—*the doorway has to open from both sides*. This sense of invulnerability, or the hiding of vulnerability through denial or pretense (or "spiritual bypass") is a hindrance to this mutuality.

In Thich Nhat Hanh's teaching and in the wisdom path of Yasodhara, the emphasis is different from the traditional Buddhist teaching in two ways:

1. *Particularity*: The emphasis is on the *particular* relationship ("I see you"). This is different from the traditional Buddhist emphasis on starting with "self and all beings," which may then manifest in particular relationships with particular people.
2. *Mutuality*: Not just the practice of offering but also of receiving. In time, both these positions drop away and there is simply *being with*—which generates cocreative movement.

The Buddha emphasized the solitary path. His dying words were said to be, "Work out your own salvation with diligence. Be a light unto yourself." In Yasodhara's story and on the Path of Right Relation, there are times when it is understood that you need not be just your own light but the light of others in order to find the way. And, sometimes you need to be a light *for* others; sharing your light with others brightens the path for all. Still, sometimes when alone in the dark, your own light makes the difference between desperation and faith—it is essential. Both the individual path and the Path of Right Relation are necessary, but each alone is not sufficient; both solitude and communion are the path.

*Being with* your own suffering allows you to be there for others, and *being with* others in their suffering allows you to be with your own. This is, at its heart, how the doorways of the path swing open from both sides. The Buddha did emphasize the importance of the monastic community and spiritual friendship, and Yasodhara added the possibility of transformation through ordinary relationships—the power of *being with* suffering together and the possibility of collective awakening.

Suffering can be a creator of true community. But the issue isn't just suffering—we all suffer; it's about *how we live and walk through it, and how we meet others in the suffering and walk on together.* If we choose to try to walk through our suffering alone, not asking for help from others, or not showing up for others, we will suffer more—and spread more suffering around. If we try to walk through our suffering with others, without a spiritual practice and path, we may become lost, confused, and dispirited. The practices described here offer ways of generating and sustaining concentration, energy, and clarity in *being with* others in suffering and release. We do not need any other technology or device; we just need to know how to use what we have—it's built into us as human beings. Just as in the Buddha's teaching on "mindfulness," it is possible to take what is naturally occurring and find the way to mindfully create pathways for mutual liberation and for the realization of right community.

This is the Path of Right Relation.

# Creating Ripe Moments: Reflections and Practices

## Ask for Help

Suffering in relationship is a part of life; you do not have to be alone in it. The way through can be with others. Honor suffering in yourself and others. Learn to ask for help, to reach out, and to be authentic about where you really are. Learn how to wait with patience, how to receive care, how to appreciate what is offered, how to receive what nourishes, and how to let go of what does not.

### 1. Reflections

The following is to be written out alone and then shared with a group of others, perhaps your *sangha* or your book-study group:

- Think of a time when you have asked for or received help—when someone met you in your time of need or your pain. What stands out about the experience?
- Think of a time when someone offered care or help, but you were unable to receive what was offered. What may have been in the way? What could you learn from this?
- Think of something that feels "large"—an impasse in an important relationship, a problem with a compulsive behavior or substance, or a physical concern not yet shared with anyone. Are you ready to ask for help? If not, what holds you back?
- Think of something that feels "small"—a cluttered closet, difficult travel plans, a problem in which you feel stuck. How do you typically work through something that baffles you? How do you practice asking for help?

## 2. Individual Meditation Practice

This is a practice of asking for help and of developing awareness of the experience in the body, mind, and heart.

- Practice sitting in silence with your back straight, hands linked, fingertips touching lightly. Bring mindful awareness to the posture of sitting and breathing in, receiving the breath, receiving the moment, and breathing out. (3–5 minutes)
- Move both hands (or one hand) to reflect a posture of asking and receiving help. You may open one or both palms in a mudra (position of hands) of symbolic opening to the universe, to another human being, and/or to the unseen energies of compassion or wisdom. Ask for help, and bring mind and body awareness to this posture. Breathe deeply into the posture. Let feelings arise and pass away, allowing yourself to relax into the openness and receptivity. (3–5 minutes)

## 3. Relational Meditation Practice

This practice grounds the action of asking for and receiving care. (To be done with another person or in pairs within a group.)

- Have one person read the directions and ring a bell at the beginning of the exercise.
- Sitting on cushions face to face, practice the mindful awareness of sitting together, eyes open, hands clasped lightly, breathing in and out, silently investigating what it's like to sit and breathe together. (3–5 minutes)
- Open your hands to reflect your own expression of asking and receiving (could be one hand reaching out, one on the heart), then breathe deeply into the posture. Contemplate the feeling

of opening and receiving in the body, mind, and heart. Feel the flow or Circle of Compassion encompassing you together, around, and between. (5 minutes)

- Share how you felt when simply experiencing the other's presence. What arose in you from the practice of opening to and receiving? (5 minutes)
- End with a moment of silence, then ring the bell to complete the exercise.

## Show Up

Be mindful of the suffering of others. Turn *toward* others' suffering rather than turning away. It's not only about doing for or feeling responsible for the other; it is simply *being with*—being present—in whatever way you can. This may or may not be expressed in direct action. Seeing, knowing, listening, caring—keep your connection to the particular details while holding a spacious awareness of the whole at the same time.

### 1. Reflections

This practice is to be written and shared with your circle, book group, or family *sangha*.

- In the past, where have I shown up for others in a significant way? In an ongoing way?
- Where may I have been less than responsive, become angry or judgmental, or turned away? Where have I felt unable to *be with*? What might have been in the way in these situations?
- What might have helped?
- Where am I called into compassionate listening and responsive action today—in my personal life and relationships?

- Where am I called into compassionate action in the larger world? In confronting suffering and injustice?
- How could I take a small or large step toward showing up?
- Who has shown up for me—whether in small or large ways—and have I expressed my gratitude?
- How can I take a step toward further expression of appreciation?

## 2. Individual Meditation Practice

- To focus on and generate care and compassion, we suggest *metta*, loving-kindness practice (wish for the other's happiness) and *karuna*, compassion practice (wish for the other's freedom from suffering). Sitting in silence in a meditation posture, think of another or others who are suffering and practice evoking these phrases in your heart: "May you be happy, may you be free from suffering, may you find a way to peace." You may use whatever phrases work for you to wish or pray for others, especially those who may be suffering. (3–5 minutes)
- Practice offering these phrases as you think of a particular person sitting across from you. Offer these phrases as wishes or prayers for their freedom and well-being. Begin with a person or group of people who are easy for you to send compassion to. Think of a person or persons who are very difficult for you to feel compassion for, and offer these phrases to them too: "May you be happy, may you be free from suffering, may you find a way to peace." (3–5 minutes)
- In meditation, imagine moving toward those you have envisioned, first the easy and then the difficult, and offer your hand to this person or persons. Meditate deeply into your *body awareness* in this posture. Notice what feelings arise and subside, and allow yourself to remain steady in the posture. (5 minutes)

## 3. Relational Meditation Practice

- In a group, practice offering and receiving these metta and karuna phrases silently to each other. (3 minutes)
- Next, designate a person to say these phrases aloud to the other(s), slowly and with feeling. Have a second speaker offer the phrases, a third speaker after that, and so on. Allow time to pause for mindfulness between each phrase; practice authentic speaking and deep listening. You may also experiment with creating your own phrases. For instance, "May you be happy, free from suffering, and may God, Love, or a Higher Power (or your particular word for the sacred) be with you." (5 minutes)
- Sitting across from each other, have one person and then the other read the guidelines of Insight Dialogue (described below) slowly and mindfully to each other. Together, contemplate each guideline for 5 minutes. (For example, you could ask: "What's it like to pause together here and now?" Do the same for the others in the Insight Dialogue—*relax, open, trust emergence, listen deeply*, and *speak the truth.*) (5 minutes)

### Insight Dialogue (ID)

Insight Dialogue is a relational meditation practice offered by Gregory Kramer within the *Theravadin* Buddhist tradition. While the full practice involves a liberating, meditative, and contemplative practice, the guidelines can also be of support to all practices that point to this *being with.*[17]

Kramer's work is a beacon for addressing inevitable suffering in relationship—perhaps especially in the West—and the end of suffering in relationship. In our relationships, there is inevitable suffering, and Kramer teaches that the cessation of suffering may also come through right or wise relationship, as in this cultivated practice.

The six guidelines of Insight Dialogue meditation support this relational mindfulness practice. Each guideline can be practiced separately, but all guidelines work together synergistically. Each person's practice directly touches and influences the others. These guidelines are fundamental for deepening presence and *being with.*

1. **Pause.** The practice of stopping the automatic and habitual movement of the mind and body, slowing down and dropping into mindfulness of the present moment. Mindfulness can be sustained and supported by each person's practice of *pause.* Even one person practicing pause can impact the whole relational encounter. Pausing—and remembering to be mindful—before, during, and after speaking is especially valuable.
2. **Relax.** Invite an opening to what is actually here in the present moment—it is an invitation to bring ease, to release stress or tension in the body-mind when possible, or to ripen into a radical acceptance of what is actually here, allowing and fully receiving what is so, turning toward what is true right now. This movement of *relax* is mutually impacting and can be mutually recognized.
3. **Open.** In the movement of relaxing, there is a natural opening to a greater spaciousness and awareness, a sense of deepening or widening, and an opening to the space between. This guideline specifically points to opening into mutuality—to the act of *opening* more fully to self, to each other, and to the relationship "between" and "around" us.
4. **Trust Emergence.** This guideline points to the awareness of the changing nature of experience and the willingness to "be in it together"—to allow what is arising to be "known" in its own time and *trust* the "not knowing," to surrendering to what is co-arising and passing away in this moment of shared human experience.

5. **Listen Deeply.** This points to mindful and heartfelt listening, the ability to *listen* to voice and words and to the meaning and music of sound—embodied, attentive, open, and fully present; there is full sensory contact. Notice when distraction, judgment, or "self-agenda" arises, and simply return to this open-minded, openhearted listening to and receiving of the voice of the other. Internal listening to oneself is also part of this mindful practice.
6. **Speak the Truth.** This guideline points to mindfulness of the physical action of speaking, of voice, of learning to align the voice to represent the actual wordless experience as it is known as closely as possible. The practice encompasses learning to recognize when what is spoken is true and what is not on the mark, and setting and re-setting the compass toward *truth*-telling. The practice also encompasses the Buddhist path factor of Right Speech—an ethical guideline toward speaking only what is true, beneficial, kind, and timely, refraining from divisive, hurtful, or idle "chatter."

While this ID practice has grown and developed within a Buddhist tradition, these guidelines point to a whole-life application: to transform all our relationships. Insight Dialogue practice can be a powerful foundation for other relational practices of clinical psychotherapy and other healing, medical, and educational practices. It is a fundamental practice for building circles and communities of awakening.

# 2

# Creating the Circle of Compassion: Finding Power in the *Sangha*

And so, Pajapati arranged for Yasodhara and all the other women of the palace to gather together at dawn in a grove of pines, shaded by the deep green of the ancient trees.

—Chapter 8, "Yasodhara's Story"

Suffering meets compassion in the circle. How is it possible to be with the immensity of suffering, bearing it together so that it can be "held" and known with awareness. *If not together, how?*

Pajapati knows that Yasodhara's grief is so deep that she cannot hold it alone—it takes a village to grieve such a traumatic loss—and the women within the palace community are emotionally touched and ready to move into some way of *being with* Yasodhara.

On the morning after Siddhartha's departure, Pajapati calls those women closest to Yasodhara to meet in the Pine Grove, and she brings Yasodhara to them. They naturally gather around her, close to her, and then Pajapati asks them to sit in a circle around Yasodhara. In a gesture of honoring and opening to her pain, they begin to chant Hindu prayers. Her tears pour forth without words.

Through the compassionate listening of the circle, Yasodhara begins to find words to speak her grief. The women continue to meet together daily. Eventually, Yasodhara moves out from the center of the circle to the circumference, to become "one among many." This represents the movement toward mutuality. She begins to see how her experience can benefit others and learns to listen deeply. Others join the circle, and over time, it enlarges, holding the "ten thousand joys and ten thousand sorrows" of the community.

Yasodhara describes how the circle of women discover their own spiritual practice: In the morning circle, they continue reciting the familiar Hindu prayers and hymns, and then each person speaks, one by one, about their challenges for the day, asking for help. In the evening circle, they express their gratitude for the help and for the day itself. This grows into a practice, a way of being together, alternating between silence and speaking in a mindful way. The practice supports and illuminates their daily lives. This circle practice starts out as ritual, and the ritual becomes a spiritual practice, which lays the groundwork for the rest of her story—the healing power of relationship and the foundation for her work as a mother, a friend, and as a participant in their shared action in the world.

Inadvertently, growing out of responding to suffering, Pajapati and Yasodhara create the foundations for a Circle of Compassion to grow, which adds to the healing not only of Yasodhara's grief, but which encompasses the larger, common circle of all the women—and eventually, men. This practice becomes a basis for awakening and liberation, rather than isolation and despair—a circle of wisdom and healing, providing a vessel for knowing, holding, and transforming the suffering.

## History of Circle Practice

The history of "circles" reaches back to ancient times—perhaps as long as 35,000 years ago, when people sat around a campfire for warmth and experienced the power of the shared ritual to create a sense of gathered energy, nurturance, and belonging. Ancient peoples across the globe developed circle practices, many of which are still alive today. Through all recorded time these circles have been practiced: from Stonehenge and Machu Picchu to Hindu and Tibetan practices and into our current time. Hindu and Tibetan *mandalas*, Sanskrit for "circles," are still being drawn in sacred painting, symbolizing cosmic and human life as integrated holistic structures organized around a unifying center. Sand *mandalas*, drawn and then erased, symbolize the sacred arising and passing away of all of life.[1]

Native American "medicine circles" gather the vital energies of the natural world to heal, to energize, and to locate the pathway to healing and empowerment for individuals and tribes. This circle represents natural and personal powers in complete balance, and show how everything is connected—part of one cosmic whole. In the Native American circles, the circle practice channels—and *is*—the "medicine." The center links the great powers and intelligence of "the Directions," whose energies can be harnessed.[2]

The art and practice of sacred circles became very popular in celebrating women's spirituality over the past decades. Drawing on ancient witchcraft or Wicca traditions, women have found a way of unifying and gathering spiritual power—energy from natural and relational sources as an alternative to the authoritarian patriarchal religious practices still dominant in world religions of our time.

Today, these healing circles can also be used to create "sacred space," to meditate together, and to create life rituals to celebrate birth, commemorate death, and every aspect in between—transitions of life, such as birthing, coming of age, divorce, illness, and surgery. They serve as a framework for honoring the forces of nature and the many levels of being.

The family itself can be considered a circle or a family *sangha*. Moments or times of grief may allow already existing groups, such as a family, to transform into Circles of Compassion. It is helpful for a family to have a place in the house to gather in this way; to sit together in silence, and then to talk mindfully about challenges that may arise, such as critical events or transitions and important individual or family decisions.

## Contemporary Circles

### AA and 12-Step Groups

There is a modern corollary to the story of Yasodhara and Pajapati: the creative and momentous response to the suffering of alcoholism and addiction that arose out of the meeting between Bill Wilson and Dr. Bob Smith on Mother's Day in 1935.[3] This was the birth of what has become one of the most significant and remarkable spiritual programs and communities in the world. It is a program without hierarchy; and it is based on circles, or group meetings. Each individual group is autonomous and completely supported by contributions and donations of its members, but is also part of a vital worldwide community.

In 1935, after a series of remarkable events, either by chance or by karma, Bill Wilson, a stockbroker from New York and a terrible drunk who, after a "flash" of insight had been "white-knuckle sober" for five months, finds himself alone in a hotel in Akron, Ohio, after a business deal had crashed—close to taking a drink. He has the remarkable realization at that moment that the only thing that can keep a drunk sober is to tell his story, truthfully, to another drunk: "I knew I needed another drunk to talk to, just as much as he needed me."[4]

Instead of picking up a drink, he picked up the phone and made ten calls. Finally, he connected with Henrietta Sieberling, a prominent woman in Akron who had been trying to help Dr. Bob Smith, a surgeon with a terrible drinking problem, to get sober. When she brought the two men together, Dr. Bob—seriously hungover—said to Bill, "I'll give you fifteen minutes—fifteen minutes, tops!"[5] They talked together for six hours, and came to see and understand their lifesaving connection, and AA was born.

What happened in that first meeting? The very same thing that, more than eighty years later, happens many thousands of times every day all over the world: when in the circle or the "fellowship" of AA, suffering meets compassion. And wisdom arises—for wisdom is the spiritual fruit of a Circle of Compassion. In AA this is now available in the "12 Steps of Recovery."

Dr. Bob intuitively understood that to stay sober, the two of them had to "pass it on to a third person." If this healing energy could be passed on to others, they could create a program (or "circle") that could be replicated and sustain itself regardless of individual personalities. Each new meeting was open to anyone who, in their words, "had the desire to stop drinking and was willing to ask for help."[6] The insight from the very beginning was that the more members and then the more groups, the greater would be the healing power of this anonymous program. And as the founders put it, "You only get to keep what you give away. Our service keeps us sober."[7] That is, in the *service* you do for others in the circle, you stay sober. The wisdom of the circle is the clear recognition, in the disease of addiction, of the danger of isolation and the healing (often lifesaving) power of authentic connection in a sustainable spiritual community.

Like Pajapati and Yasodhara, these two men set in motion a relational formation and healing practice that can accomplish together what an individual alone cannot. Two clear examples of extraordinary individuals on their solo paths who have created disciples and *sanghas*, of course, are the Buddha and Jesus. What Bill and Bob discovered is a different path through the "and" of their mutual relation.

There's no great and heroic "One" at the top; the awakened being is the relation, the awakening "We"—the Fellowship itself.

Twelve-step meetings of all kinds are found all over the world—hundreds of thousands of meetings a week (50,000 in the New York City area alone). Members continue to break through the prison walls of self-will run riot—out of the bondage of self—and into authentic connection by "coming clean" about their lives and their suffering. These are the practices:

1. The gathering, the group coming together, forming a circle here called "the fellowship" or "the meeting" or "the group"; the meeting is in real time—the present moment—and is also repeated over time, daily or weekly.
2. As you step into and speak in the circle, you break the barriers of social convention and self-deception, learning the practice of authenticity and deep listening ("Identify, don't compare"). An honest sharing, telling your story, speaking the truth as it comes alive in the moment.

Like the Quakers, who find the spirit present "when two or more are gathered in stillness," AA groups are guided by "group conscience"—a wisdom that emerges in the circle practice of the spiritual path of the 12 Steps. The energy of "joining," of coming into right relation, releases an energy that is often experienced or named as "spirit."

Some religions promise heaven; AA promises release from hell.

It also promises an opportunity to find the steps on this wisdom path to a way of life based on ethical and spiritual principles and practices.

It's only by continuing to remember "I am an alcoholic," and by asking and receiving help that one remains in recovery, in sobriety. Sobriety is defined as not drinking, but it also refers to the spiritual state generated and sustained in the circle. It is only realized "one day at a time," contingent on daily practice of the 12 Steps and "right relation" with the fellowship of AA. It is suggested that members in the morning "ask for help for one day of sobriety," and at night "offer gratitude for a day of sobriety."

Bill Wilson, a Christian, was well-read in many religious traditions, among them Buddhism. The 12 Steps of AA are a *spiritual* path—a fellowship of *spiritual community* or circle. The 12th Step says: "Having had a spiritual awakening as a result of these Steps, we tried to carry this message to those who still suffer." This assures that the "hand of AA will be available always to reach out to those who still suffer—to meet suffering with compassion. It is a holistic program, as the disease of alcoholism has three aspects—physical, psychological, and spiritual—and must be addressed in all three aspects.

Prolonged isolation from this group energy and practice is seen to set the individual back into the limited and delusional, self-centered thought and action of the alcoholic—the unaided, disconnected, isolated self. Long-term sobriety depends on maintaining this "fit spiritual condition" of connection and full participation in the fellowship. Practicing such connection on a regular basis becomes the foundation for asking for help when conditions become dire or begin to trigger the addiction vortex.

## Grief Circles

There is a contemporary movement in mental health hospitals and community centers to create circles or groups for those dealing with sudden or traumatic loss. Some have lost a baby or child suddenly, to violence, illness, or suicide. Others have lost loved ones gradually with lingering illness or injury. Many have been helped through the long sorrow of a chronically suffering loved one—parent, partner, or friend. The hospice movement is available almost everywhere today, to support the dying and their families.

The grief circle is one that, again, weaves each of the separate, unbearable journeys into a tapestry of the basic human experience of vulnerability, of horrific and traumatic loss. The power of facing the unbearable and unspeakable together reassures each person of being part of something greater than the prison of their own pain. As acceptance and humility grow over time, healing can occur. In the grief circle there is a time and a place for the depth of experience to be spoken and held, with no rules about doing it in the right way, or to "get over it already." It takes as long as it takes, sometimes a lifetime.

This echoes the Buddha's story of the Mustard Seed as well as what Yasodhara experiences once she joins the circle as a member, hearing and sharing the details of the individual stories of others. She comes to appreciate the uniqueness of each, and at the same time finds some underlying current of what is common, beyond all differences. In this case, what feels like the extraordinary becomes ordinary. And the ordinary extraordinary. Members begin to feel that they "belong," no longer alone, apart, isolated; and no longer "strange" or "weird," or beyond the pale of the human.

Emotional isolation or lack of connection during the grieving process has devastating consequences. It is known today to be a source of illness: high blood pressure, chronic depression, substance abuse, and cardiac problems. Psychologists point to our "cultural intolerance" of painful emotions, especially for men, which are necessary to experience for healing from traumatic loss.[8]

The growing new field of social neuroscience reflects increasing attention to the investigation of the effects of social isolation on morbidity and mortality rates in medical illnesses as diverse as cancer, cardiovascular and autoimmune disease, and many other syndromes.[9] Social/emotional connections mediate the effect of stress across the entire life span. Perceived isolation or loneliness has been shown to be a risk factor for hypertension, slower wound healing and poor sleep efficiency, while social connectedness is correlated with lower levels of autonomic activity (such as lower blood pressure), better immuno-surveillance, and lower basal levels of stress hormones.

The power of grief and healing circles in providing such mind-body "connection" has just begun to be recognized and is not yet fully understood, nor optimally utilized. It is quite likely that, looking back on this nascent exploration of the healing power of connection on the immune system, we may currently be glimpsing only the tip of the iceberg of the healing that can manifest out of profound spiritual connection.

## Ripe Moments: John's Story[10]

John had lived with and cared for his wife Kelly for almost eighteen years after her first diagnosis of breast cancer, following the birth of their second child. After a remission lasting five years, Kelly had a recurrence, which soon metastasized to her bones, and then to her brain. Against all odds, after being given a two-year survival date, she lived an additional thirteen years—saw her son graduate from high school and her daughter graduate from college—but died almost immediately after these events. The cancer hospital suggested that John meet with the social worker for grief counseling, which he did for about a month. He thought this was helpful, and she suggested joining a group of men and women who had lost spouses to cancer in the prime of their lives. As a man—a high-powered, successful CEO—he felt initially less able to be open and expressive of feelings, but quickly found the atmosphere safe and warm enough to be able to show his grief and to cry for the first time with others.

"Again and again, when people told the stories of their loss, my own feelings resonated with theirs. I learned to be able to be with the others and my own feelings at the same time—something I'd never ever experienced before. The culture wants you to be functionally 'normal' as quickly as possible, and people say the most offensive things, like 'she's in a better place now' (that's not easy for an agnostic like me!) or voicing their assurance that 'I' would 'get back to normal soon.'"

In the group, John was able to share the unexpected moments of profound grief that erupted sometimes out of nowhere and the annoyances about the absurd things people said to him—and how enraged this made him. He shared his experiences with people on the outside not knowing what to say, creating awkward silences so that he would then feel that he had to take care of them. These experiences were shared by all the group's participants and they could laugh together about them. The comic moments in the face of the horror of the whole dying process—all the medical and care details they shared and found to be in common—turned out to be okay, even healing.

Talking about things that had never been able to be verbalized—the burdens of keeping honest feelings from spouses and family, and now sharing this with the group, was profoundly helpful. John went on, "The circle transformed the idea of time—not to 'before' and 'after'—but to trusting the process: not trying to rush it or slow it down, just letting it be as it was, following along organically. For me the kinds of experiences I had through the dying process and afterward, when juxtaposed with my perception of what was normal, left me really worrying: am I crazy? Am I sane? The emotional rollercoaster—I'd burst out crying and have to walk out of business meetings or family gatherings—the intensity and, at times, the numbness and paralysis left me worrying about whether I was still sane."

He considered this: "What I found out from the group—and all of us found out—was that healing wasn't linear, it was more like a spiral; and it wasn't about each of us alone but was part of the normal human experience in extremis that we were sharing. It was a huge relief. It wasn't only about me; it was about my being human. Rather than feeling alone, I opened up to new possibilities for relationship I'd never imagined before."

## Facing-Cancer Groups

The healing in the medical-diagnosis groups is not just psychological or psychospiritual, it is also physical, as there is no body-mind split. There are healing or "medical" effects of the power of the circle, and medical outcomes that impact mortality and morbidity. As Dr. Amy Banks, a noted psychopharmacologist from Boston and a pioneer in the field of "relational neuroscience," put it: "If the power of connection and relationship could be bottled or made into a pill, the pharmaceutical company that did so would become the richest in the world."[11]

In one leading cancer center, people diagnosed and dealing with cancer can join a cancer support group for those first getting the diagnosis and dealing with the shock, disbelief, fear, and stigma. The circles emphasize learning about the disease, treatment, and resources. The goal is helping to make one's way through the maze of early medical treatment, and getting a treatment plan established.

Those who feel that the depth of their experience is not being held in monthly groups, can join an ongoing "facing-cancer group." Members are men and women with every kind of cancer diagnosis, at all stages. The groups may go on for years, and some of the original members may no longer be alive. One member told us that he had lived through twenty-one deaths in his group over eight years. There are other long-term survivors still in the group, who continue to feel that this group has been the most powerful and transforming experience of their lives—perhaps a key to their survival.

## Ripe Moments: Martha's Story[12]

Martha, a fifty-four-year-old mother of two who worked in the film industry, was diagnosed with stage-one breast cancer. Her psychotherapist referred her to a local wellness center, and she joined a breast cancer support group.

Martha's decision to have a double mastectomy—because her mother had died of breast cancer and her father had died of lung cancer—was a positive prevention step for her but still an extremely traumatic physical loss. She felt the depth of her experience was not being held in the monthly group, and found her way into an ongoing facing-cancer group. The group had already been meeting for five years, and only two of the original members were still in the group. The leader was a cancer survivor herself. Martha came to feel that this group was transformative for her.

"The level of honesty and intimacy was stunning—the commitment to *being with* each other's suffering. The intimacy—talking about body parts and losses and disfigurations, how the cancer impacted our relationships and sexuality, how we felt marginalized in the culture, and how we were facing metastasis, recurrence, and death. For me," she said, "it was also facing survivorship and understanding my survivor's guilt. In the circle, this guilt turned to profound gratitude for life and a desire to help others. Speaking in the group was like a call and response—sharing the suffering in the face of understanding, compassion, and a growing faith that empowerment was possible at every stage and level of illness."

For Martha, the facing-cancer group helped her face her fears, making them less overwhelming and hindering. "My fears actually got much more concrete and articulated in the group. I was terrified of metastasis, yet here was another person who had metastatic cancer and she was someone I deeply care about and love. We were standing with her in the experience. This made it all much less terrifying to me. . . . I saw that the group experience empowered me to speak out in other situations without shame about having cancer and to speak to the power of the shared journey and the possibilities of the human spirit in facing suffering. I survived and left the group after seven years. I now call myself a 'cancer warrior' in the world."

The highlights of this healing circle are many. Even through members dying, the power of the group was sustained. After the leader died, another staff person took her place and the group continued. One of the qualities of a healing circle is that it can sustain itself through and beyond individual sufferings, and may survive beyond individual deaths. What was remarkable about this facing-cancer group was that it held each participant in the circle through the progression of the disease, from early diagnosis and treatment to recurrence and death. The whole life cycle of *being with* this disease was represented and recalled realistically by all, so that the nameless fears, the sense of doom, the terror of suffering and of death was held in the group. To encompass these truths, the group reached a depth and dimension some would describe as deeply sacred and fundamental to the human spirit.

## Circles of Spiritual Awakening

Circles have the potential to touch this transformative, transitional space. Between ordinary space and time and ways of being, the circle is a vessel for what we have come to name as *spiritual*. What do we mean by spiritual? For some it is about union or communion with Love, Truth, God, or some other conception of a power greater than the self—the spirit of the universe, universal consciousness, awareness, or the whole of nature itself.

When you step into a spiritual circle, you access a sacred space and receive gifts from the natural world, all that lives, breathes, loves, sings—the unending harmony of being. This may be a powerful force, a subtle energy, or an array of gateways between worlds seen and unseen. The natural energies of life come forth. Yasodhara's circle was on the ground—literally touching the earth—containing wind, fire, water, and the deep green of the ancient trees reaching high into the air. The humans of her time and of all ages have reached out in sorrow and called forth the elements of nature, focusing and saturating the natural energy for the humans gathered there. It's not that you lose yourself, rather *you gain access to a full realization of who and what you and we really are*. You realize what Thich Nhat Hanh calls "interbeing," the interconnectedness of all beings, and the power which flows from that. This is not only spiritual realization but that which gives energy to move into right action in the world—to join with and help others. (We will return to spiritual circles and contemporary examples of these communities in chapter 7.)

## Qualities of a Healing Circle, or *Sangha*

It is an ancient relational formation with no beginning or endpoint.

- Each point on the circle is equidistant from and held together by the center.
- Each person can be seen by all others—on the same level on the ground; there is no hierarchy and no one is "above" another.
- The circle can always enlarge and become more inclusive.
- It becomes a container, and when the circle is dispersed, the individuals who emerge are touched and changed—the group energy now resides in each person.
- Each person contributes to the circle and helps magnify the strength of the whole. Each person draws on all the power, wisdom, compassion, and healing provided by the circle. With this, the circle is transformed into a sacred space.
- It is predictable and ongoing, and can open to add new members or to lose members, enduring because it is greater than any one person. It has a shape, a form, and a momentum of its own. While it doesn't depend on particular individuals, each member is equally important.
- Through the coming together in ordinary time there's a touching of a new sense of timelessness and spaciousness. The Australian aborigines call this "the Dreamtime:" everything of the natural and spiritual world is a source that actualizes collective healing. At the same time the circle "grounds" and "settles" the members.

- Mutuality is fundamental. There is an equality of members, everyone is giving and receiving as the need arises. There is room for all. No one is an insider or an outsider.
- Ritual for morning and evening circles. Ritual relies on a shared intention, of agreements between members to practice together. Morning prayers—sharing the intention for the day; evening thanks—sharing the gratitude for the day.
- Speaking and listening become spiritual practices that need cultivation, awareness, and care. The ritual becomes a spiritual practice, as all learn how to listen and respond—to call forth by deep listening and then to respond in careful speech, in kind. A time and place of refuge, it reliably transforms everyday social conversation—news and gossip and jokes and banter—to the expression of essential, core experience. It relies on the great human gift of voice to transmit our experience person to person in the ripe field of compassion. This is the essence of healing, both for the group and for the individual. As each person speaks, you can almost see the light pouring toward that person; and their voices speaking the truth into the compassionate listening radiates to the others, then back to the speaker. This is true mutuality: the relational principle of listening and speaking as spiritual practice co-arises with each other. We hear each other in speech, and speaking truth opens the being of the listener; there is profound receptivity and resonance.

As anyone who has participated in a healing circle knows, when we step into the circle and practice in this way, we come to realize who and how we truly are. This is our "Yasodhara/Pajapati/Mustard-Seed Nature." This is also called our "Buddha Nature," Thich Nhat Hanh's "interbeing," or the "Net of Indra"—the ancient Hindu metaphor where each being is a jewel reflecting all others—a realization and experience of "interconnectiveness" as separation and isolation melt away. There is a basic sense of breaking out of isolation into the unseen but immediately recognized truth of interbeing. There's an energy released which is available to all when we step into alignment with our true nature in Right Relation and Community.[13]

## CREATING RIPE MOMENTS: REFLECTIONS AND PRACTICES

### Finding a Circle of Compassion and Healing

All of us, at different times in our lives, could benefit from participating in a healing circle. Sometimes the need is urgent and desperate, and moves us beyond our typical "automatic" habits that may preclude seeking help, companionship, and spiritual empowerment. Sometimes the need is not so acute, and it may be harder to be open, and yet a healing circle may well help.

#### 1. Reflections for Writing and Group Sharing

To be written and shared within your circle, spiritual community, or Family *Sangha*.

- When experiencing something difficult or challenging in your life, have you asked the question: *How would it help me to find a circle of people focused on the same or similar issue?* Has this been part of your life experience?
- Is there something in your life right now that would benefit from your participation in a circle?
- If you have sought and not found one, can you imagine creating one?

- What steps could you take in your relationships, family, or communities?

## 2. Individual Meditation Practice

- Find and create a meditation space in your home or office. Sitting on a chair or cushion, imagine a circle of loved ones around you—alive or not—including parents, grandparents, influential teachers, friends, pets, and important symbols of nature. Let these surround you in compassionate love, and support your awakening.
- Practice entering this circle and, breathing in, draw on the love and energy. Breathing out, contribute your love and care to the whole. Notice any resistance, and let it melt away for these few moments.
- Breathe in this way for 5 to 20 minutes. End the practice with a silent offering of gratitude.
- If it is possible, create an actual circle around your chair or cushion, or an altar of photos or elements of nature or any symbols of what you want to include in your circle practice.

## 3. Relational Meditation Practice

- Sit in meditation with others in a circle, eyes open or closed. This can be the meeting place of the family *sangha*. In silence, practice opening to the circle, allowing yourself to feel connected, part of, belonging to, totally open to being loved, illuminated, and empowered. Allow the "boundaries" to become fluid and try allowing the circle to become your collective "body." As any feelings, thoughts, distractions, or resistances to the practice occur, simply notice, and then bring care and compassion to these obstacles. In this way, the resistance can be a source of energy or suffering that can also be included in the circle. It allows you to be more fully connected.

- Practice in silence for 5 to 10 minutes, alternating between awareness of your own body, the collective body, and even the larger circle of all beings within which this circle exists.
- Speak truthfully and listen deeply. Each person in turn (2 minutes each) can share something of this experience to the group. Notice the quality of sharing and listening that enlivens, that breathes spirit and energy into the circle.

## Call Forth Community

Real communities and possible connections are all around you, at many different levels. You may need to call them forth to respond to particular suffering, to organize a community of compassionate action around ones in need. This might involve helping to organize a community of support around a friend in the midst of chemotherapy or after the death of a family member. It might involve finding a way to provide food and clothing to a community devastated by a national disaster. Realize that what you are doing is an act of faith in the power of interconnectedness, and turning *toward* the great compassion and wisdom of the community.

## 1. Reflections for Writing and Group Sharing

- Have I participated in mobilizing a community around someone or ones who suffer?
- Have I been able to participate as fully as possible in such a community or have I turned away?
- How might I have been a more dedicated member of a significant community in my life?
- What in the past or present holds me back from service?

- What would help me to move into action? What commitment can I make?

## 2. Individual Visualization Practice

- In your mind's eye evoke Kwan Yin, a goddess with a hundred arms and an eye in the palm of each hand. Imagine yourself god- or goddess-like with a hundred arms. Breathe deeply into this image. Allow yourself to experience the strength and power of the image in your body. (3–5 minutes)
- Feel the presence of the hundred arms and hands working with you. Let the image be one of power, harmony, and bright compassion; breathe deeply into this image. Think of a person you would like to show up for in your life, and imagine offering your hands of compassionate service as part of the hundred to that person or persons or community. (3–5 minutes)

## 3. Relational Meditation Practice

- Try His Holiness the Dalai Lama's "Smiling Practice: Creating Community with a Simple Smile": In any circle or group, simply ask each person to smile at all the others (in no specific order) and to simply receive the smile. Notice how the quality of connection in community changes with this simple practice. (5 minutes)
- In dyads, with eyes closed and then open, meditate on *being with* each other, held by the larger circle. Meditate on the circle as a community aligned in purpose, for service. (3–5 minutes)
- Each person, in turn, shares their experience of these practices, speaking carefully and mindfully, and listening deeply. (3–5 minutes)

# Part II

# The Path of Devotion: Accompanying Others through the Circle of Life

*There can never be deep peace between two spirits, never mutual respect, until, in their dialogue, each stands for the whole world.*

—**Ralph Waldo Emerson**

*Every aspect of human life, as well as the life of every species and ecosystem on Earth, is composed of interactive, organic relationships, which are always changing creatively and are alive with responsiveness. It is not merely a matter of having relationships but being relationships. As the interactive relationships that constitute the world respond to what is happening from moment-to-moment, a dynamic state of emergence brings into being new patterns. This is the relational reality in and around us. Nothing in the entire universe is completely static or exists outside of this vast web of creative, responsive relationship.*

—**Charlene Spretnak**, *Relational Reality*

# 3

# BIRTHING AND NURTURING THE NEW

> Accompanied by the circle of women—mothers, grandmothers, sisters, and friends—Yasodhara began to turn fully toward her baby and to "come forth" as a mother.
>
> —Chapter 12, "Yasodhara's Story"

Yasodhara's story is one of joy and great suffering. Through the birth of her child and her husband leaving, with the accompaniment of Pajapati and her circle of women, Yasodhara experiences what, in the Buddhist tradition, are called life's "ten thousand joys and ten thousand sorrows." Her Path of Right Relation takes her on the journey of accompanying others through the circle of life, from birth to death. This chapter focuses on the first arc of this path: the experience of birth and parenting—the *being with* new life arising. In this way, her story is every mother's story; the experiences of birth and nurturing new life are, at heart, basic human stories of joy and sorrow. Almost everyone, whether a parent or not, has experience working as an educator, a healer, a nurse, a caregiver, or a therapist, supporting the growth and healing of others.

Siddhartha's birth story reflects the pairing of birth and loss, as his biological mother, Maya, died seven days after his birth. His father, the king, turned the newborn Siddhartha over to Pajapati, Maya's sister, to raise him as her own. So, in his story as well, birth and death, joy and sorrow are linked.

It is part of the human experience to have suffering along with joy. When the suffering is denied or bypassed, the potential for true spiritual growth is lost—and more suffering occurs, and often leads to isolation and depression. The cultural idea that you are "supposed" to be only happy, positive, and optimistic, especially as new parents, can become a burden—and then the burden itself may be denied. When suffering cannot be shared in relationship, it leads to isolation from authentic connection and may lead to further withdrawal. Extreme isolation for new parents can have terrible outcomes: domestic abuse, child abuse, divorce, and even suicide. There is perhaps no more intense time of life when extreme joy and extreme suffering coexist than in early parenting. So many young mothers and fathers feel guilt and personal insufficiency when they experience the exhaustion, overwhelming demands, and doubt about their own competencies, so natural at the beginning. Parenting is a steep learning curve, and shame and doubt may keep new parents from reaching out and asking for the help they need.

In the understanding of impermanence there is, always, in the arising, the passing away. As Thich Nhat Hanh puts it, "in the flower is the compost, and in the compost is the flower."[1] In the beginning is the end; in birth, there is death. In the circle of life, there is always the birth of the new in the death of the old, and the death of the old in the birth of the new; they "inter-are." It can be as simple as the realization that the baby is a part of a new generation that will, if all goes well, outlive you. And as you are with this baby from the first moment of life, if you are fortunate, this baby will be with you—perhaps at your bedside—at the end of your life.

This circle of life is inherently relational; it is not about individuals alone.

The hope for the redemption of suffering in a new baby may lead us to deny our own and then the actual sufferings of the child. What we want most is to prevent and to protect our child from all suffering. Of course, this is impossible. This is the first *koan* of parenthood. We want to shield our child from all suffering, and we know we cannot. One of the important tasks of parents is to learn to *be with* the suffering of the child—to help them learn that this, too, is a part of life and can be shared. Siddhartha's father tried to keep his son in a bubble of comfort and pleasure to prevent him from feeling and witnessing suffering. The effect was that, when he saw it, it became the center of his life's mission to understand and help to liberate himself and others. Most parents learn this lesson eventually, but it is a hard one to accept. Like Siddhartha's father, we see what contemporary writers describe as "helicopter" parents, who hover and protect their children from suffering or any personal challenge that may seem risky or potentially moving them "off track." In our time, there is a cultural ideology of splitting off birth and early childhood as joyful times, and old age and death as sorrowful; while in fact, joy and sorrow always arise together in the natural order.

*Being with* suffering in the child is one of the most challenging aspects of parenting, as is helping children to be with their own suffering and with others', in growth-fostering ways. The focus of Yasodhara's story is the ordinary relational Path of She Who Stays, who participates in the growth and new arising of life in the child. She makes the commitment to stay and come face to face with her suffering for the sake of her son. She is called forth in meeting and *growing with* her child. After the loss of her husband, Yasodhara struggles to "stay present" in the face of grief and isolation, but with others—Pajapati and the circle of women—she begins to turn toward life and toward her child, to make the commitment to be there for Rahula. Despite—or perhaps because of—her suffering, she intuitively takes this vow:

> This became her sacred work—struggling to not let her own grief and anger get in the way of mothering this precious being. Yasodhara made a vow to stay alive, vitally alive and present and responsible, for her son and to her son—*no matter what*. (Chapter 12, page 41)

This ordinary pathway, as old as humanity itself and as essential for the continuation of human life, has extraordinary potential for the birth of the spirit.

When this pathway is honored and illuminated in all its complexity, beauty, and staying power, its potential for real awakening can be realized. It's a path that starts with a particular person in ordinary life, but through the community of others, the path can open to a wiser way of living, with greater compassion for all of life and deep appreciation of the universality of human suffering. Without a spiritual community, suffering can lead to greater isolation and self-centered despair, or perhaps a search for others to blame: "How could this happen to *me*?" "Who is to blame?"

## The Path of Devotion

For Yasodhara on the ordinary Path of She Who Stays, these are the conditions for the extraordinary to occur:

- Devotion reflects an ardent dedication or loyalty, a commitment or vow. In Yasodhara's case, to be with others as a beneficial presence. This devotion has a dimension of reverence. This devotional path is not just to serve great teachers or gurus, but ordinary human beings. A parent's vow to lifelong devotion—to meet their children at an appropriate level of care to the best of one's ability for the whole of life—is a mighty life commitment. It is often hidden, invisible, and unnamed. This vow can be made fully intentional and witnessed by the family and community. It can become a spiritual vow and a foundation for growth through intentional spiritual practice.

- Clarity about the beauty of the intention must also include recognition that repeated practice and progress is necessary, and at the times when it seems very difficult, it is not a sign of failure. In a sense, we always fail, but failure can be a signpost to asking for help, learning, and refining your practice.
- The commitment or vow to *being with* these particular others involves showing up through joy and sorrow, recognizing and supporting the coming forth of their unique particularity.
- The devotion to the particular other(s) opens the doorway to the greater community who share this practice.
- This can occur most likely when there is a spiritual path, as well as a compassionate community to support this practice.
- Economic resources and privilege are helpful but by no means sufficient. At times, they can become obstacles. The devotional path might not open even if you are a prince or princess but might open up in refugee camps, where a fierce mother, grateful for food, clothing, safety, and shelter, finds a person or a community. If they create a Circle of Compassion, they may not only endure but prevail together.

## The Relational Practice of Parenting

As the voices of mothers have begun to be more represented in literature, mothering is being seen not simply as instinctual nurturance but as an elegant, intelligent, and evolving relational practice. The philosopher Sarah Ruddick describes the complexity of maternal thought, which leads to maternal "praxis" or practice.[2] As fathers fully join in this work, it can then be called "the relational practice of parenting." Parental thought and relational practice is three-fold in intention:

1. To preserve and protect life
2. To develop individual strengths and gifts
3. To socialize the child within culture standards

These often present conflicting and challenging choices, which may require balancing over time. Making choices with an awareness of the inherent contradictions can be a helpful framework for the complexity of parenting. Very often these conflicts and choices remain obscure, unnamed, leaving parents feeling less clarity and strength in their decision-making. Clarifying the role of relational "practice not perfection" is useful, and parent groups can be very helpful in supporting this.

When these contradictory practices are not clarified, parents—especially mothers—can begin to feel inadequate, insufficient, and even harmful. The ideology of "mother blaming" has been prevalent over the last century in America. It is often mothers who have internalized the image of "bad mother." This leads to overt or subtle self-blaming by mothers themselves as well as their children, teachers, other professionals, and, sadly, even other mothers. Rather than recognizing the absence of a community of care and shared purpose in supporting childcare, mothers feel a pervasive sense of personal limitation and insufficiency.

Dr. Jean Baker Miller in 1990 suggested that we declare a moratorium on mother-blaming, in order to be more creative and thoughtful in our clinical formulations and psychotherapy.[3] Decades later, the challenge is as fresh and the need is as great. Images of "good" and "bad" mothers still abound in therapy, in the media, and in the culture as a whole. Recently the challenges of being a "good mother" have been relabeled with armies of "tiger moms" and "helicopter moms"—new labels and descriptions seem to arise in every generation. Ironically, these "supermom" labels distort the *real* strengths and capacities of mothers as real allies and advocates in partnership with their children, over life.

This is true for fathers as well. The antidote to mother-blaming is not father-blaming.

These formulations draw attention away from the cultural and contextual sources, and place all responsibility for suffering on the nuclear family. Dr. Miller, in her 1978 book *Toward a New Psychology of Women*, described the actual relational practice of mothering in a new way. There is a condition of "temporary inequality," where the more powerful person (mother or father) uses her or his power to enhance the power of the other (child). The overall direction of growth, then, is toward "full mutuality and not separation."[4]

Relational-cultural theory supports the idea that helping the child toward adulthood *does not* involve a break in relationship. Rather it involves the movement toward greater authenticity, and *the possibility of more, and even more fully mutual, relationship*.

This relational practice is fundamental and applicable to all forms of nurturing and devotional practices for parents, teachers, healers, and mental health professionals. This is the model of building shared power, or *power with*. The intention is toward right relation: mutuality, partnership, and the creation of a stronger relationship, growth into connection. This model is a healthy alternative to the dominant-power model in our world today, *power over*. This power-over model has been used to characterize traditional father-son relationships. Freud imagined in his "Oedipus Complex" how initially the father overpowers the son, and then the son retaliates as an adult by overpowering that father and gaining power over others as well. The ideology of power over—dominance and hierarchy—is still firmly entrenched domestically and globally, and underlies many of our political as well as corporate models of hierarchy, with one strong president or CEO "on top." Mutuality or partnership models are healthier, more sustainable, and ultimately, more powerful. But they are a threat to the dominant group in control of virtually all our political and cultural institutions. "Power over" causes "blowback"—at worst the unrest, terrorism, and violence of the disempowered person or group. Alternatively, the collective power of nondominant or so-called "minority" groups can be an untapped resource for change to this model of shared power, arising from the spiritual and transformative power of shared suffering.

In the power-over model, power is conceived as "being in a person" ("Hillary Clinton is a powerful woman") or their network ("Henry Kissinger has a powerful network"). The relational model is a *power with* model, suggesting something more akin to what actually can happen, at best: when two or more people meet in right relation, the *power arises in the connecting. Both or all people feel more empowered.* This is the power of the circle and is at the heart of the power with, or *power together*, path.

Riane Eisler in *The Chalice and the Blade* has traced the roots of what she has named the "partnership model"—early pre-patriarchal religious traditions of "the Sacred Feminine." Her partnership model also describes this remarkable shared power of cooperative action of the collective. This power arises out of the deeply shared intention and values.

Jean Baker Miller has described how one interacts with another so as to foster their development or to increase the power of the other and, ultimately, to build mutual relationships. Meeting the new leads to mutual growth: as the child grows, the mother (or father) grows, and vice versa. The ongoing birth of the mother (or father) occurs when the growth of new life is fully met, moment-to-moment, throughout life.

In the *spiritual* dimension, the joy of living into the "new" creates an energy available to all. This is almost always experienced by parents when a miracle happens with their child—when the child somehow or other suddenly begins to walk! How did this happen? Times of birth and growth bring us close to the "miracle of life," the mystery of the unknown inspires all wonder and gratitude. These experiences take us through the door of the ordinary to the appreciation of the sacred dimension of life. A spiritual path in community creates the ripe conditions for this naturally occurring joy and appreciation to be sustained and cultivated more consistently.

The growth of the child fuels the growth of the parents and vice versa. Spiritually, at the same time that there is a deepening of mutual growth, there's an increasing awareness of the practice of letting go. Each creative moment is fluid, and requires the devotion of both "staying" and "holding" the relationship, as well as releasing and "letting go." This is the spiritual Path of She Who Stays, who nurtures life in its arising, and lets go in its passing.

This is the second *koan* of parenting as a spiritual-relational practice: "the holding and releasing occur together in a moment, co-arising, moment-to-moment, through the whole of life."

## Exceptional Mothering

Suffering cannot be denied, but has to be woven skillfully into the fabric of both joy and sorrow. Vicky's story exemplifies this challenge. She gave birth to twins, a boy and a girl. The girl died shortly after birth, and the boy twin was totally healthy. The capacity to hold both the joy and the suffering is challenging. Like Yasodhara, Vicki had to lean into the joy, and at the same time, live with the loss; she had to stay present with the child who lived while mourning the child who died. Only in the Circle of Compassion can everything be held. This is the collective foundation for any one person trying to hold these seemingly impossible contradictions. It is a complexity at the heart of life, one of the great tasks to embrace.

This is the third *koan* of parenting: "to become a parent is to have your heart walking around outside your body."

There is perhaps no greater insecurity or experience of lack of control than in the most important relationships in life. The death of a child changes life forever.

There is a saying, often spoken by those who have come through difficult times: "Whatever doesn't kill you makes you stronger." In fact, suffering does "kill" some people, yet also makes others stronger. It's not an either/or, all or nothing. Parents come to realize this and are often balancing on the razor edge of being overwhelmed and/or strengthened by the challenges of parenting—feeling completely vulnerable and powerless over their children's lives, illnesses, and deaths.

A wise mother said: "You never get over a child's death; you just begin to live a new life that encompasses this reality."

Many mothers and fathers who have traveled a difficult road with their children over a long period of time—perhaps due to a severe illness or disability—say, "It's the worst thing that ever happened, but—and I never thought I would say this—it's turned out to be the most important thing in my life." How many times have we heard that?! It is the best testimony to the empowerment and spiritual growth that can come from facing into the suffering together. In some cases, the child becomes the teacher in this devotional practice where the mutuality is so illuminated.

## Ripe Moments: Miriam's Story

Our friend Miriam had three children. Her first child had severe congenital medical problems and lingered in the hospital for two months before he finally died. The second child was perfectly healthy.[5]

The third was born with severe developmental disabilities, undiagnosable by teams of doctors over many years. Her symptoms were chronic hypotonia (low muscle tone), extreme vulnerabilities to repeated fractures and illnesses of all kinds, and major learning disabilities. Miriam and her husband Roger's devoted attention and sacrifice—physically, emotionally, and financially—took an enormous toll on their family life.

There's no romance in living such a marginalized life, advocating every day for a child who is so different. On the other hand, their experience with this child has been deeply enriching. In Miriam's words:

> Esther herself is the best source of whatever courage and resistance I muster in the challenge of mothering her. She has taught me acceptance and gratitude for each moment in a way that has brought a very special kind of joy into my life. She has freed me from the shackles of a driven, achievement orientation . . . Esther teaches me the value of a life, a value that has nothing to do with what she can give me by way of reflecting back my own ego. I am rarely proud of her in the normal way in which people narcissistically take credit for their children's accomplishments. When she sings her heart out at a musical recital, it is not her near-perfect pitch that I take pride in. What I feel is a sense of gratitude for the amazing beauty of her spirit, and the way it comes through her in song, warming the hearts of those who hear. Everything Esther is she has made herself—against tremendous odds. It is not pride I feel, but genuine respect for who she is as a person. The flip side of Esther's special needs are her special gifts: open-hearted generosity of spirit, compassion, emotional wisdom, and joy in the midst of liberation and suffering. She is a continual source of delight and spiritual sustenance in my life. I am blessed to be her mother.[6]

## The Importance of Other Mothers

In our circle, I had other mothers and grandmothers and aunts and servants, and this *sangha* held me, and I them, on our path together.

> Walking a compassionate wisdom path together. This is what makes the ordinary extraordinary. (Chapter 15, page 49)

Psychologist Shelly Taylor and others have described an alternative survival strategy or response to stress for women. They have shown that instead of the "fight or flight" response more typical of men, women show a "tend and befriend" response to stress (perhaps under the influence of oxytocin).[7] This caring-and-befriending response is more likely to insure survival of the young since it creates a shared community of care.

For Yasodhara to walk the spiritual path of devotion, she herself needs the accompaniment of others, especially other mothers and older mothers. The path of caring for children must be shared, not simply in the practical sense, ("It takes a village . . ."), but also in the spiritual sense—the sense of collective care and the creation of a loving circle around each mother and child. Contemporary grandparents often are central in creating this circle, holding both their adult children and grandchildren together at the center of their hearts and homes.

Sarah Hrdy, a social anthropologist, has suggested that in the biological evolution of the human species, the potential for collective and relational intelligence grew out of the necessity of shared childcare. The care and protection of children became the responsibility of the group of "other mothers together." This culture's overemphasis on the bond with one biological mother within the nuclear family is at odds with this optimal "shared" responsibility. In other cultural groups, greater collectivity is assumed by extended family: grandparents, aunts, sisters, and neighbors.[8]

Patricia Hill Collins writes about a language in the African American community for "blood mothers" and "other-mothers." In Latino culture, there are *madres de sangre* (blood mothers) and *madres de crianza* (childrearing mothers).[9] In these cultures, the necessity and value of other mothers is deeply held. In Western culture, there is perhaps no other time when the isolation within the nuclear family is more harmful than in early parenting. It is not only the overwhelming demands of childcare that lead to isolation but the overpowering sense of sole responsibility—the lack of psychological and spiritual supports. One young mother in a mothers' group described her yearning for other mothers and other families to share: "We desperately need each other—yet the lack of time, and my fear and shame in asking for help, [has] kept me silent and apart."[10]

This is a time when there is great need for the young parents to be cared for themselves. It is a difficult time to ask for help because one feels that one should already know these things; it is also hard to commit time to self-care and cultivating relationships. As Shem says in *The House of God*, in relation to the situation with doctors: "How can you care for others if no one cares for you?"[11] And yet, that is often the reality of the situation.

In our time, there are many ways to find a greater circle of other parents. Church and other religious groups, Buddhist *sanghas*, even social media offer many opportunities to join with others. Buddha Moms has appeared as a recent website, and many opportunities for mindful parenting groups have begun; it's still necessary for individual mothers to reach out and find others to create circles of care. Parents need to create communities with other families—children and parents together—to break down the isolation, and to provide the opportunity for special relationships to grow between children and other adults.

The optimal development of the circle of other mothers is a blessing for a child too—to have more than one mother. Author and psychoanalyst Clarissa Pinkola Estes: "You are born to one mother, and if you are lucky, you will have more than one; and among them, you will find most of what you really need."[12]

Pajapati is an adoptive mother or a *madre de crianza*, a childrearing mother. The assumption that the bond of a child with an adoptive mother is "less than" that of a biological child, or that adoption is always about "traumatic loss," permeates our culture. It challenges the real experience and strengths of mothers and children who deviate from the so-called "normal."

## Buddha Moms, Parenting as a Spiritual Path

> Yasodhara was sad but also flushed with delight—to have found a way to watch with her son the crucial people in his life as they moved around under his hands, the boy creating stories full of adventure and honor and anger and the cutting off of heads; him flying through the air like his hero, Lord Rama, The Blue-Skinned God, who ruled over the whole wide world! She had found a shared language between mother and child; and in it, she could listen and be with his suffering. It was being created between mother and son, a "Right Dialogue" for the two of them together that she could use to prepare him for Siddhartha's return. (Chapter 18, page 58)

Parents, teachers, and therapists can support the spiritual life of children. Children are often seen as "naturally awake," joyful, curious, and creative. Spiritual connection with children fosters spiritual awakening in both child and parent together. Walking in the natural world, imaginary play, and simple ordinary tasks of life can be transformed with mindfulness. Two wonderful resources for these practices are Susan Kaiser Greenland's *The Mindful Child* and Christopher Willard's *Child's Mind*.[13]

Never underestimate the joy, and never underestimate the suffering of this path of parenting. Even at the darkest time, the gift of desperation can ripen into a spiritual moment—even an awakening. The perils from the extreme conditions of intense suffering in relation to a child or others are often exacerbated by the relentless action of our minds in shame, doubt, and worry. We are often caught in the lure of imagining the future, the net of memory that pulls us away from the simplicity of the present moment with our child. Or we are swept up in the rush of feelings, trapped in fear or desire, held back from the creative practice of meeting the perils of suffering and even the joy. This is the essence of relational practice that can lead to awakening and transformation. You become more of who you are by fully meeting the new arising in the other. This is the heart of the relational practice of parenting. This is the creative energy of new beginnings.

## CREATING RIPE MOMENTS: REFLECTIONS AND PRACTICES

### 1. Reflections

Questions for individual writing and/or discussion in groups:

- What are your devotional vows and commitments, and to whom?
- Who has witnessed these, if anyone?
- If you're a parent, what are your strengths and weaknesses?
- Who has been there for you on your path of parenting?
- Do you have a community of other parents?
- What community do you need to find or develop to support your particular challenges?
- What would you wish for in the form of teacher, guide, mentor, community, practical support?
- Can you think of a moment or interaction in your own life as a parent that has transformed your perspective or energy—a moment of awakening?
- Who and what are you grateful for in this parenting practice? Write a "gratitude list."

## 2. Individual Meditation Practice

- *Being with* the arising of the new: sit in meditation or silence as you watch the sun rise, beginning the day. Observe all the energies of beginnings—the light, the form, the shadows, the colors, the movements of the sun rays rising; notice, too, these rays and the sense of their fading. Impermanence. (For the last "circle of life" chapter, "Staying With," we'll do the same with a sunset.)
- Every morning, at the beginning of your day, offer the following phrases of the heart to yourself and to your child. You may sit alone or hold your child as you meditate, or you may find your own phrases that best express your wishes.

    - "A lotus to you, a Buddha to be."
    - "May you live with joy; may your suffering be the fertile ground of awakening; may we be grateful for this day, for each other, for all the blessings of this life."
    - "May we and all beings be happy and joyful; may we and all beings be free from suffering; may we and all beings live in peace and harmony."

## 3. Relational Meditation Practice

- At any moment in the day, in the midst of any activity or interaction, pause to be with and simply remember to practice: "Pause, Relax, Open, Smile." Practice this with your child, your partner in parenting, to yourself, and to all parents everywhere. (See Insight Dialogue guidelines on page 136.)
- Extended Family *Sangha*: notice any opportunity for connection with other families and for growing an intentional extended family *sangha*. Make it part of your devotional prac-

tice to nurture the growth and sustenance of such communities/ *sanghas*.

- Invite another family to partner with yours in specific ways:

    - Be there for each other in emergencies, and make agreements to call on each other anytime, day or night, as needed.
    - Share a meal or an activity as families regularly, perhaps once a month.
    - Meet in circle together as adults, and include your children at an appropriate level of participation.

# 4

# The Flowering of Mutuality: Spiritual Friendships, Couples Partnerships

Spiritual friendship is the whole of the holy life.
—The Buddha, in Yasodhara's Story, Chapter 24

Yasodhara has a need for a special friend. Pajapati is a mother figure; and at first, in Yasodhara's intense grief, it is Pajapati who comes toward her. But as the meetings in the circle progress, and she starts to heal and sit with others, she finds Nayla, a special person—a spiritual sister around the same age whose baby had died.

Nayla is one who, because of class differences (a palace worker and a princess) Yasodhara would not ordinarily befriend. But grief may cut through the structures binding relationships in the palace by class. Listening to Nayla's story in the circle, Yasodhara approaches her and they begin to talk—the two of them connecting in the circle, then meeting outside. The particular shared details of their experience become the rich soil of their friendship. This is the start of a special, spiritual friendship between them, held in the larger circle.

Yasodhara's friendship with Channa is also remarkable—not only in terms of class but also gender. Even today, male-female and cross-class friendships can be difficult to maintain. Yasodhara and Channa share the bond of suffering around Siddhartha, and both are members of the circle *sangha*, a spiritual community.

Yasodhara and Nayla, and the others as well, apply the wisdom of the circle to their daily lives. The women's relational practice—as mothers, daughters, sisters, or friends—comes alive in the circle as a sustaining and developing daily practice of mutual awakening. Together, in special friendships, they face what the Buddha would come to call "the worldly winds" that toss and turn and twist each of their lives, finding similarities and differences—all strengthening their practice and path. The challenges of the day are shared and become opportunities for spiritual growth. Such friendships are the quintessence of mutual relational development and become illuminated through this sense of mutual recognition, and the alignment of spiritual intention and aspiration. Mutuality often flowers in midlife.

In spiritual friendship, we commit to the awakening of one's self, the other, and the relationship. It is a way of creating a vehicle for mutual awakening, grounded in intentional practice—steps taken through focused attention to the details, not only the great aspirations but the facts of daily life. This is the practice of seeing—and keeping—the particulars of this spiritual friendship as doorways opening to the whole. Sustaining such friendships challenge the social structures that work to separate us.

A metaphor for the relational path could be a garden. There is planting, nurturing, and cultivating in a garden; and the haphazard and the chance become part of the whole. Plants, like humans, bud, bloom, flower, fruit, and die. Each grows separately aboveground but roots intermingle and are mutually impacted. Sometimes, it is far easier for one friend to see deeply into the true nature of the other. Such friendship cuts through the limited self-images of each, the mental constructs we develop to see ourselves. Thich Nhat Hanh has, for many years, used the metaphor of a garden to describe the "interbeing" of all things: "Awareness that in the compost we see the flower, and in the flower we see the compost."[1]

The first part of this chapter describes the unique flowering of women's spiritual friendships. We also see beautiful examples of men awakening together, for example, in AA and other 12-step groups, or within religious and spiritual communities. Fathers sharing parenting responsibilities and fathers getting together with other fathers can also evolve to encompass the spiritual. This paradigm of fully mutual relationships can potentially hold for siblings, such as sisters who become "soul" friends, but the extra emotional baggage for siblings makes this rare. It is inspiring and powerful when it does happen. Heterosexual spiritual friendships can be more challenging, both because of gender differences in many spheres and the question of sexual intimacy.

In the Buddhist tradition, these friendships are called *kalyana mitra*, specifically created to support each person's growth on the spiritual, meditative path. Bhikkhu Bodhi calls them "horizontal relationships of equals," with a shared dedication and commitment to spiritual goals.[2] In the Christian tradition, the Celtic words for spiritual friendship in Christ are *cara anam*.

This is a special part of Buddist practice, distinct from the monk-teacher relationship, which is more "vertical," with less mutuality, at least at the beginning. Both spiritual friendships and couples are an example—on the Path of Accompanying Others—of the possibility of full mutuality of adult relationships. We will describe two forms: spiritual friendships and couples partnerships. Although there are obvious differences, both share a spiritual core. Couples partnerships, when at their best, rest on the foundation of spiritual friendship.

## Spiritual Friendships

Although the traditional bonds of family in Western culture are established through sexual partnerships in nuclear families, sometimes it is the friendships among women that are most sustaining and enduring. As Ellen Goodman and Patricia O'Brien wrote in their book, *I Know Just What You Mean: The Power of Friendship in Women's Lives*:

> Friendship matters to women: it matters a lot. Women today—with lives often in transition—depend on friends more than ever. Many who believed that family was the center of life, with every myth and fairy tale having the same happily-ever-after ending, now know that friends may be the difference between a lonely weekend and a lively one. As they turn over the Big Birthdays, women are taking deep breaths and looking around at the other women who are their fellow travelers, and saying—sometimes for the first time—this person is important to my life; indeed, this may be the most sustaining relationship of all.[3]

This isn't to say that friendship doesn't come with contradictions; they can be as complex and as entangled as any other relationship.

The notion that friends are "family by choice" can be magical. Yet there is still a sense that family lasts, while friends come and go, and that moves and transitions challenge friendships. We don't always fully acknowledge the value of friendships—the wisdom and love that can be grown and cultivated together over time, and the sustaining value of friendship in our lives. It is important to begin to acknowledge the potential for awakening in spiritual friendships.

The first step is recognizing the potential of the ordinary—of this shared commitment to accompanying each other through joys and challenges—and of sustained dialogue. This nourishes compassion, the potential for learning, and the discovery of the wisdom that illuminates the shared journey through life.

Yasodhara is sustained by her relationship with Pajapati, held in the circle of women, but her ongoing friendship and weekly meeting with her special friend in the midst of daily life is a beacon of spiritual support and a vehicle for awakening. As Yasodhara develops her capacity for relationship, we see the flowering of her friendships with Channa and Nayla in particular, but with many others along the way. She learns to value and strengthen these relationships that had always been possible but were often overlooked or taken for granted. With this new awareness of the great value of those in her community, she "pours" herself into every interaction, bringing her full presence to each relationship, and creating intentional structures of "meetings" that support and promote the deepening of connection.

## Ripe Moments: Janet and Kathy's Story[4]

Janet had been given Kathy's name by a friend as someone who knew about meditation. Janet was about to go on her first retreat to the Insight Meditation Center (IMS) in Barre, Massachusetts, and needed some guidance on what to expect on a two-week silent retreat. Out of that first meeting had grown an intentional friendship—committed to supporting each other's spiritual exploration and growth.

"I remember feeling a deep respect and awareness of our cultural and family differences," said Janet. Kathy Dyer was from a large, Roman Catholic, Irish family of seven children (five girls, two boys), and Janet from a secular Jewish family, an only child. "These huge differences have brought different perspectives, and resources to our relationship. . . . At that time, in 1980, I was deeply involved with the small group of women at the Stone Center who were creating a relational theory of women's psychological development—exploring the hidden power of the net of relationships and the energy and growth potential of 'movement in relation.' We were discussing the power of mutuality, authenticity, and empathy in the building and sustaining of relationships.

"I immediately sensed in Kathy a deep spirituality, a quiet intelligence, and an untapped aspiration for supporting and promoting healing relationships in families and organizations. We were both in the early stages of new spiritual explorations and a deeply shared 12-step spiritual community, which has sustained us now for three decades. We soon discovered the seeds of a new energy and exploration with each other and the challenge to bring together the power of friendship with spiritual wisdom and practice. These are the roots that have sustained the form and practice of our spiritual friendship for thirty years.

"We quickly decided to meet and meditate together in silence, and to begin a formal practice of speaking and listening to each other 'on our cushions.' We called this our 'I am' practice, giving voice to our deepest authenticity and spiritual experience. This weekly practice of meeting in silence and then hearing each other into authentic speech became the first step of a shared commitment to creating an intentional relationship dedicated to spiritual awakening. Without realizing the incredible vow we were making to each other, we established a foundation for a spiritual friendship that has spanned a remarkable time in both our lives, with huge life challenges, other relational changes, and now, the challenge of living in different locations.

"On a retreat in 1982 at IMS, we found a small pamphlet written by Joseph Havens, *Relationship as Yoga*.[5] He put relationship at the center of spiritual growth—a vehicle for the yoga of awakening. Naming this as a spiritual path had enormous meaning for the development of our friendship. We each wrote an inspired description of our individual life purposes and aspirations and declared our witness and commitment to our own and each other's awakening.

"In 1983, Vimala Thakar, an Indian meditation teacher, visited Boston and we were both deeply touched by her teaching. She described the spiritual journey as a process of 'self-education,' the study of life and living, and dedicating one's life to 'spiritual enquiry'; to learning about living a life of simplicity in harmony with the natural wholeness—the inter-relatedness—of all life. Living as an enquirer and dedicating one's self to 'learning from life, the Great Teacher,' as part of the organic interrelatedness of the cosmos,

Vimala stressed the 'scientific' study of life and living. She taught meditation as the state of observation, a new dimension of silence that requires as a foundation a daily life of discipline: precision about sleep, food, how one uses one's time, life energy, and resources.[6] *Living*, she would often say, *is learning*. We undertook this process of life examination, exploration of the wholeness and holiness of every aspect of life, and a dedication to learning an 'alternative way of living.' Together, we began to craft life questions, and daily and weekly reviews.

"The first questions we worked with for many years:

1. How can we live a nonviolent lifestyle dedicated to peace-building in daily life, in all our relationships, and globally?
2. How can we best use our power in relation?
3. How can we stay in enquiry, in the spirit of learning?
4. How to work skillfully with relational pain, impasses, disconnects, distractions?
5. How can we bring attention and loving-kindness to self-care?
6. What are the amends we need to make?
7. How do we learn humility and practice forgiveness?

"Our shared decision to commit to this partnership has become a treasure of this life as we continue our journey into aging. Over the years, in the turmoil of life, one of us has called the other feeling lost and said, 'Please help me remember who I am—what is important. Help me find the path here.' We hold these memories for each other and support each other's spiritual practice: 'You are the guardian of my solitude.'

"Recognizing how difficult it is to lead a spiritually centered life in the midst of this materialist world—with the pace of life and media, information and technology intrusions, the overall stress and tensions of our lives—we have gratitude for the generosity of spirit for the gifts of this relationship; the importance of regular nourishing; the necessity of each contributing her other spiritual resources, and holding each other in compassionate loving and forgiveness—while still holding ourselves and each other accountable and responsible."

## Qualities of Spiritual Friendships

- *Cultivating and deepening friendships*: In life, we let different relationships flower as they organically unfold, but also seek ways to develop more intentional ways of initiating and supporting the development of friendship.
- *Sharing spiritual community*: Finding relationships within spiritual community, which can develop from a base of shared values. Sometimes, we need friends to help create a new community or circle together.
- *Sharing intentional friendship*: It is helpful to write and speak to each other the intention of the friendship, the purpose and shared aspiration, the nature of the commitment to each other, perhaps taking devotional vows of friendship. In some *sanghas*, the commitment to spiritual friendship takes place in a special ceremony witnessed publicly by the whole community.
- *Creating structure*: Sacred space, time, activities. For example, a day or a morning set aside for spiritual friendship, to listen deeply to each other (perhaps each person speaking for a certain period of time, on the "cushion" or in a special place of meeting); make a special place of meeting and agree to set periods of time (daily, weekly, monthly, etc.).
- *Committing to self and each other, and to the "We"*: This commitment is organic, but also intentional. It is supported through regular meetings, shared practices, and the cultivation of the spiritual "We"—greater than both persons.
- *Learning together*: Conflicts, disconnects, misunderstandings—all these are part of the process and inevitable. Interest

in differences can become a resource in making amends and practicing forgiveness. Friends negotiate changes over time, place, age, and life crises.

- *Become listening and speaking partners*: Deep mindful listening—nonjudgmental, concentrated, and uninterrupted—and authentic speaking are fundamental aspects of such a friendship. This great human gift of speaking and listening is so often squandered in social chatter, gossip, and superficial conversation. In spiritual relationships, these gifts support the opportunity to deepen and touch into core truths through emerging dialogue: Right Speech and Right Listening.
- *Creating service projects*: Each person and the relationship are supported through service projects. Alone or together, expressing values in action, encouraging courageous "speaking up" together, and taking action in the world.
- *Work*: Enquiring together in addressing the whole of life, helping to clarify "right livelihood"; to bring awareness to money, status, and other cravings; to recognize that "cracking the chronics" of habit patterns can require the ongoing accompaniment and support of a friend and community; to see that each of us has special gifts and special disabilities; to honor areas of vulnerability and to pay persistent attention to these.
- *Maintaining ongoing practice and learning as fundamentals*: Spiritual relationship depends on consistent relational practice; we can *learn* through our practice that challenges truly are opportunities for learning; and enquiring—"being in the question"—together.
- *Honoring the fruits of relational practice*: Recognize the value of friendship and the way it has changed the world. Long ongoing conversations, depth of connection, shared commitments—all can have a huge impact on individuals and on the world. There

are countless examples, such as the sustained friendship of Susan B. Anthony and Elizabeth Cady Stanton, which held the women's suffrage movement through the 1920s. A less well-known example was the friendship between Rachel Carson and Dorothy Freeman. The correspondence between these women suggests how deeply Rachel was inspired, accompanied, and supported in her important pioneering environmental work by this vital—but "hidden"—friendship.

## Couples Partnerships

> She felt he was seeing into the depth of her struggle and the light of her spiritual attainment. And she saw so clearly that they were sharing a moment suddenly lightened with awareness itself, in and from them both. A moment of profound meeting and *mutual* recognition. It was recognizable to her, resonating with the moments of mutual understanding she had shared with the women in the circle: *I seeing him; he seeing me; each of us seeing the other being seen. Infinitely resonating between us, time before and beyond time.* (Chapter 22, pages 79–80)

At the core of any spiritual friendship and vital couples partnership is a spiritual path and spiritual community, underlying the spiritual "we." While there are many differences between friends and couples, couples that survive are those more likely to embrace this core and do the work of renewing and sustaining their spiritual "we." One difference is the "official" bond between couples: the legal documents and societal recognition, the exclusive sexual boundaries, and boundaries on cross-gender relationships outside of the marriage. A couple is often more excluding, in the sense that while a spiritual friendship can include other spiritual friends, couples often become isolated from forming deep relationships with other couples.

The joys of couples are plentiful: new love, commitment, wedding ceremonies, creating families, a deeply shared path through life. At times, however, when members of a couple would want to be most loving and supportive, they cannot—especially if there is a shared loss or traumatic stress. There can be huge pain and loss in our lives, which need to be held within our couples partnerships. Couples can become quite isolated—sometimes desperately so—in carrying the burden of this pain, and need to be part of a large community or Circle of Compassion together. Challenges arise around anger, sexuality, money, and difficulty with other family members. When these issues cannot be talked about openly, shared and held with others, they create unmanageable burdens for the couple. Without spiritual community, this can lead to great unhappiness, lethal conflict, domestic abuse, or divorce. King Suddhodana and Queen Pajapati's unbridgeable conflict around the return of Siddhartha could only be bridged in the context of the larger circle, with the initiation of Yasodhara.

## The Perils for Couples

The common predicament in our culture is a couple walled off from other couples and, in our fragmented society, from extended family and friends. A life partnership is a journey together, in the company of others, sharing the "ten thousand joys and ten thousand sorrows."

There is a common saying: "No one knows what really goes on in a marriage." In the couples groups we have worked with, men and women frequently say, "We have many friends, and family, but we have no one with whom we can—both of us together—truly share what's really happening in our marriage."

The perils for couples in our culture are well known: huge expectations for constant care and connection, the deep need for open-hearted help and love from each other. These inflated expectations of what each person and the individual couple "we" can provide often put too much focus on the partnership, on what we are getting from (and hopefully giving to) that partner. This creates conditions where it is hard to allow for vulnerability or limitations, to accept the other for who he or she is, with compassion. Impasses can grow and then crystallize rapidly from the smallest event: leaving the cap off the toothpaste, a chance glance, or a harsh word. The relationship constricts into a smaller and smaller space, filling with tension and impermeability.

There are other significant destructive habit patterns:

- *Becoming adversaries, not allies*: losing the sense of "being on the same side"; however, "being on the same side against the rest of the world" will never work in the long run.
- *Invisibility of differences*: not seeing clearly or appreciating the source of the difference, in gender, culture, ethnicity, etc., and learning to use difference as a resource for the relationships; this is true for all couples, heterosexual-straight and gay-lesbian. Gender differences can be especially difficult for heterosexual couples, while other differences and sources of social oppression may be more at the center for other couples.
- *Absence of awareness of the larger forces acting on the couple*: What seem to be "our problems alone, and unique," are in fact often shared by couples in general.
- *Absence of a shared purpose—especially of a shared spiritual purpose*: not only something within the individual couple, but of a shared purpose in the larger world, often expressed in partnership with other couples as part of shared spiritual communities or *sanghas*.

## The Spiritual Challenge for Couples

Commitment to any spiritual path requires ferocity of purpose and finding a shared spiritual practice. Keeping in mind the shared purpose, even reminding the other person of it, in the midst of life's storms.

The overarching practice for a couple is to create a spiritual "we": creating this together and holding it together as a spiritual practice. This often rests on a shared path of spiritual aspiration, with a commitment to the relationship as the vehicle.

The challenge is to find a way to "awaken together." Couples may have had naturally occurring "moments" of such openings, such enlarged connections to each other and to the greater world. These moments of deep connection and "mutual recognition," as that one moment between Yasodhara and Siddhartha, are intensely personal: both seeing the other and both feeling deeply seen. At the same time, such a moment opens a doorway to connection with the whole of life: seeing deeply into our "true nature" and this shared human experience. This doorway opens through the particular to the whole, to the realization of the deep, interconnected reality of being in this mystery together as fellow travelers on the path. We have this brief chance in life to love and support each other.

What can help us find this spirit, and then keep this spirit alive and present in the day-to-day details, especially in stressful, exhausting, and demanding times? We all have seen how tragedy and hard times in a couple—illness, death, tragic accidents—either tear a couple apart, often leading to divorce, or bring them closer together, depending on the presence and awareness of the larger spirit, the spiritual "we" and a path and practice that can support it.

What are the ripe conditions for such a spiritual "we" to emerge? How do we expand the relationship to the spiritual dimension? How can we use our differences to begin to open to a larger circle? How does a relationship become a vehicle for shared spiritual awakening?

One way to begin the dialogue beyond the couple dyad is to open to a larger circle. An example of this builds on our many years of work, with over twenty thousand men and women, boys and girls, in our gender dialogues, which we wrote about in *We Have to Talk: Healing Dialogues between Women and Men.*[7]

Our clinical work with heterosexual couples began with gender dialogues. We are using this as one example of difference which almost everyone is familiar with—and at times has suffered with. Gender is one example, but any difference can be approached in this way.

## Couples Groups: Opening through Difference to Shared Awakening

In Yasodhara's story, there are the seeds of cross-gender relationships, the most actualized with Channa, but also Suddhodana. In our time, "single" mothers have a much greater opportunity for cross-gender relationships. There can be mutually supportive relationships with both women and men.

After our decade of working in the peace movement in the 1980s, bringing together groups from the United States and Russia to promote mutual understanding through cross-cultural dialogue, we began to conduct cross-gender dialogues, considering gender as a cultural divide. This involved bringing men and women together in groups with the assumption that gender operates like different subcultures within the larger culture. We did this to engage with group differences, to work with prototypical relational impasses, and to build connection within and across gender groups in the service of supporting breakthroughs into mutuality. "Group" differences meant that no individual would ever be fully defined by these differences, but could not help but be impacted by them.

These dialogues proved to be so valuable that we used them as a centerpiece for couples groups. These were attended by six-to-eight couples at a time.

While many couples struggle alone with these gender issues, we felt that they could best be worked on in larger groups, where individuals can experience themselves as supported by a group and where collective intelligence would work more effectively. The power of group dialogue is extraordinary. When this power can be channeled toward mutual understanding and deeper relational connection, all participants can experience the transformation, and the energy becomes available in their individual lives and relationships.

## Circles of Men, Circles of Women: Opening to the Spirit Together

The workshops were designed to first foster mutual relations within gender groups, and then, with men and women in dialogue with each other, to work with differences to create mutual connection.

First, each gender group met alone: the men with Sam, the women with Janet. Each gender group then broke out into smaller groups (of three or four) to come up with consensus answers to three questions:

1. What are three strengths the other gender group brings to relationships?
2. What do you most want to understand about the other gender group?
3. What do you most want the other gender group to understand about you?

Working on these questions in small same-gender groups, both the men's and women's groups became more connected—more energized and "present" in the room, enlivened and curious. There was disagreement among participants, and the challenge of acknowledging and representing difference (not denying or suppressing or "giving up" in the face of these) was reinforced as a fundamental challenge of healthy relationships. Although both the women's and men's groups eventually felt connected, at first the men were much less willing to open up in an authentic way. The women were immediately energized and relieved to have a chance to share their experiences in relationships with men.

In Sam's first meeting in the circle of men, something remarkable happened. The conversation in the large men's group soon settled upon an important, shared—and previously hidden, even secret—experience. The men began to talk about their interactions with women, when a woman approached them wanting to deepen the connection with them. In the approaching, the men were often overcome with a sense of dread. To a woman asking him, "What are you feeling, darling?" one man described the feeling as "an icy fist squeezing my heart," and the thought: "Nothing good can come of my going into this; it's just a matter of how bad it will be 'til it's over. And it will never be over!" As the woman kept inviting a response, the man kept withdrawing further, until there was distant silence, or an eruption of anger, and the relationship crashed.

We named this "male relational dread."

Most of the men, including Sam himself, had a striking sense that what they had seen as their *own* problem or failure or defect, or even a "neurosis," or a "psychopathology"—a deep sense that "something is really wrong with me"—to their surprise found that it was *a common feeling of many of the men in the group*! It wasn't *each man's failing; it was part of the normal life of many men*. It came along the cultural development of men in this society. This realization was a huge relief—to move this from pathology to normalcy. With this realization, the men relaxed, relieved, felt a lifting of shame, seeing this as "merely human, for us men."

Over and over, this transformation took place in the men's circles, often based around naming and sharing their different and varying degrees of relational dread. Later, we would see this as the men's part of a relational impasse with women: the "Dread/Yearning Impasse." An example is a couple on a beach, after a picnic. They are feeling connected, and the woman yearns to feel even more connected:

"What are you feeling, dear?" she asks.

The man is startled and says nothing.

"Can you tell me?"

"I . . . I don't know," he says, as dread starts to appear, an icy fist in his gut.

"Sure you do, hon. Can you tell me?"

The sense of dread is now overwhelming, and to try to keep control, the man says, "Don't . . . spoil . . . it."

Angrily, the woman says, "Oh, *I'm* spoiling it?!"

Total disconnection.

Understanding this "dread" together brought ease to the men as they faced the next challenge: moving back into dialogue with the women. There was an almost palpable sense of liberation and enhanced connection. They actually became eager to bring this back to the women in the cross-gender dialogue. What happened in that moment in the larger circle was the opportunity—offered to most of the men for the first time—to speak their experience openly, authentically. It was only by first coming together in a safe place with other men and talking truthfully about their own experience that they took this risk in the larger group.

## Widening the Circle: Men and Women Together

Next, we brought the same-gender groups back together, in a circle facing each other across the room. We then asked them to read the answers to the three questions that each of the small groups had completed:

### Question One: *What are three strengths the other gender group brings to relationships?*

**Women's answers:** Caretaking; deep loyalties; true humor when it's funny and not used as a put-down or escape; lifting heavy objects; removing dead animals from the attic; focusing on one thing at a time; can let things go and move on; freedom from the bog of emotions so they can skim across the top.

**Men's answers:** Capacity for feeling and empathy; speaking emotional truth; interest in working on relationships; seeing both sides of a situation; ability to do more than one thing at a time; ability to listen well, in a nonjudgmental way; organization of the social stuff; creation of community.

Dialogue about these answers to the first question was usually animated, intense, and appreciative—and irritation was expressed, as well. There was a palpable sense of fear and dread and anger. Intense feelings and incendiary comments were part of the dialogue.

### Question Two: *What do you most want to understand about the other gender group?*

**Women's answers:** What's going *on* in there? What moves you deeply? Do men feel? And if so, how and what? What do sports really mean? What do jokes really mean? Are men lonely? What would it take to get men to open up? Why won't men go to doctors or ask for directions? Why can't you reach out when you're hurting? What goes on in men's friendships with men? How do you get through the day without intimacy? Is life worthwhile for men?

**Men's answers:** What do you want from us? Why is what I do never enough? Why so many "whys" for us? Why do you demand that I be vulnerable and then see it as a weakness? What's so important to women about connection? How do you come to personalize relational failure to such a degree? How do you care so much without losing yourself? Why do you always bring up the past? Why do you always say you want sensitive guys and go for the macho jerks?

These dialogues soon provoked discomfort in the men, and this led to their describing what they were feeling and had just discovered and named: male relational dread. As they did so, the women nodded in recognition, smiled, and even laughed at the humor in the men's descriptions. They asked more and more questions of the men—which led to more and more dread. This was an all-too-familiar vicious circle ending in disconnection, for most of the men and women. This led to the women describing how they have a similar deep feeling in close relationship, of *yearning*. "It's not just a yearning," one woman said, "it's a *burning* yearning." They yearn to deepen the connection, which then seems to bring on dread. As one woman put it, "We know that look: when your eyes go blank and everything turns to ice, and the walls go up! Now we understand it a little better."

It was the first time that many of them had been able to name this—the moments when yearning meets dread, and leads to an impasse. We pointed out how this was a "relational" impasse; it didn't get activated in the man or woman alone but only in the give-and-take of relationship. The movement toward connection in the women provoked the men's dread and their movement away. The impasse is not in each person alone but *in the connecting*.

The impasses in the groups of men and women facing each other reflected the experiences of the same three relational impasses in many of the individual couples: (1) Dread/Yearning; (2) Product/Process (women more into Process, men into Product), and (3) Power Over/Power With (men Power Over, women more Power With). Often, it seemed like the circle was about to fracture and fall apart.

Yet, in ten years of work with thousands of people worldwide, the groups never gave up. The desire for connection, the support of the leaders, and the structure of the dialogue carried them through.

The conflict and sense of impasse inevitably gave way to acceptance, interest, curiosity, and humor. The group moved between polite surface connection; escalating disconnections; impasses; small breakthroughs; more challenge; and more passionate expression of yearning, anger, frustration, and grief in the struggle for mutuality—for each to feel heard and held. Through this movement, we supported a "healthy engagement with difference"; a "facing into" rather than retreating or fighting, promoting authentic contact with what was actually happening, and allowing different voices to shape new and creative insights and ideas for action.

The principles of mutuality were present:

- *Mutual engagement*: process of active relational engagement, struggle, interaction around difference and individual contributions.
- *Mutual authenticity and mutual empathy*: process of alive, real, present-moment truth-telling and empathic responsiveness; movement toward each other's experience, with each person and group feeling "real, heard, and held."
- *Mutual empowerment*: empowering the movement from "I" versus "You" to "We."

It is from this sense of opening into a more spacious, energized, loving way of "being together" in the "we"—of alignment of purpose and presence; of the breakthrough beyond boundaries of self, separation, and isolation into a new level of being and being together—that the heart of awakening together into our fundamental connectedness occurs.

It is often through engagement with difference, with speaking authentically—even the difficult truths being heard, received, and "held" in the whole—that something essential and spacious, beyond and holding, without lethal conflict, can be realized.

And in each dialogue, to a greater or lesser extent, something else happened: there was a palpable shift in the room. The "felt experience" of this shift was described by the men and women as: "Release, comfort, caring, safety, sharing, peaceful, easy, enjoyment of different styles, hopefulness, mutual nurturance, energy, movement, insight, softening, appropriate confrontation, dynamic process, clearer recognition of others' experience."

We called this "the shift to mutuality," or "the expansion into the We."

There was a clear, palpable breakthrough into a dimension of greater spaciousness, with a shared sense of a greater freedom and ease. A kind of "click" of mutual connection.

Only after this shift had taken place could the most difficult subjects be worked on. The issues brought up previously, that had led to the impasses, were often the ones that the group "goes back over" with a new fresh sense of really attending, responding, ruthlessly encountering the psychological facts without the burden of judgment or a need to "agree" or "disagree"—or even "agree to disagree"—and with an authentic desire to understand. It was amazing to us how the same questions to each other between the men and women that had brought hostile silence now brought animated discussion. Humor, as well as wisdom and compassion, was much in evidence.

### Question Three: *What do you most want the other gender group to understand about you?*

At the end, the men and women read to each other their answers. Both groups had the answer: "We are not your enemy."

Some answers from the women, spoken slowly and softly, and with great feeling: "My way is not wrong, just different; we are angry because we are hurt; I just want you to be there; I am a human being too; we want to share, not take over; we're not experts in relationship either."

From the men, also, now, with a remarkable openness, vulnerability, and feeling: "I want to change; we care about relationships too; the heavy burden placed on men to be successful and not look foolish; understand our relational yearnings, our grief over losses; I will come back after I go away."

And then there was silence.

Sensing this new spaciousness and shared compassion for each other, it was a silence of gratitude and understanding.

Many of the women, and some men, had tears in their eyes. In the stillness, no one spoke for a time. Finally, one woman said, "There's a glow now. You gave us the other half of the string, and now we can make a tie."

We learned a profound lesson: By giving the men and women the chance, in a safe holding circle, to name and engage with their differences respectfully, there will be a shift, an expansion into mutuality. All will feel more connected to each other *and* more themselves. When members of a couple experience this way of engaging in dialogues it can become a way of *being with* each other within their particular couple. Our hope for the joy and wisdom of couples was affirmed.

## From the Psychological to the Spiritual "We"

Couples who have this dialogue experience in the larger group can learn to bring this to their couples relationship. Having been accompanied in the dialogue with others of their gender group and then breaking through to a larger circle brings new energy to the couple. The possibility of these breakthrough moments can become a resource to building a spiritual "We," and put in place intentional structures to support its restorative power and continuity over time.

The couples in our couples groups began to work at home to use this energy and structure of the larger group to build their spiritual "We." Here are some of the steps we suggested they take, many of which are applicable to all couples working to create a spiritual partnership. The key is to find community to support and sustain these practices:

1. Write a relational purpose statement: What are our spiritual aspirations for the relationship?
2. What are our vows and commitments we are making to each other? These can then be witnessed by the larger group.
3. What are some simple phrases or *mantras* to remind ourselves of these commitments? One couple said, "We do it together."
4. Write out a relational inventory of each person and the relationship around specific spiritual qualities.
5. Make specific amends to each other for past mistakes that have created suffering.
6. Find practices to work on forgiveness as an ongoing process, asking for forgiveness and offering it to self and each other.
7. How can we support each other's self-care?
8. Create an intentional plan and structure for ongoing "meetings" and spiritual practice together. Like the circle practice in chapter 2, begin with prayer and meditation, find rituals and practices that support the relationship for a vehicle as awakening.
9. What is our spiritual community? How can we find or create an ongoing process for sharing as a couple and tapping into the power of the Circle of Compassion together?

## Our Shared Journey: Creating a Four-Way Circle

These are all steps we personally have taken together. In retrospect we were ready, when the opportunity arose, to reach out to join another couple, and to suggest we all join together to work on some of these questions.

Frankie Moore Lappe and Dick Rowe became friends of ours about seven years ago. For the first two years of the relationship we met occasionally for dinner. As the friendship developed, our foursome began to change into something else. As we became closer, we shared issues within our couple relationships and in our very different areas of creative work. Over time, we found a deeper sense of shared purpose in the world—each in our different ways and together in our couples—and committed to bringing our individual and couples' vision of education, democracy, meditation, and spirituality, and our writing out into the world. The four of us made an explicit intentional agreement to use the relationship as a vehicle for inspiration and liberation.

The structure: almost always it was around dinner, though every few months we would meet for a whole morning. In each gathering, we would listen deeply as one by one each person spoke about whatever they chose for about twenty minutes. After that, all would respond. Sometimes, if there was a crisis, one of us would be at the center of the discussion. We have been meeting for about five years now. We've also found deeper common purpose, celebrating events in each other's lives, and recently, have been experimenting by taking action: how we can bring the power of this foursome into the world. To our surprise and delight, this simple meeting of the four of us over the years has led not only to a sense of closeness, care, and love, but each of our considerable concrete efforts to bring our vision out into the world has been strengthened and fulfilled.

All of us recognize how very rare and precious this is for us as couples. It's even become more and more possible to get a "same day" call to get together to do so—both for fun and in crisis. It is a gift.

## Creating Ripe Moments: Reflections and Practices

### Spiritual Friendships

#### 1. Reflections

To be written and shared within your circle, spiritual community, or *sangha*.

- Write a relational inventory, past and present: What are the important relationships in my life today? How are they helpful or hurtful? How could I honor and celebrate these more fully?
- What are my strengths and weaknesses as a spiritual friend?
- How could I make my current relationships more intentional as spiritual friendships? What is my own aspiration and willingness to grow a spiritual friendship with another?
- What are the obstacles in my life and in my ways of relating?
- Choices in relationship: How might I choose to deepen relationships where I feel there is spiritual potential? How might I approach this?
- Is there someone who is part of a spiritual community with whom I share spiritual aspirations who I might invite to explore greater intentionality in spiritual practice?
- Might we go on a retreat together as a step toward developing a friendship?

## 2. Individual Meditation Practice

- Create a gallery of photographs of important spiritual friends and relationships in your life: children, parents, mentors, spiritual teachers, pets, special places in nature. Sitting in meditation, surround yourself with this gallery. Gaze and appreciate each and all of these beings around you. Allow the energy and vitality of the relationships to be felt and sit in meditation, in the flow of these many connections.
- In any moment, practice opening to others—friends, strangers, pets, plants, minerals—taking a moment to pause, feel the relational presence, breathe deeply, and consciously generate heartfelt warmth of care, gratitude, friendship flowing between, and the internal expression of love.

## 3. Relational Meditation Practice

- Think of someone you might ask to join you in exploring spiritual friendships. Maybe just a request for sharing a quiet morning or afternoon, set aside for reflection and practice. Express your own aspiration for spiritual friendship. Allow the relationship to develop slowly and organically, but also be willing to take the risk of expressing your own aspiration for spiritual friendship.

# Couples Partnerships

## 1. Reflections for Writing and Sharing with Partners or Couples Group

- What is the *purpose* of our relationship? What are our individual spiritual aspirations, our aspirations for our partnership?

- How can we support each other spiritually?
- How can we support the relationship?
- What are our commitments and vows to each other?
- What is our spiritual community? Could we join or grow such a community together?
- Do we have a spiritual intention and practice that supports our relationship?
- What are our differences that create disconnections? How can they be better used as a creative resource?
- Are there any amends we would like to make to each other?
- Do we have structures—time, space, ritual—that support our spiritual journey?
- Can we find another couple or couples to create an intentional circle of spiritual friendship?

## 2. Relational Meditation Practice

- Create a sacred space and a ritual practice for speaking your vows and commitments—perhaps two meditation cushions in a special corner of the house.
- Spiritual check-in: in any moment of life, either partner can ask for a spiritual check-in. Ask each other, "Where are we? Are we in deep alignment with our purpose? What would help us get there?"
- Practice "beginning anew" in the sacred space. On a regular basis, speak your gratitude to your partner—what are you most grateful for in each other at this moment? Each person speaks what was received. Is there anything that needs to be let go of? Are there amends to be made?
- *Mantras*: you can write your own *mantras* that are shorthand for your commitments and vows; or you might try using those from chapter 1: Four Love *Mantras* (reading slowly

to each other; these can be used anytime during the day, as appropriate):

- "Dear one, I am really here for you."
- "Dear one, I know that you are here, and it makes me very happy."
- "Dear one, I see that you are suffering, and that is why I am here for you."
- "Dear One, I am suffering; please help me."[8]

- Cultivate relational mindfulness: breathe together for ten minutes. Sit in silence, facing each other, with eyes closed. Be mindful and attentive to breathing in and breathing out—eyes open, attending to the in- and out-breath of your partner as well as your own. Sit in silence, just breathing together. (5–10 minutes) Share the experience in simple words, listening deeply and speaking the truth from the heart.

# 5

# The Path of "Staying With" Through Illness, Old Age, and Death

> Yasodhara began to understand that her devotional practice to her son and with the others in her circle could expand to encompass the arising of life to the vanishing of life, the letting in and the letting go, the *being with* birth and the *being with* death, the first in-breath to the last out-breath—the whole universal circle of life.
>
> —Chapter 13, "Yasodhara's Story"

Yasodhara, She Who Stays, accompanies loved ones through illness, old age, and death, what the Buddha called "the heavenly messengers" that started him out on his journey to find liberation from suffering. In Yasodhara's story and in our own contemporary stories, we are called to face these "heavenly messengers" together, as most of us have to do, in relation to others we love. These journeys of staying through to the end have perils and great possibilities.

The messengers are "heavenly" because they wake us up to the deepest realities of suffering in life, which sometimes we feel we can't bear. When met with love and wisdom—as Yasodhara does in the

Circle of Compassion—they can lead to deeply precious, even transformative experiences. The devotional commitment to stay with, to stay "through the dark night," to stay to the end and beyond, is often filled with sorrow, suffering, and times of resistance, yet may bring moments of surprising joy and freedom. Even with material resources and sufficient medical care, this requires courage, staying power, and community.

Yasodhara has her whole community with her as she cares for her aging mother through illness and death. This relational practice is woven into her whole life as she mothers her young son and practices, daily, in her circle of care. This life moment, of caring for a child and an aging parent, is familiar to many of us. And with Pajapati, Yasodhara has the privilege of being in a *sangha* and in profound connection to Pajapati through her dying process. Their mutual love, and the shared journey to the very end, allows Yasodhara to *be with* fully, to listen and receive Pajapati's final gift—the completion of their relationship and the honoring of Yasodhara's path.

## The Path of Staying With

"In the position of caring for both my child and my mother," Yasodhara said, "I made a vow to be a beneficial presence for these particular others on this shared life journey. And I understood how this vow resonated with the lives of the other women in our circle—this journey that is the core and span of each and every life. The unique yet ordinary stories of the women *accompanying* parents, children, husbands, and friends through life had a universal resonance: the life journey of accompaniment—*walking with* as a relational practice, from birth to death—became a spiritual path, the ordinary devotional path held in the larger circle." (Chapter 13, page 45)

If these were monastic vows, perhaps to a guru, they might be honored and celebrated. In the stories that follow there are vows similar to Yasodhara's, made by ordinary people in their life journeys, relational vows to stay through illness, old age, and death. These are normal, but often private and hidden, vows of care and commitment that underlie our staying present in our closest relationships in life. They are usually not heralded or recorded in any public way, but frequently are steps on the path of awakening in relationship. They may arise in the turmoil and desperation of relationships—sometimes surprising the person who makes the commitment, who takes the vow. And they may arise in the mutuality of the relationship. These vows or spiritual intentions "to stay" can be a resource, when one feels at his or her wit's end, to gain strength, spirit, and compassion. This is another example of "the gift of desperation." In our lives, close relationships are complex, ambivalent, and often create significant suffering. Taking such a vow to "stay" must support a person's staying in Right Relation—attending to the care of the other and care of the self, and held in a larger community. Sometimes a relationship is too abusive to stay close, and may require the help of others recruited from a distance. It may also be important to find the "emotional distance" at which empathy can be maintained.

These contemporary stories are ordinary examples of "staying through" the passages of illness, old age, and death—with love. While each of them reveals, to a greater or lesser extent, the possibilities of mutual transformation, the perils in each story are significant, and the way through can be treacherous. But something extraordinary shines through the stories.

The characteristics of the practice of "Staying With":

- It is often filled with critical choice-points along the way.

- There is no blueprint for this process; it's a pathless path. You sometimes have to see what doesn't work, in order to find your way.
- No one gets it right all the time; it's an emergent process and always "messy."
- The issue is not only what you do, it's what you do next—how you stay through it.
- This is very difficult to do alone—a friend or friends, a community, and a circle of care is essential, and you never know who might show up. Reaching out in dire times brings compassionate people who have gone through something similar, either as hospice workers or caregivers in their families; someone who shows up randomly or unexpectedly may be woven into the circle if we stay open.
- There's something about "staying" that benefits almost anyone who does stay. People in this process often say, at the end, "I never could have imagined saying this, but what we went through was an opportunity, a privilege—even a blessing. One of the most important times of my life."
- Even though the adult child can become the parent, as a "role reversal," this is never a total reversal; at unexpected moments, the mother may come alive as "the mother" again.
- Especially in dire moments, there can be mutual healing. In both giving and receiving, and when there is surrender, these opposites fall away: giving is receiving and receiving is giving; and together, they become part of a shared dance.
- In the practice of staying through, it is not only about caring but also about *attuning*: a process of tuning up and tuning in to the unique moments and turning points of these relationships—*getting to the surprisingly mutual moments* that can move those involved to extraordinary places. The spiritual aliveness—in both younger and older—is awakened. Staying

can lead to unexpected and transformative endings, often laced with heightened intensity and deep calm at the same time.

## Ripe Moments: Diane's Story[1]

"Long ago, I had vowed to be there for her as she had been there for me." When asked about the intense care and devotion to her mother in the last three years of her mother's life, Diane called it "a blessing." Her last memory of her mother's death was holding her hand in silence: though her mother had lost the ability to speak, she managed to say, "More than words." Diane and her mother realized that this was part of what she was saying in full—"I love you more than words can say."

As her mother and father were aging, her mother, Florence, became increasingly ill. Her father's denial of her mother's illness, and his inability to care for her, became increasingly painful for Diane. During one hospitalization for her mother's chronic pulmonary disease, Diane called in a social worker and staged an intervention to separate her parents so her mother could be appropriately cared for—a very bold move from someone who had never openly challenged the power structure in her family. Diane took her mother home with her for a few months while they tried to figure out how best to care for her.

Although she had a lifelong sense of an underlying "unconditional love" from her mother, in this last time period together, she felt this could be actively experienced—and named—between them. While living together, they had many conversations about past times and family history. Diane eventually moved her mother into a beautiful apartment in a retirement community close by. Her father refused to move there with her—his pride had been challenged. He died, rather suddenly, a year later, having reconciled with Florence but never living together with her again. Diane's mother lived a happy first year with many friends, visited regularly by her children and grandchildren, and finally had the space that had been denied her for many decades.

That Diane was able to give time and this beautiful space to her mother was an extraordinary joy for her. Her mother expressed great appreciation for her "new life" and her daughter's care. In the next two years, her mother declined in health, and it was at this same point that Diane's daughter was having her first child. It was a difficult pregnancy, and Diane was torn between her daughter's needs and her mother's needs. Florence said, "I just want to live to hold my great-grandson so he will know he had a great-grandmother who loved him." After a difficult birth and slow recovery, the needs of her mother and daughter created a conflict that was agonizing for Diane.

One day during that time, Florence said, "Let's call in hospice. It's time to go." This was an abrupt change in direction after two years of seeking every kind of medical help. It took a lot of courage on Diane's part to listen to her mother and follow her instructions around dying. Florence stopped eating and eventually took to her bed, which was next to a large window looking out over an apple orchard.

Diane described the end as a culmination of this very close time. They would walk slowly together, when her mother still was able, and during the walks, her mother would take her hand, which she had never done before. "Breaking the physical barrier between us," Diane put it. In her room, too, Diane would sit and hold her mother's hand. They were surrounded by loving friends and family and caregivers, but the centrality of their mother-daughter bond was evident.

What became clear after her death was that Florence had understood Diane being caught between mothering her own daughter and tending to her mother. Diane wondered later if her mother had made the decision that it was time for her to release Diane. There was a delicate mutuality in the letting go—in spirit and in action—on both sides.

In this story of Diane and Florence, it's clear what neither of them knew fully at the time. Though each of them felt they were making decisions alone, Diane realized afterward that a deeper, more transformative mutuality had been present than she had quite understood. At the same time, as they passed through exhausting crises and impossible decisions, the process of letting her mother go and her mother letting go into death was filled with exquisite love and mutuality to the last moment.

## Ripe Moments: Ellen's Story[2]

This practice of *staying with* may change everything for the rest of your life. Our friend Ellen Goodman had a full life as a much-lauded journalist and a well-appreciated mother, grandmother, wife, good friend, and daughter. Over many years, she was the primary caretaker for her widowed mother. The last ten years of her mother's life were spent in a facility for dementia; she had very little awareness of her situation, and Ellen had to make many medical, caregiving, and legal decisions for her mother over and over without really knowing what her mother would have wanted. This commitment to care was treacherous, confusing, uncharted, and lasted for many years.

"In all our years together," Ellen said, "we talked about everything except one thing: how she wanted to live at the end of her life. I realized only after her death how much easier it would have been if I had heard her voice in my ear as these decisions had to be made."

These agonizing years before her mother's death ultimately transformed her life's work. Ellen founded The Conversation Project, dedicated to helping people talk about their wishes for end-of-life care.[3] Noting that ours is a culture of denial of death, Ellen is now working to change the culture and to help people start these conversations over the dinner table, with their children, spouses, doctors, and lawyers: "Not to wait until the end to try to figure this out without the benefit of this ongoing conversation."

Ellen is devoting herself to nothing short of major cultural transformation. The impact on the survivor's life can be life-changing. While some of the stories—as with Yasodhara and Pajapati—reflect a deeply mutual process, Ellen's story did not appear to be. Nevertheless, by staying to the end, she still found a way to make meaning out of this experience with her mother, and to redeem the suffering in the relationship over the long, slow dying process.

## Ripe Moments: Janet's Story[4]

As I write this, I am more than seven years into living this journey myself. Seven years ago my ninety-two-year-old father, living independently with my mother, was diagnosed with lung cancer, and died within the year. When he went into hospice, my mother was hospitalized with a life-threatening infection—she was brought in a wheelchair to his bedside to say good-bye to him. She survived, and lived for six more years—to 101—a thousand miles away from me, in Florida. She passed her 101st birthday. I was her sole family support—her legal, medical, and caregiving "manager."

One of the great (and shameful) terrors of my life as a young child had been the thought of losing my mother; I simply could not imagine how I would survive. This fear was in the background of my adolescent and young-adult years; and I remember in my forties, on my first solo meditation retreat—being on a path on an ocean beach, contemplating my relationship to my parents—when the words formed in my heart: "I will be there."

This was the moment that I made my first conscious devotional vow—to give back what I had been given, to face into the truth of impermanence and mortality, and to "show up" for my parents in aging and death. It was a moment of faith and strength in my own capacity to be present and to make such a commitment. I can see now that making such a commitment to a partner and to a child formed the basis for this radical spiritual turning.

As my father died, I made the commitment to him to take care of my mother, one which has graced—and haunted—the last six years. As I look back today, I am grateful for the love and support in many forms that I have drawn on—one book stands out vividly. It was given to me by my dear friend and meditation teacher, Trudy Goodman: *Circles of Care: How to Set Up Quality Home Care for Our Elders*, by Ann Cason, an inspired Buddhist guide to working with aging elders.

Ann Cason and Victoria Howard created a Home Health Care agency together—Dana Home Health—in Boulder, Colorado, in the 1970s that was dedicated to helping seniors remain in their own homes. Cason's many years of experience working with elders and their families are beautifully described—particularly offering the relational practice of creating and nurturing "circles of care" around elders. This work has provided me with an image that has inspired and sustained my own relational practice with my mother through these years. It helped me to put energy into creating such a circle, and working diligently to care for the circle and tend to the relationships between all who were part of it. Times of burnout, frustration, and interpersonal stress characterized the life of the circle. It greatly helped me to have this creative image of the circle of care to visualize and practice as I lived through this very challenging time. This circle sustained me and came into its full expression and illumination at the time of my mother's recent death a few months ago. I had the sense that the light of the circle, which had been cultivated and sustained over seven years, was visible and shining—creating a protective, loving shield around my mother and me over the last days of her life.

## The Circle of Care

> Care is not just one person doing something for another, the attention has to be in creating an environment in which all the members of the circle take care of one another.—Ann Cason, *Circles of Care*[5]

Ann Cason describes a humane, illuminating, and meditative approach to being with and caring for elders. This is an institutional practice (as in her home-health agency as a geriatric-care manager), which provides an exemplary vision for healthcare and geriatric, end-of-life service. Like the Hospice Movement, it provides an alternative to the cultural madness of our current health care system. It offers families and patients an integrated holistic approach to end-of-life care, where healers, caregivers, families, friends, and others can work together to support each other in a web of care, compassion, and dignity. This model of Circles of Care and the Hospice Model are beautiful examples of the natural, holistic, complementary bridge between the personal/familial, and the professional medical practitioners, and integrated relational practice worthy of the vision of Yasodhara's Path of Right Relation.

Fundamentally, Cason's circles of care are created as vehicles for caregiving and encompass the physical details of caregiving, as well as spanning psychological, relational, emotional, and spiritual aspects.

The first task is to establish a current plan of care.[6] Then the beginning of a circle of care around the elder can be created. This is a living, breathing, ever-changing circle, made up of family members, friends, service providers, and any seemingly random persons who enter, some "invisible" team members, ultimately spanning human and "other-than-human" realms—the natural world, pets, the sun and the moon and the stars.

Cason writes, "Creating a circle of care is like working on a puzzle. It takes diligence as well as bursts of inspiration: keeping the atmosphere light, warm, friendly, and accommodating."[7]

Often, from a closed-in, isolated system, there can be expansion into greater inclusion and connectedness—reaching beyond the limits of each person alone. All participants in the circle can access greater energy and resources by tapping into the greater power, intelligence, connection, love, and wisdom that become remarkably available to all. This team of very particular people can become a vehicle to touch into a universal experience of connectedness with the whole circle of life and the webs of care and love and kindness that weave the "invisible thread that connects us all." The practice of the circle is concrete, organizing basic physical care—food, bathing, environmental safety, monitoring doctor's orders and visits, etc., in a spirit of dignity, order, kindness, and mindfulness/awareness.

This creation of a field of attentiveness, concentration, compassion, and relaxation establishes a meditative field within, among, and around all circle participants. This field is the ground and the sky established to accompany elders on the journey of aging and death, a journey Cason describes as a major life shift:

"The elder is required to go from doing into being. Old age requires a change of pace. It may come on gradually as energy and memory decline or it may come abruptly with illness or loss of a mate. The atmosphere turns gray and heavy; the ground is littered with shards of broken dreams."[8]

Keeping spirits up through this journey is crucial:

"Old age itself is fairly simple, but what goes on around it is complex. It takes a great deal of energy, discipline, and joy on the part of caregivers to keep from sinking into a state of mind that yields to despair and feels burdened."[9]

When adult children and their parents feel part of and supported by such a circle, this provides maximum support for their being present and actively participating in the current situation. This creates auspicious conditions for potential transformation for both elders and their adult children.

Circles of Care can create the support that helps people relax, accept, and let go of the old—the relational patterns and obstacles in the way—and move forward to connect with and be together in the new, the "present moment." It is saying "yes" to the spirit of the moment.

This represents a different view of aging. As a society, we privilege beginnings, and fear and stigmatize endings. Cason describes a beautiful reframe to this: "The ebbing of the life force is a genuine and precious part of our shared journey, hard to fathom. Elders can become "teachers," and model this journey for the next generation."[10]

A major principle of Circles of Care for everyone involved is the flow of energy, insight, and changing and fluid capacities, which can hold despair, grief, fatigue, fear, irritation, and overwhelm. Each person can feel supported and cared for. The terrible conflicts between "self-care" and "other-care"—between the sick, aging, or dying, and the caretakers—can drop away in the circle, as care is not a zero-sum resource, but generated and regenerated in the circle, when it is working optimally.

## Ripe Moments: Olivia's Story[11]

Most of these stories have been about adults with their elders. A remarkable story is of a couple going through this together, with a shared spiritual practice, and with as much mutuality as the illness and dying could allow.

In her book, *Ten Thousand Joys and Ten Thousand Sorrows: A Couples' Journey Through Alzheimer's*, spiritual teacher Olivia Hoblitzelle describes elegantly the six-year journey with her husband Hob, from his diagnosis with Alzheimer's to his death. Both Olivia and Hob were *dharma* teachers and both had strong meditation practices.

"Determined to live the experience consciously and lovingly, we regarded this—the final challenge of our relationship—as an opportunity for opening to the unknown, for learning, and above all for deepening in love."[12]

This is the ultimate expression of *The Buddha's Wife*, in terms of a journey together toward awakening, in facing illness, old age, and death. As Olivia wrote:

> The compelling question is: How do we accept the process of aging, diminishment, and loss? In the case of dementia, how do we find meaning amidst what appears to be a ruthless and meaningless pro-

cess; is it possible to find something redeeming while living with a heartbreaking illness? Hob and I lived tenderly with these questions. This book shares some of the ways we found peace with them.[13]

Olivia described her path:

I surprised even myself by my determination to make his last years as smooth and happy as possible. I was his fierce protector and his advocate. We were in different stages of the life-cycle—his life was winding down; I was vibrant and fully engaged in a life that seemed to extend into the future. Had I not felt that destiny had handed us this journey to do together, I might have resented being thrust into the caregiving role. Certainly there were times when I felt burdened, but the depth of our journey together, over thirty-five years, far outweighed our feelings. It fired my commitment and sustained me.[14]

They built on their long relationship and shared commitment to spiritual practice. Their Tibetan teacher had helped them by saying, "Even the little things, see them as an opportunity, a meditation, a blessing, as spiritual practice; if you use hardships in a proper way, they can bring inner peace."[15] This became a guide for both of them.

The process was mutual. Hob also made a commitment to face this chapter with openness, as if exploring a new territory for living: new lessons, new landscapes and sounds and sights, and—for he had been a devoted college English professor as well as a meditation teacher—new ways of teaching and learning. He also continued, at moments, to take care of Olivia. In lucid moments, surprisingly he would ask about her experience, and once said firmly, "Don't sacrifice yourself for me."[16]

Olivia continued to make "turnings" in her practice, according to his stage of illness. In the end she realized that she had to help him let go, and to be with him through that final moment—and then even beyond that. She promised him at the end that she would write this book and continue to share his voice and their experience to benefit so many others going through such a profoundly difficult journey. The book offers a path of hope and grace in the face of life's greatest and most terrifying and somber challenges.

## CREATING RIPE MOMENTS: REFLECTIONS AND MEDITATIONS

### Taking Vows

Commitment to *being with*, and staying through, illness, old age, and death involves recognizing the wonder of this path, the extraordinary intelligence, the wisdom, and the heart in the daily work of this practice. This is a commitment—a choice beyond attachment or obligation—to be present and to stay through, no matter what. This is an aim or an aspiration. We recognize that we can never achieve it fully, or always gracefully—we are all merely "human." It is simply what we are aiming for. A huge amount of self-compassion is necessary to walk this path and to accept our limitations. It is essential to make conscious the intention, and to be sure that right relation does not violate care for self. It may be that taking a vow to oneself is also necessary.

### In Community

Having family, friends, or a community who recognize the extraordinary work of this loving, devotional path and provide practices to support this work is vital. A wisdom path supports "wise" suffering—the turning of suffering, as it meets compassion, into understanding, awareness, and a deepening sense of the interrelationship of all beings. A compassionate community that appreciates the complexity of this path supports all those walking this path together.

## What Are the Perils?

Create an inventory of your own personal perils and the possible perils of meeting them.

- Isolation
- Loneliness and the sense of oppression (the opposite of freedom)—the feeling of having no choice in frustrating obligations
- Lack of resources and poverty; lack of adequate medical, nursing, and household care
- Drugs, substance abuse, and depression—either for parents and/or adult children
- Unmanageable, severely debilitating illness—psychological and/or physical, in either the elder or the adult child, or both

## 1. Reflections to Be Written and Shared with Your Circle, or "Family *Sangha*."

- What formative experiences have you had with illness, old age, and death?
- What role models have you had—teachers, grandparents, friends—and what about these has been positive or negative? What end-of-life stories have inspired you?
- What are your commitments now? What do you imagine they will be in the future, and how are you preparing for them?
- What are the obstacles in your way of staying through illness, old age, and death—as a caregiver and as an elder?
- Have you had conversations with those who are ill, aging, or dying about their wishes or fears about end-of-life decisions? Have you been able to share your wishes, fears, and concerns?

- Do you experience extreme conflicts between your own and others' needs? What would help you? What would help the relationship?
- What is your current community or what community do you need to develop?
- What qualities would you like to develop to support you in your practice of staying with?

## 2. Individual Meditation Practice

- Sit in meditation or silence while watching the sunset. Observe all the energies of endings: the light, the form, the shadows, the colors, the movements in the sky. Observe impermanence.
- Meditate on a circle of care: Imagine a loving circle of light and warmth all around you and your loved one. Feel the strength and power of the loving community there to support and ease stress. Let the suffering be transformed into light, and illuminate the relationship and the Circle of Compassion around you.
- As your *metta* practice, offer the phrases of loving-kindness and compassion to yourself, to the elder, and to the relationship. In your heart, cultivate loving-kindness and compassion with this wish, or blessing: "May you be happy; may you be free from suffering; may we live and die in peace."

## 3. Relational Meditation Practice

- Mindful breathing: Sit in a chair or next to a bedside of someone ill, aging, or dying. Gently align your breathing with that of the other. You can either do this silently or ask the other person if they'd like to do some breathing together. You might want to breathe out with a sigh or an "ahh," allowing the out-breath to release stress and tension. Simply aligning the breathing is an easy way to practice *being with*.

- *Mantra* practice: Try to find a simple word (or words) that can be used through illness or death—words that have been said in the spirit of the relationship—and try to use them frequently, either in your heart or out loud, offering them at important times. Phrases like "No words" or "Just love" can come to have very evocative meanings as the person declines, as these few words can come to represent the whole relationship.
- A simple mindful moment of *being with*: Pause, relax, open into the relationship; then smile to yourself, to the other, and to the whole universe, and feel the whole universe holding you.
- Making amends and asking forgiveness: You may want to do this formally or informally. Think about what you want to have out of the way between you and the other person, and take the time to make amends and ask forgiveness. Practice self-forgiveness, and accept that the other person may or may not choose to reciprocate.

# Part III

# Widening Circles, Ripples of Change

*No one of us on this earth—past, present, future—has the power to overcome despair, brokenness, and violation. Only together, hands joined and bodies leaning into one another, is there hope for this world and any of us in it.*

—**Carter Heyward,** *Touching Our Strength*

*The Great Turning is a name for the essential adventure of our time: the shift from an industrial-growth society to a life-sustaining society. To see this as the larger context of our lives clears the vision and summons our courage.*

—**Joanna Macy,** *Stories of the Great Turning*

# 6

# Creating Circles of Peace, Diversity, Restorative Justice

> The able men were still gone, off to war. This was, strangely, a blessing—a rare chance to see the power of the women's circle expanding beyond our own power. It was an opportunity for the women to explore this new way of making peace and solving problems.
>
> —Kisa Gotami, in Chapter 25 of "Yasodhara's Story"

This chapter represents the flowering of the Path of Right Relation and peace-building as it meets the challenges of our time. Relational practices are resources for creating peace, social justice, and social healing. The sacred circle, initially growing out of a response of compassion meeting suffering, and then as the circle of care holding the devotional practice of accompanying others through life, now becomes a resource for peace building and "going forth" as a community movement.

As it is written in Book One of Yasodhara's story, a neighboring palace community, Kalayana, is drawn into a war, with the men far away in battle, and the remaining community of women, elders, and children descending into struggle, chaos, and division. Messengers are sent to Yasodhara's community to ask for help. Pajapati asks the king if they might go, and he agrees, "Yes, we'll send you, the women of our Sakya clan." Their decision is to respond together, as a circle, rather than sending one or two.

Pajapati and Yasodhara and the others travel together to Kalayana and create a circle with the women in the village. They share their relational practices: a shared prayer and silence to begin. Each person is invited to speak their truth with others in deep listening, each voice "heard" and held by all. Into this space, divisions, differences, and conflicts can be engaged respectfully, and strategies for meeting these challenges can be suggested, and agreements made to try to put into action. The Sakyan women agree to return at a regular time to Kalayana to follow the difficulties through to a hoped-for peace and reconciliation. None of the able-bodied men are left in the village, and the young, old, and others who cannot fight, come to respect what the women are doing, and some join in. In the absence of the usual power structure, power over—the warriors and chieftains in control—things have fallen into chaos and struggle, and the Sakyan women offer a new power structure to the whole village: a model of power with, based on collective "gathering" and collaborative problem solving.

Over time, not without conflict and difficulty, there emerges a shift to a new way of meeting the conflict and suffering, through building "right" or "wise" relation—dialogue, sacred ritual and prayer and meditation, "staying" through the conflict and process. Often, nearly consensual decisions, "facing" difference and "staying" through conflict, are reached. The circle of women is at the core of this shift in the village.

As the new Kalayana village group is growing stronger and more empowered, Yasodhara and Pajapati and the other Sakyan women are surprised and grateful for how this circle has taken hold. There is great joy in being able to share their vision with the Kalyans, who are so different in their culture and practices. They grow even stronger in their practice and in developing the sense of service. They are awed to see the value their path can have for others, that it can be passed on and that everyone is strengthened through the further "widening of the circle."

The principles they discover are the fundamentals for the flowering of this "hidden path" in our time. The relational practices have now grown to be a vibrant, worldwide resource for cultural change, peace-building, and social justice.

These discoveries are of great value, and they feel valued as "messengers." They show that inclusive circles can ripple out more and more widely—and the widening increases their power. Their discoveries:

- Showing up together
- Widening the circle, opening to the new—new culture, new voices
- Inclusion and creatively metabolizing differences, allowing something new to emerge
- Holding division and conflict—moving through it and beyond it—to reconciliation; moving through disconnections to new connection and restoration of community
- Developing new rituals and practices along the way
- Grouping and regrouping; the process of reconnecting, gathering again at regular intervals; the circle becoming an ongoing "relational practice"
- Working with conflict, disconnection, and burnout as challenges to widening the circle
- Showing up together lays the foundations for going forth together; "deep" or "beloved" community is touched, realized,

and recognized, offering a glimpse of profound interconnection, or interbeing.

## Diversity in Community: Inclusion and Engagement

One of the great cultural challenges of our time is to widen our circles and spiritual communities to become welcoming and affirming to diverse groups and to foster continuity of awareness of the suffering and oppression of exclusion, subordination, and marginalization. Open and continuous engagement among particular groups is necessary, especially where it has been the privilege of the dominant group to render the experience of the oppressed group invisible, devalued, or repressed, such as with white racial privilege or white male-gender privilege.

The work of fostering awareness of privilege and the reaching out and empowerment of nondominant groups is necessary to embrace inclusivity and nonseparation. For opening and widening our spiritual communities and for engaging directly with the suffering of oppression and invisibility, the shared intention of compassionate action and transformation must be strongly held.

One of the foremost Buddhist communities, Spirit Rock Meditation Center in California, has undertaken this initiative very seriously for many years and has become a beacon and model for this work. In 2001, the Board of Spirit Rock wrote a Diversity Program Initiative, which has guided the work of the community since then—with varying degrees of progress along the way.

The Statement of Intention:

> To ensure that Spirit Rock is accessible and welcoming to all people who wish to participate in the *sangha*, regardless of ethnic origin, race, culture background, socio-economic class, age, gender, sexual orientation, or physical ability. Our purpose is to

> awaken and sustain an engaged exploration into the many levels of seen and unseen separation among the Spirit Rock community using the fundamental joining of our *dharma* practice.[1]

This initiative, to challenge separation and to cultivate honest engagement requires diligent effort in supporting healing or freedom from the *dukkha* (suffering) of racism and oppression.

This practice of diversity is undertaken as a *fundamental* grounding of the dharma practice of the community. It involves making the invisible suffering of oppression more visible to the whole community and active engagement of the whole with this undertaking of inclusivity and healing. In this spirit, Spirit Rock has undertaken creating a matrix of programs and retreats for specific groups, e.g., people of color. It has worked on building cultural competency at every level and has changed the membership of the Board of Teaching Council to be more fully representative of nondominant groups. It has reached out to members of unrepresented communities and in unserved populations (such as inner city, rural, prison, elderly, homeless, addicts, adolescents, Native American nations), and brought members into leadership positions in both teaching and administrative positions.

Larry Yang of the East Bay Meditation Center in Oakland, California and Gina Sharpe of the Insight Meditation Center in New York City, have been guiding teachers for this initiative and have made enormous contributions to keeping the diversity practice alive and center in the wider *Vipassana* Buddhist communities. We see this as a great contribution of American teachers to the evolution of Buddhism in the West. America, by virtue of its "melting pot" status and its horrendous history in its treatment of Native peoples, African Americans, and other ethnic groups, needs to play a unique role in this powerful work of building awareness, creating opportunities for grappling and struggling with these differences through dialogue, healing, and reconciliation in the service of inclusivity and the widening of *sangha*.

This is a particular challenge to spiritual communities, which point to a universal absolute, beyond this worldly substrate of human experience—to appreciate the separation and oppression within their own communities and to appreciate that this *dialogue work is in itself a pathway to liberation—not separate from but a legitimate way of opening the dharma doorway wide—to all.*

In one diversity dialogue, a white woman said to the white men, "If you don't see yourself as a 'white man,' you don't really see yourself."

The man replied, "If you *only* see me as a white man, you don't really see me."[2]

Both are true. This reflects the crucial *dharma* doorway of the particular held in awareness of the whole, and Yasodhara's path of wise relation.

The spiritual pathway to the growth and power of "widening and deepening" relationships and communities, which have been divided by unequal power, oppression, and unseen suffering, is a deep expression/realization of Yasodhara's Path of Awakening within, through, and toward inclusive community.

## Ripe Moments: Betty's Story[3]

In our time, many women—and men—have embraced this relational path. In our country, African-American and Native-American cultures have seeded it. The women's movement and peace movement have drawn from this. We are discovering how the power of relational practices and the realization of deep community can become a resource for peacemaking, social justice, and social healing.

Our friend Betty J. Burkes is an educator and "relational activist" who grew up with "the power of circles in my blood." Born into an African-American community in Malvern, Ohio, her grandparents, along with many others who were descendants of slaves, had emigrated North from the South, to work at a brick-making plant. They formed a community which was held together by the church and by the collective sense that this community was necessary for them to survive. This sense of community created a protective "shield" which operated in the harsh conditions. Betty felt this implanted within her a deeply collective experience of "being part of"—of "belonging to community"—as her earliest sense of herself. Her first memory was of sitting on the floor close to her grandmother in a women's quilting circle. The quilting was practical—sewing clothes and warm quilts against the Northern cold for the families—and discussion ranged from when to plant and when to harvest, when and where to meet and offer help to each other, stories about fishing, cooking, relationships, affirming the art of storytelling. As the threads of fabric were woven, the threads of community were strengthened.

The women were also weaving together, and attending to problems or disconnections in the community—a single mother who needed food, an abused woman with an alcoholic husband—they would try to come up with ways of solving these problems. The implicit idea was that individuals were responsible for the community, and the community was responsible for the needs of the individuals—that there was a central core of movement toward mutuality. As problems were attended to, the fabric of the community was strengthened and empowered.

Where things were frayed or torn, they were mended and formed into new patterns, just as the beautiful quilts they were creating. "To a little girl," she said, "the work of the women was compelling, exciting, and very real. I felt a heightened sense of aliveness and presence there—that what was happening really mattered."

Developing out of her work in education with children, in Berkeley California, in the Peace Corps in Ethiopia, and the creative arts in England, Betty began leading workshops for children of all ages on Cape Cod called "Play Fair." These provided opportunities for children to build skills in non-violent, cooperative, and creative arts and game-playing activities. This took her into deeper questions of how to build "peace cultures," nonviolent alternatives to the dominant militaristic and consumer-driven cultures. And it led to her sense of the power of education, especially with young children, to promote cultures of peace and "launch" peacemakers out into the world.

As part of her commitment to peace education, she joined the local community of the Women's International League for Peace and Freedom, and became president of this global organization for several years. Betty believes and lives the power of "beloved community," where all life is valued and human interactions are guided by equality, kindness, and compassion. She also believes the structures of power can be transformed through nonviolence and education that promotes inquiry and investigation, patience, and love. Peace is achievable through honest dialogue, relational practice, and self-reflection. This became fundamental to her political action, which we have come to call *relational activism*.

Betty built directly on these experiences to work for global peace education in countries and communities that had been devastated by, and were recovering from, war. She worked as a peace educator coordinator with the United Nations Department of Disarmament in Albania, Peru, Cambodia, and Niger. In this work she helped create circles of community leaders to enquire deeply about what cultural resources for peace-building already existed and to develop a curriculum to promote peace education on a national level. These circles of leaders have gone on to create curricula that have been implemented in each country. Betty is currently working on building peace culture through community-building and circles to empower young people in New Orleans to "rethink" their schools and their educational system following Hurricane Katrina. The young people are learning to use their voices to advocate for equality and quality education based on human values, based on the conviction that they *together* have the power to change the educational system they inhabit.

Betty's personal story has been shaped by her community experience as a child, and her openness to embrace and be embraced by the many communities in which she has participated along the way. She deeply believes in the human capacity to build communities of love and justice. She describes the spiritual dimensions of sacred circles as follows:

- Respect and affirm wisdom already present in individuals, groups, and cultures
- Promote an inquiry process that opens a meditative space
- Allow deep listening to happen
- Create capacity for inner silence and silence together
- Foster the experience of our "many-ness" and our "one-ness"
- Cultivate connection at deeper, more intuitive levels
- Contribute to repairing outer conditions and circumstances

## Peacemaking Circles

The Quakers, or Society of Friends, have long relied on the practice of open dialogue in "listening" circles, the practice of sitting in silence until a person comes forth and shares from the heart, and is met with deep listening:

- A practice of spiritual gathering and worship
- A way of uncovering collective wisdom and power
- A way of discernment for personal and social action based on "group conscience"

In the past few decades, the power of circles has been described and utilized as a basis for peacemaking circles of many kinds.[4] Circles are an alternative process of communication, based on traditional discussion and healing practices of aboriginal peoples in Canada and the southwestern United States. Circles have been adapted but maintain these essential features:

- Everyone in the circle is equal and has equal opportunity to speak.
- Decisions are made by consensus.
- Everyone agrees to abide by guidelines established by the group itself, based on shared values, in order to work toward a common goal.

Additionally, circles are established as "sacred spaces; circles are opened and closed with words of reflection, prayer, and poetry, and people may be invited to symbolically cleanse themselves before entering the circle."[5]

In circles, participants are invited to "step into" an extraordinary space, which invites a deeper sense of authenticity, truth-telling, inquiry, discovery, witnessing, and deep listening. Through the collective wisdom that emerges, action strategies can emerge as well—this is the power of the path, of a new power emerging from the realization of deep community or connection.

Circles can serve different purposes. There are support circles, listening circles, dialogue circles (see "gender dialogues," later in this chapter), school-based circles, healing circles, circles to build relationships and promote peace in communities, and healing circles of all kinds.

Originating in the 1970s as mediation processes between victims and offenders, through the 1990s the "Restorative Justice" Movement has broadened to include restorative circles including friends, families, and communities. This work is based on the recognition that humans are more satisfied, cooperative, and more likely to change when engaging in restorative, participatory power with relational practices, rather than punitive or authoritative power over—or even a more permissive, paternalistic *power for*—practice.

The most crucial function of "restorative practices" that restore or repair or reconnect is the restoring and cultivating of relationships and community.[6] Circles are based on restorative practice. In restorative justice, circles provide a vehicle for "fair process," where the harm caused for individuals and communities can be named, and apologies and amends can be made directly to the victims. The suffering of all parties is witnessed, a full range of strong feelings expressed, and the needs of individuals and the community can be heard and attended to.

Rather than punishing by extruding the perpetrator from the community (by banishment, incarceration, or death, for example) the work of reintegrating and rehabilitating can be done, and each participant and the circle as a whole can be "re-called" and grown through the process. Reconvening the circle after the initial meeting(s) provides for accountability and continuity and a process that ultimately restores and deepens the bonds of each to all, and all to each. The underlying principle here is that communities as well as the individuals are harmed when there is a violation of any member, and the community is responsible and capable of healing and self-restoration.

## Ripe Moments: Judith's Story[7]

Judith Thompson has devoted her whole life to the study and practice of social healing and transformation. A tall and graceful blond woman born into privilege in the 1950s, Judith has always been deeply aware of the suffering of oppression in both dominant and marginalized culture groups. In her life, she has been called forth to participate in many forms of social healing and peace-building through creating and being part of processes of "participatory discovery," an opening deeply to authentic and passionate truth-telling and deep listening in the service of "waging peace."

In 1984, she and Arn Chorn-Pond, a young Cambodian who had personally witnessed the killing fields of the Khmer Rouge, created Children of War, a program which offered young people from war-torn communities a way to come together, share the depth of their experiences, witness and relate tales of the horrific suffering each had known, and to "hear each other into speech and action." The goal was to empower a new generation of activists and peacemakers.

Judith was a Peace Fellow at the Bunting Institute at Radcliffe, and worked at the Center for Social Change in Cambridge, Massachusetts. For her PhD thesis in 2002, she studied "The Role of Compassion in Social Healing." Judith has spoken and written powerfully about the "spiritual energies of compassion," which can generate—and be generated through—the relational practices of "social healing." When members of cultural and national groups (Israelis and Palestinians, for example) can find pathways to break through seemingly intractable disconnects and relational impasses created by past wounds, atrocities, traumas, and deeply engrained historical narratives of "victimhood," seemingly impossible relationships can be forged as a basis for bridging and healing the profound national or group wounds.

In 2002, she convened a three-day circle at the Boston Ikeda Center in Cambridge, Massachusetts, bringing together Palestinian and Israeli, Northern Ireland Catholic and Protestant, children of Holocaust survivors and of Nazi Youth, Serbian, Rwandan, Cambodian, South African, African American, Native American—all survivors and peacemakers, gathered in a sacred circle. They were given the time and space to enquire together, to tell their stories through sacred symbolic objects they had brought to place on the altar, to witness each other's suffering and healing, to experience the sacred power of opening and forgiveness, and to awaken and spark the imagination of what is possible in healing and transformation in the world.

Judith honors the power of compassion to break through divisions and separations and the power of circle and participatory dialogue to heal and transform the most devastating disconnections in modern human history. In the process, she points to the power of breaking through separation and division and tapping into deep connection, and deep community; the energy and joy that are released in the joining or restoration of relationship. This is the energy, the movement that taps our "human resources" for deeper—and wider—healing. The peace-building can radiate into the world through the faith and *practice of relational activism.*

## The Karuna Center for Peacebuilding

Paula Green founded the Karuna Center for Peacebuilding in Western Massachusetts in 1994. She shares this depth of faith in the practice of deep dialogue. The Karuna Center is "committed to the development and implementation of innovative, sustainable strategies for conflict transformation and community reconciliation in societies where ethnic, religious, sectarian, or political conflict threatens the possibility of a healthy and inclusive democracy and sustainable development."[8] Karuna has now worked in over twenty-five conflict-torn countries on four continents, and works at multiple levels—with government ministries and parliaments, community leaders and grassroots groups—to promote genuine dialogue, cooperative problem-solving, and nonviolent solutions to community problems.

*Karuna* is the Pāli word for "compassion." Paula is a Buddhist who has taught at many Buddhist centers nationally and internationally. She is part of the Buddhist Peace Fellowship—Thich Nhat Hanh was one of the founders. She has joined other spiritual pioneers in focusing the attention of Buddhists toward compassionate action in response to the suffering of our world, at greater levels than simply as individuals in private internal realms. Paula's work is grounded in the power of generating compassion to meet and respond to suffering.

The essence of her work is, simply put: *to use the power of compassion to transform conflict by transforming relationships.*

# CREATING RIPE MOMENTS: REFLECTIONS AND PRACTICES

## 1. Reflections

The following questions are for individuals but are particularly valuable to discuss in a group.

- Think of all the groups you are part of. Include race, gender, sexual preference, socioeconomic class, ethnicity, religion, nationality, age, body capability, and so forth; while certain groups are more central, all are operative; and you are a part of each.
- Notice which groups you most identify with and those with which you identify the least. Consider how this reflects on your life and communities.
- What are the joys and sorrows, privileges and limitations of being part of these groups?
- How has this social and cultural location shaped your identity, your view of others, and your worldview? How might you be unaware of this?
- How are you working toward greater awareness and openness in your life?
- What intentional communities could support this work?
- Does your spiritual path in community support this level of practice?
- What do you need to do to continue to expand this work in your life? What are the obstacles and what are the resources you can offer?
- What are some personal or cultural amends you would like to make? Where would you wish to have amends made to you? How would you respond?

## 2. Individual Meditation Practice

Creating Circles of Diversity (Please put aside at least two hours for this exercise.)

- Create an intentional structure within your circle, *sangha*, or Family *Sangha*, and a special time devoted to cross-cultural dialogue. (Keep in mind that a group's level of diversity enriches the dialogue.) Choose one or two relevant areas to begin with—race and gender, for example.
- Using the four questions below, write out answers and then read them to each other, either alone or with others who shared the same identity:
  - What do you see as the strengths and privileges of your group? The other group?
  - What do you most want to understand about the other group?
  - What do you most want the other group to understand about you?
  - What would you need to create to participate in a circle of right relation with the other?
- Ring the bell to open the circle.
- Practice deep listening, and pause before responding. First, speak back only what has been heard. Practice the guidelines of Insight Dialogue within the circle. (See page 136)
- Allow space for curiosity and deepening of your responses through dialogue.
- Identify impasses as they arise, and simply name them as not yet worked on but still acknowledged.
- Accept the work as far as it can go. Express appreciation and acceptance, appreciating that this can only be "lived" into—

that we must learn to live with uncertainty, confusion, and "not-yet-knowing."

- Set a date to reconvene in further discussion.
- Express gratitude to each other for the willingness to face into difficult territory and to open these dialogues.
- Ring the bell to close the circle at a designated time.

### 3. Relational Meditation Practice

- At the end of the circle of diversity, ring the bell. Sit in the circle in silence for 5 to 10 minutes.
- Allow the words to settle, and simply bring awareness to the energy and insight arising in the circle. Breathe deeply. Continue to practice, internally: Pause. Relax. Open. Trust Emergence.
- Offer the *metta* phrases of loving-kindness in your heart to everyone in the circle. Speak them to each other.
- Ring the bell to end.

# 7

# Going Forth Together: Communities of Awakening

A new monastic community of women was formed alongside the men's *sangha*. Word spread like the monsoon rains that the queen and princess, and many other noble women and their servants, had joined the Buddha's *sangha*—something, as yet, unheard of!

—Chapter 27, "Yasodhara's Story"

The community of Sakyan women, through Pajapati, twice asks the Buddha if they can "go forth" and become ordained in the monastic community. The third time, Pajapati requests that Ananda, the Buddha's cousin and close attendant, petition the Buddha on the women's behalf. All three times, the Buddha says no. The women then decide to go forth without permission. Heads shaven, with begging bowls, they walk together to the Buddha's *sangha*.

Ananda comes to ask the Buddha again, as the women are fast approaching. As the Buddha is deliberating, he informs him that the women are already at the gates. The Buddha, although hesitant, finally agrees—but designates strict rules for establishing a women's monastic *sangha*. These rules are set in place to protect the women and perhaps to protect the monks from sexual temptation. The rules are also to keep order and preserve the male hierarchy, which is the cultural order of the time. The women somewhat reluctantly agree to these rules, and the new community of "almswomen" or nuns is established. Pajapati becomes the leader. It is said she advances spiritually and becomes enlightened and then brings many other women into the community. (This is described in the *Therigatha*—a collection of writings and poems of the first nuns. Yasodhara is hardly mentioned in this literature.)

In Book One—our imagined story—Pajapati on her deathbed reconnects with Yasodhara in remembering their journey together. As they realize that their relational pathway to awakening is being lost in the Buddha's *sangha*, Pajapati realizes that Yasodhara can never fully attain enlightenment because she cannot fully receive the Buddha as her teacher. She is still married to Siddhartha and cannot reconcile the Buddha's claim to have "gone beyond" that part of him. Pajapati wants to give Yasodhara the gift of full awakening and realizes that Yasodhara needs to have her story and her path affirmed before she can fully be released, to let go. Both come to see that many others may be left behind unless they name and affirm their pathway as an opening toward spiritual liberation.

The Sakyan women actually walk a revolutionary path. As a community, a sacred circle—having "gone together" to do service and to widen their circle of peace, they ripened into spiritual maturity to "go forth" together in the holy life—and not alone. Before this the act of spiritual awakening is described as an individual event—as the Buddha experiences it—alone in the wilderness. While the Buddha spends most of his life, before and after this event, in community, this moment of awakening is always imagined as the awakening of One—in solitary struggle with *mara* (demons), blossoming into total freedom and awakening, which can then become a teaching to transmit to others.

The women enter the community as a circle. Rather than leaving home alone, they leave *together*—actually in an act of community solidarity and resistance, a "Yes!" to the Buddha's "No."

At Pajapati's deathbed, there is an attempt to tell the whole story. We have the sense that, and imagine that, at some point in time this went underground, although often recalled and remembered over the hundreds of years that the community was in practice—when the nuns' practice remained vibrant and intact. Somewhere in the 2,500-year history of *Theravadin* Buddism the original unbroken lineage of nuns died out. Historians suggest that the ordaining of nuns stopped after about 1,500 years. To this day it has not been formerly re-established once again—women nuns are not invited to full ordination. As the flowering of the Relational Path is happening in our time, so is the movement (although still controversial) to reestablish the opportunity for full ordination of nuns in the monastic community.

As His Holiness the Dalai Lama said at a recent conference in Hamburg, Germany, on this issue: "If he was alive today, I believe the Buddha would be for it. But I myself cannot say. I am not a Buddha."[1]

## Spiritual Awakening Together

> We lived on and worked together, until our traveling *sangha* of women, traveling with the Buddha, was thriving. Together, we tried to join our own wisdom and practices with the monastic rites and practices of the Buddha, expanding both paths so that there was something of a joining of the best practices and teachings of each. (Chapter 28, page 103)

While the Awakened One still remains the mythic heroic story of our spiritual traditions, there is a contemporary recognition of the power and centrality of *sangha*, of community—in our time. Thich

Nhat Hanh has sounded the call in his deeply prophetic teaching: "The next Buddha may be the *sangha*."[2]

This suggests that the community itself is called to go forth, to fully awaken and transmit in a new way. Thich Nhat Hanh fully recognizes the primary importance of *sangha* for his Western students. In the West, he acknowledges, there is vast suffering of isolation and separation, psychological alienation from family and community—and he understands that "learning to be and see with *sangha* eyes" is of primary importance.[3]

He and others (such as David Loy) appreciate the powerful qualities of the Western cultural context, particularly in America, fueled by:

- Greed (consumerism and wealth addiction)
- Hatred (guns, violence, and profound conflict and division)
- Delusion (refuge in separation, extreme blinding self-centeredness, and technological and corporate values—above human values)[4]

Resisting these individual and collective "poisons" (Thich Nhat Hanh's term) can best be achieved in powerful community, not by an individual alone.[5]

Finally, Thich Nhat Hanh, as he faces his own death (as did the Buddha), has recognized the need for his teachings to be held and sustained in the communities he has created around him—without the power residing in one teacher. He calls for the next Buddha to be *sangha*, a community of spiritual awakening, the work of "*awakening community*," to be the focus of his lay and monastic students.[6]

"Awakening community" implies a double doorway: an awakening of the community to its own powerful nature of interbeing and interconnectedness, and also of becoming a vehicle of awakening for those who enter. Thich Nhat Hanh is working on ways to grow his communities toward sustained awakening.

Thich Nhat Hanh speaks about the absolute priority of building the strengths of the *sangha*:

> We can take refuge in the *sangha* in order to succeed in our practice. . . . The *sangha* has a collective energy. Without this energy, the practice of individual transformation is not easy. . . . Any group of people can practice as a community determined to live in harmony and awareness, committed to going together in the direction of peace, joy, and freedom . . . Together we benefit from each others' strengths and learn from each others' weaknesses. A family is a *sangha*, the members of a monastic and lay practice center are a *sangha*, even the U.N. is a *sangha*![7]

He goes on to describe this:

> A *sangha* is a family, a spiritual family connected by practices of mindfulness, concentration, and insight. The *sangha* may be Buddhist or non-Buddhist, so long as it is a community that walks the path of liberation together. . . . Our success or failure as practitioners, our happiness in life, depends on whether we have this capacity for *sangha* building. . . . Our *sangha* body is going forward on the path of practice and its eyes are able to direct us.[8]

When we refer to seeing through *sangha eyes*, we mean the insight and vision of the collective body. Although the contribution of everyone's insight is necessary, it is not just a simple adding-up of individual insights. *The collective insight has a strength, a wisdom, and a vitality of its own which surpasses any individual insight.*[9] We learn to use the eyes of the *sangha* as our own. We need to hear the truth about ourselves as others see it, always practicing in the spirit of compassion. The energy of the *sangha* has the capacity to protect and transform us. As a member, we each have to make our contribution. *Sangha*-building is "the most precious work a monk, nun, or layperson can do."[10] We each have to work on ourselves to become what Thich Nhat Hanh called a "good enough" member, and to continue to support and grow "good enough" community.

Thich Nhat Hanh has begun to develop relational practices that awaken and reawaken his communities. From "Straw Over Mud" (peace-building practices to reestablish the community through conflict and vision) to "Beginning Anew" (practices bringing the community into the present moment, releasing old perceptions and resentments), "Watering the Seeds" (harnessing the power of community to affirm and recognize individuals for their gifts and service), and "Second Body" (each person watching out for and caring for—with special attention—one other community member).[11] Thich Nhat Hanh draws on and refreshes for our time the spirit of the Buddha's teachings on monastic life.

In Thich Nhat Hanh's words: "Awakening community can be a vehicle for spiritual awakening to the fundamental truth of nonseparation, of a fully interdependent reality beyond delusions of separation and a new experience of time and space and identity."

## Aspects of Spiritual Awakening across Spiritual Paths

- Acceptance of the limitations and suffering of the "self"—challenging the delusion of separation and personal control over this human life; cultivating humility
- "Coming forth" out of isolation
- Opening to a new way of being in the world—of *being with* a wider circle of practitioners, fellows, meditators, and family members
- Holding together in communities of compassion, care, wisdom, and love that meet and share suffering

- Allowing this new power, energy, and wisdom of the whole to infuse one's being in the world
- Finding a new happiness, a new peace, and a new freedom in relationship and community
- Sharing, transmitting, and passing on this new way of being to others by working to build inclusive, widening circles
- Taking action with the priority of strengthening communities; relationships and *sangha* "come first"

## The Net of Indra

This great Hindu image of interconnectedness is a beautiful representation of an awakening community. Each node of the web is a shining gem, connected to all others, some closer, some further away. Each reflects all the others. Each is illuminated by the whole, and the light of each one is reflected in all others and the whole. The net is illuminated—a "field of light," energy, love, and awareness. This image is just a moment in time. As the community awakens it is emergent, moment-to-moment, arising anew and vanishing again. Paradoxically the net is always there, and though we may feel apart or lost, it is a web—in Joanna Macy's words—"out of which we can never fall."[12]

## Contemporary Spiritual Communities of Awakening

### Buddhist Communities

Many Buddhist communities are prioritizing the work of building *sangha*. The Spirit Rock meditation center in California has begun a "community *dharma* leadership program" to support leaders who are committed to community building. Insight meditation teacher Eugene Cash has suggested reordering the Triple Gems to put "*sangha* first"—*sangha*, *dharma*, Buddha—to "re-balance what has been taught as the priority of the Awakened One."[13]

We have already mentioned the enormous energy being released in building a worldwide *sangha* within the Thich Nhat Hanh community. This is the traditional four-fold community of monks, nuns, laymen, and laywomen. Another large and growing Japanese Nichiren Buddhist community is Soka Gakkai. This huge international community is dedicated to achieving positive change in individual lives and in society as a whole.

**Insight Dialogue**

Gregory Kramer has inspired a worldwide community based on the teaching and practice of Insight Dialogue, teaching a fully engaged co-meditative practice, including deep listening and right speech. This practice is built on three pillars: the meditative "mind" cultivated in relationship, the wisdom teaching of the Buddha *dharma*, and the powers of relationship—all synergistically working together. The worldwide Insight Dialogue community is investigating and witnessing the as-yet untapped power of relationship in cultivating the factors of awakening together. This shared path can be directly experienced and known in relation. It is within this community of practice that the power of silent, internal meditative practice, interwoven with engaged co-meditative practice, is being manifested and realized as a full expression of the dharma.[14]

**Twelve-Step Fellowship/Community**

In hundreds of thousands of meetings every day across the world, members of 12-Step communities practice deep listening and speaking their truth in large and small groups. Each member is invited to tell his or her story to speak their truth, and in doing so renewing their commitment to sobriety and strengthening their connection with the fellowship. This is simultaneously doing service and helping others to stay sober. Each meeting, in its own particular way, touches into and illuminates the healing powers of a vibrant global community of awakening. Stepping into the circle, which deepens "through prayer and meditation" (Step 11), each person can access the compassion and wisdom of the 12-Step fellowship and each can offer the hand of AA or other anonymous 12-Step communities to anyone who still suffers. Step 12 states: "Having had a spiritual awakening as the result of these Steps, we tried to carry this message to alcoholics and to practice these principles in all our affairs."

## Joanna Macy: Practices that Reconnect the *Sangha* of All Beings

Joanna Macy's life work, over six decades, is one of the most powerful examples of the flowering of this hidden relational pathway coming to life in our own time. Trained as a scholar in the Western educational system as a social activist and as a dedicated Buddhist, Joanna describes the "Great Turning" happening among us—as the "Industrial Growth Society" is collapsing and a whole new evolving spirituality, and way of being and being together, is arising, coming to life. She has developed a new view of reality based on "deep ecology, systems thinking, and the resurgence of non-dual spirituality." These three streams attest to our mutual belonging in the whole of life: past, present, and future; and "to the power within us for the healing of the world."[15]

Joanna describes her work as "helping to discover our innate connections and the self-healing power in the web of life." She is a prophet of this new evolving/emerging "life-sustaining culture."[16] She helps create communities of awakening as vehicles to bring people into this new culture. She teaches the work that reconnects to large and small groups around the world, designed to provide people the opportunity to experience and share their innermost responses to "the present condition of our world." Our profound connection to life encompasses deep grief, fear, anger, great despair, and sorrow for our world, which can only be held by larger community. It is simply too much for any one of us. Experienced in the larger web, the power of our love and connection to this world and to the planet we share with all beings can become the passion and energy to activate and clarify our individual and shared role in the "Great Turning" and the healing of our planet.

Joanna's workshops are dedicated "communities of awakening," to bring people out of despair, isolation, and paralysis into the inspiring vital web of the *Sangha* of All Beings of the natural world, human and greater than human, and to reach beyond the traditional experiences of time and space. She offers practices that stir and allow our innate connections with each other to be animated, and the self-healing powers in the web of life to "come to life," take hold and shape the evolution of this "life-sustaining culture." Joanna has described herself as a "social mystic"—we might say a "relational mystic"—who is imbued with spiritual power and prophetic passion when fully engaged within such communities of awakening.

She describes the foundations of life-sustaining cultures:

- Our earth is alive; it is our larger body.
- Our true nature is far more ancient and encompassing than the "separate self" defined by habit and society.
- Our experience or moral pain for our world springs from the interconnectedness of all beings—from which arises our power to act on their behalf.

- "Unblocking" occurs when our pain for the world is not only intellectually validated, but also deeply experienced, together. This experience animates the web of our interconnectedness and strengthens and sustains it.
- When we reconnect with life by willingly enduring our pain for the suffering, the mind retrieves its natural clarity.
- The experience of reconnection with the earth community *arouses our desire to act on its behalf.*
- Action, based on love and sustained in community, can be personal, familial, or social.[17]

## The Council of All Beings

One such culture-building practice is the ritual of convening a "Council of All Beings." Created as a sacred council or circle, a number of humans are seated in the center. The other participants are representing—even channeling—the wisdom and insights of other species (snow owl, titmouse, squirrel, eagle) or natural beings (mountains, grass, rivers). The participants allow another being to choose to speak through them. Each human may wear the mask or simply speak in the voice of this other being. Each offers their natural wisdom to the human species. Each speaks to how humans are causing suffering and offers their unique energies to support and encourage humans to act responsibly in the healing of the world.[18]

The ritual of Council is dramatized, participants receiving the wisdom of species through deep listening, and then offering their responses and commitments to be witnessed by the Council.

This type of ritual and ceremony reminds us of our commitment to work toward healing our world, revitalizes energies beyond despair, paralysis, and isolation, and rekindles the passion for purpose, love, and deep understanding that becomes available when we "realize" in actual experience our fundamental connectedness.

# CREATING RIPE MOMENTS: REFLECTIONS AND PRACTICES

## 1. Reflections

To be written and shared within your circle, spiritual community, or family *sangha*.

- Have you had any experience of feeling yourself part of an awakening community?
- How and where does this experience arise for you? In nature? In special moments? In community: family, work, spiritual community?
- Is there a community you have imagined joining? What could be in the way?
- How might you "come forth" more fully into your current *sangha*? Can you imagine becoming a leader or activist in this way? It can be in your own family *sangha*, or in spiritual or social justice communities.

## 2. Individual Meditation Practice

Practicing the work of becoming a good enough community member.

- Make an inventory of personal qualities or past actions that you are still carrying which have harmed yourself or others. Share this with another person. Make any amends you feel ready to make, and ask for forgiveness.
- As forgiveness practices, repeat the following phrases internally, or directly speaking to another:

*May I ask for your forgiveness for any harm I may have done,*
*Intentionally or unintentionally.*
*May you allow me to be a student of life and make mistakes;*
*And if you cannot forgive me now, may you forgive me in the future.*

*May I forgive you*
*For any harm you may have done,*
*Intentionally or unintentionally.*
*May I allow you to be a student of life and make mistakes;*
*And if I cannot forgive you now, may I forgive you in the future.*

*May I forgive myself*
*For any harm I may have done,*
*Intentionally or unintentionally.*
*May I allow myself to be a student of life and make mistakes;*
*And if I cannot forgive myself now, may I forgive myself in the future.*[19]

- Make an inventory of your self-care practice and share it with another person in your community. State your aspiration and realistic commitments to self-care and community care. Report back to the person(s) with whom you have shared this inventory on a regular basis.

### 3. Relational Meditation Practice

- Family *Sangha*: create family or group rituals. For example, saying grace at the beginning of a meal, which may be simply holding hands, taking three breaths, and offering a family prayer or aspiration. Or take a moment to express gratitude to each other during family time.

- Create an intentional structure to support a group in order to grow into a community of awakening—a family *sangha*, work-group, spiritual community, social or political action group. Here are some steps to take, to begin:

  - Designate a particular time period and set it aside.
  - Designate a particular place—this could be a meditation room or cushions set up in a quiet room—a room that has come to be a "refuge" for family.
  - Begin and end with prayer, meditation, or a ritual such as lighting a candle.
  - Pose a particular question, issue, or theme.
  - Speak of family issues and challenges: deaths—including deaths of pets; conflicts to be resolved; decisions that need to be made; peace-building within the family or larger community or world; or spiritual renewal.
  - Alternate silence and speaking; each person in turn practicing speaking their truth and deep listening.
  - Designate a next time to gather again together.
  - Close with a "loving-kindness" or "gratitude" ritual—using these words in shared speech.

- "Beginning Anew," a renewal practice for communities:

  - Gather everyone in the circle, and designate one cushion as the spotlight;
  - Each person has their turn on the spotlight cushion (2 to 5 minutes).
  - Everyone speaks in turn to what they have appreciated about the person in the spotlight.
  - Any difficulties that can be released are spoken and let go.
  - The spotlight person has a chance to respond to the whole group, expressing gratitude for the community.

# 8

# Conclusion: A Path of Awakening Together—Becoming Relational Activists

"Hear it, remember it, and pass it on!" Thus I have heard.
—Kisa Gotami, in Chapter 30 of "Yasodhara's Story"

You are part of the circle. We invite you to pass it on and become a relational activist in your life in this fragmenting, hurting world. Yasodhara's story is our story—"uncovering" the extraordinary potential of relationship to support a path of awakening; to liberate from the "prison of delusion" and the suffering of isolation and separation.

And to become a vehicle for deep learning and spiritual awakening.

To see with *sangha* eyes.

To see together what cannot be seen alone.

To bear together what cannot be borne alone.

To face—the only way possible to face—the immensity of lethal division and violence and threat to our world: to meet the challenge of climate change, terrorism, consumerism, gun violence, and the growing inequality in our country. We must become "global citizens" of "the *sangha* of all beings," including those born and to be born, those dead and gone before, human and greater than human—part of this living planet and this living universe.

If not together, how?

Together, now, we have walked the path with Yasodhara. If it resonates with who you are, with what is important in your life, pass it on!

## Becoming a Relational Activist

Vimala Thakar said, "We must learn to live together in this new dimension of relationship."[1] Living into the moment, right now, wherever you are, you can choose to be ready to do your part to strengthen and illuminate this path. It is grounded in the simple and profound practice of *being with*: accompanying others in the circle of life, committing to relationship. We can become relational activists in each moment in our close-at-hand relationships, and as activists for social justice and global healing. Each moment of awakening opens to our true nature—our relational being. In the light of this knowing, there can be a moment of action in relation: opening, joining, sustaining, and growing the circle of care and compassion. There is intentionality and devotion to particular relationships and the communities of our lives. There can be shared resistance and the challenging of injustice, both close at hand and in the larger world.

Relational spiritual practice can be at the core of our lives as we become "good enough" members of each community in which we participate: friendships; partnerships; families; and spiritual, religious, or social action communities. We can practice right relation in all.

## Attributes of a Relational Activist

1. Visionary *and* realistic
2. Faithful to the vision

3. Evolutionary
4. Committed to right relation:

    - On the shared path
    - *Being with*
    - Accompanying others
    - Mutual presence
    - Awakening together
    - Widening circles of care and compassion

5. Coming Forth into Right Relation:

    - Asking for help
    - Showing up for others (and self)
    - Mobilizing community
    - Participating in *sangha* or community
    - Becoming allies and partners
    - Resisting demonization of "other(s)"
    - Living into *non-separation*
    - Learning to see with *sangha* eyes
    - Resisting disconnection and violation
    - Building new connections through ruptures

## Relational Spiritual Practices on the Path

- Vows or commitments
- Devotional practice
- Circle practice
- Deep listening, right speech
- Caring for self and others, and relationships
- Making amends
- Forgiveness practice

- Creating intentional supports for creating relationships for spiritual awakening

Relational activism is "living into right relation" as a way of being and a way of living, glimpsing moments of awakening together. We aspire—are faithful to—devoting our lives to bringing forth this experience, sometimes against all odds. A relational activist is evolutionary—he or she "sees" what is not yet actualized and works to bring it forth, to realize it. A relational activist understands that only together can we fully live and tap into the power and wisdom of the *sangha* of all beings. Faith, ferocity of purpose, courage, patience, and forgiveness are required to keep on keeping on, living through the "not-yet moments."

Betty Burkes describes this practice as "living the change you want to see," offering a "seat" in the widening circle to all. She is both a visionary and a relational realist, knowing well the actuality of racism, militarism, structural violence, corporate greed, politics of hatred and delusion, and the turning away from the facts of environmental degradation. Betty shares with relational activist Joanna Macy, Carter Heyward, Frances Moore Lappé, Martin Sheen, Patch Adams, and Bill McKibben among others, the hope and faith in the possibility of the "Great Turning." These relational activists live their lives grounded in this faith, seeking friendships with others from all walks of life in the spirit of becoming "allies," grounded in compassion for change.

## Ripe Moments: Meryl's Story[2]

Meryl was in her fifties, a mother of six, in a marriage for three decades. Her husband was diagnosed with metastatic lung cancer, and, at this time, took the opportunity to "come out" as a gay man, leaving their home and marriage. The bottom fell out. She felt total despair, disempowered, and paralyzed. She would later come to describe this as the "gift of desperation."

Two years later, Meryl invited twenty women, including Janet, to a gathering in a private room at a local restaurant. She called this "a sisterhood celebration." She wanted to have a ritual to celebrate the women who had walked with her through desperate times and into her new life. While she now had the devotion of her grown children, a challenging career, and a male partner with whom she was living in a newly bought home, this intentional gathering was for her sisterhood. The women she invited were a mix of very close friends with whom she was in daily contact and others who had offered something special along the way. Sister, cousin, long-time best friend from elementary school, hairdresser, other mothers, as well as those who knew her at a much greater distance but had been with her in special moments that "saved her life" and were "signposts on her path."

Meryl was an unlikely "feminist," not someone who previously might have gathered people in this way. At the restaurant, she spoke to each of us in turn about the particular moments shared—moments when she had felt understood and challenged to go forth into the new. She spoke with great care about the particular importance of each person. In her own way, she had become a relational activist!

Everyone at the gathering was deeply touched, moved by Meryl's expression of gratitude and honoring. There was a sense that the circle that had been woven around her over these two years was being realized—illuminated—in the present moment. Each person felt the privilege of having been "called forth," of "becoming more of who they were," in meeting Meryl in this difficult time. We all felt a sense of the circle. The fabric of the community that had been woven over time was now lit up, visible, tangible to all.

It was a moment of grace, filled with love and a deep sense of powerful bonds—threads of interconnection between all, many of whom had never met before.

There was a sense of peace, a stillness, and yet a powerful energetic movement—a "living field"; a changing, vibrant sense of life. There was a heightened awareness of feeling deeply alive, awed, and inspired together.

When the evening ended, we all walked back into our daily lives changed and strengthened.

This mutual awakening—this quickening and liberating of spirit—was felt by all. Each person contributed, participated, and was transformed through this moment of grounded community, "knowing deeply in the field of love." It was a moment of recognition, realized *together*. Each, and all, sensed our spirits to be stronger, with renewed faith in the power of life. We left the circle affirmed—as relational activists.

And there was the sense that each of us was part of many circles that probably overlapped in ways we could not see. Each circle could be seen as containing the whole of life—the ancestors and the future generations that would be impacted by these, the "chance" moments that, woven together, formed the circle that not only held and sustained new life but allowed the old to fall away with little residue of resentment. The circle held a sadness, a poignancy, a hope, a resolute strength and power, a great rejoicing and appreciation of the creative possibilities and tragedies of this human life. Each at the center and in the web of the whole.

And I almost hadn't gone. I was too tired, and it was a long drive. I didn't know Meryl all that well. But I had promised a friend I would drive with her, so I felt I had to go.

Often, we *don't* fully "come forth" when called. We don't show up; we don't ask for help, gather the circle, act with faith in life's possibilities. We can always make a slight bend or stretch, a small effort to show up.

All are part of the Great Turning.

## Help Is Always with You: An Encounter with a *Bodhisattva*

Almost all of us have had the experience of having a chance encounter when we least expect it—but are perhaps ready for it—with a person we meet briefly who says or does something that reveals great understanding and compassion. These can be humble or much-learned people. We have come to understand these beings as *bodhisattvas*—living their lives in obscurity, perhaps, who through their own suffering have learned how to show up for others. They themselves may not even realize this—their hearts are just dedicated, naturally, to helping others or to creating moments of connection that awaken us.

New York City seems to have a preponderance of these street *bodhisattvas*. Perhaps it's the necessity of getting along in such an overwhelming environment, where, as one person said to us, "It sucks, but we're all in it together." Sometimes they merely help out a little—like when they see you are lost in the subway or on the street; other times, when you are passing by. They are often there when you need them, but you don't know it yet. Sometimes they connect with humor; other times, they stop you in your tracks with their wisdom. It becomes a "a moment on the path of awakening."

One day, we were in New York, rushing along Tenth Street to an important meeting. We were carrying heavy bags and sweating in the hot day. Just as we were passing a stoop where an African American man was sitting, he called out:

"Help for a homeless Vietnam Vet?"

We gestured no, and walked on. He called out, "Man, you two are in a hurry!"

We looked back, and gestured yes we were.

He said, "You too *old* to be in a hurry!"

This stopped us in our tracks. We three were held together in a moment. We were startled, and then all laughed together. How right he was! It changed us, and we still use his words to remember this message in times of stress. And he got help as well—the money he was asking for—and a wonderful joy in the moment together, being received and appreciated.

We call these moments "*Hey, wait a second!*" *moments.* We pass by someone in need or don't drive to a gathering—and only later do we ask ourselves, *Hey, wait a second. Why did I pass by? Why didn't I show up?*

Yasodhara calls us to act more fully into this relational activism. It's close at hand, every day, in all of our lives—especially if we are ready and living life in earnest. We can act with faith and intention, creating ripe conditions, but the alive and deeply beloved community can only be realized in grace.

We can never *make* it happen.

It occurs all around us, all the time.

## How Good It Is

How good it is to act with an awareness of the whole world!

Empathy is to the particular, as compassion is to the whole.

If you're a global relational activist, every relationship is important. Even the smallest action—your heart opening, your hand reaching out, asking a question, listening, *staying one more moment*—it's always possible, for both individuals and communities, to reach out to others. And it's always possible in each of our family *sanghas.*

What we really hope, more than anything else, is that this book can be an inspiration for those whose lives are dedicated to relational practice, and for whom this work is essential. We are continually co-creating faith and can only continue if, moment-to-moment, on Yasodhara's Path, we hold in our hearts the experience and vision of awakening together.

That is what relational activists are—and do.

That's the inspiration in the beginning, the middle, and the end of each relational moment. In the "hello," the "staying," and the "goodbye." And while there will come a time when we will no longer be alive in our circles—our families, friends, *sanghas*, communities—the circles will remember, and go on awakening together.

# ACKNOWLEDGMENTS


It is with deep gratitude and appreciation that we acknowledge all the beings who have helped bring this book into the light—those seen and unseen, in this world today and gone beyond.

**To our teachers: deep bow to you!**

Vimala Thakar, Joanna Macy, Thich Nhat Hanh, Jean Baker Miller, Gregory Kramer, Sri Nisargadatta Maharaj, Larry Rosenberg, Jack Kornfield, Sharon Salzberg, Phyllis Hicks, Pema Chodron, Surya Das, Bhikkhu Bodhi, Gina Sharpe, Tara Brach, Sally Duncan, Bill W. and Dr. Bob

**To all our friends on the path: gratitude for each moment of support and encouragement, and for "getting it."**

Diane Aronson, Nancy Beardall, Tara Brach, Deborah Berger, Betty Burkes, Stephanie Covington, Michelle D'Amico, Surya Das, Nina Dabek, Kathleen Dyer, Natalie Eldridge, Leslie Epstein, Michael

Fredrickson, Susanne Fairclough, Mary Lou Fanelli, Christopher Germer, Trudy Goodman, Cathleen Grant, Paula Green, Kevin Griffin, Carter Heyward, Phyllis Hicks, Olivia Hoblitzelle, Annie Hoffman, Cathy Hoffman, Melinda and Parkman Howe, Judy Jordan, Joan Klagsburn, Frances Moore Lappé, Peg McAdam, Joanna Macy, Darla Martin, Florence Meleo-Meyer, Nancy Menard, Stephanie Morgan, Susan Morgan, Denis Noble, Pamela Petinatti, Susan Pollak, Irving Reich, Cia Ricco, Christina Robb, Patty Rosenblatt, Richard Rowe, Steve Schaffran, Elyse Simon, Jackie Simonis, Susan Solomon-Shaderowfsky, Martin Sheen, Barbara Sternfeld, Jaylene Summers, Amma Thanasanti, Judith Thompson, Ferris Urbanowski, Mark and Barbara Vonnegut, Karen Waconda, Mary Watkins, Kaethe Weingarten, Lila Kate Wheeler

**To Jan's beloved communities: many thanks to all my *dharma* sisters and brothers. I could not do it alone!**

- **Metta Insight Dialogue Teacher Community**—especially Gregory Kramer, Phyllis Hicks, Sharon Beckman-Brindley, Mary Burns, Gary Steinberg, Lori Ebert, Fabio Giommi, Antonella Commellato, Bhante Sukacitto, Bart van Melik, Patricia Genoud, Anne Michel, Florence Meleo-Meyer, Nic Redfern, Rosalie Dores, Yowon Choi, Jill Shepherd, Beth Faria
- **Institute for Meditation and Psychotherapy** (Cambridge, Massachusetts)—especially Trudy Goodman, Susan Pollak, Chris Germer, Ron Siegal, Paul Fulton, Tom Pedulla, Bill and Susan Morgan, Charles Styron, Sara Lazar, Mark Sorenson, Nayla Khoury, Andrew Olendski
- **CDL3 at Spirit Rock Meditation Center** (Where the project began!)—especially Gina Sharp, Tara Brach, Darla Martin, Karen Waconda, each of you!

- **Jean Baker Miller Training Institute** (Wellesley College)—especially Jean Baker Miller, Irene Stiver, Judy Jordan, Natalie Eldridge, Wendy Rosen, Sandy Kaplan, Cynthia Garcia Coll, Carolyn Swift
- **Worldwide 12-Step Fellowship**—our eternal gratitude. You are the living realization of this Path—As Anytime Anywhere around the world, the hand is extended

**To those of you who share our obsession with all things relational**

Jean Baker Miller, Judy Jordan, Martin Buber, Carter Heyward, Kathy Dyer, Gregory Kramer

**To Jan's special groups: special thanks for your accompaniments**

Monday Night Theory Group, Buddhist 12-Step, Monday Noon Meeting, Unreasonable Women, Mother's Group, China 2, Sunday Art and Soul Sangha, Relational Insight Meditation team

**To our colleagues who live this path wholeheartedly: you have deeply inspired us!**

Ethel Gates, Take Care Home Health, Susan Pollak, Carter Heyward, Kathy Dyer, Diane Aronson, Phyllis Hicks, Olivia Hoblitzelle, Ferris Urbanowski, Ann Cason, Betty Burkes, Lucille Stott

**To Kwan Yin, Chinese Goddess Mother, and to all the other mothers in who have walked the path of motherhood together: gratitude for your accompaniment**

Christina Robb, Mary Watkins, Beth Shipley, Erica Bronstein, Kaethe Weingarten, Jackie Simonis, Nancy Beardall, Joan Goldberg, Julie Landau-Taylor, Susan Solomon-Schaderowfsky, Betsy Smith, Natalie Eldredge, Deborah Hirshland, Kate Straus, Kate Seidman

**To beloved anonymous friends and clients: with special gratitude and love as we have walked this life path together for decades!**

**To the team that made this book possible: deep appreciation to you all!**

Our persistent agent, Deidre Mullane, who helped develop the book proposal; our wonderful editor, Rosemary Ahern; Emily Han at Beyond Words for her sensitivity, insight, and editorial brilliance; Emily and Henry Covey for their partnership and editorial skill

**To our parents and grandparents: thank you for your love and courage.**

Rosalie and Alexander Surrey, Rose and Sigmund Bergman, Katie and Morris Susserman, Anne and Frank Goldblum

**To our beloved Katie Chun: you have lived through this book, and have been our heart and inspiration to keep on keeping on!**

**To Stephen, life partner, coparent, coconspirator, coauthor:**

Gratitude and awe beyond words for your accompaniment in walking this path together. Your unwavering enthusiasm, brilliance, and creativity through all the messiness—the light shines!

**To Janet, total partner, great mother, group-former, dialoguer, beacon of empathy:**

From the first time we met, the most relational person I've ever known. Your brilliance brought the vision of this book to us; your deep faith and practice and tenaciousness brought it to fruition. I, too, am in awe of you and in love with you; and I apologize for the messiness as I applaud the creativity, and send you loving-kindness and gratitude always.

# NOTES

## A word on language—the vitality of the gerund:

As many Buddhist teachers have said, "the word is not the thing." One of the most difficult things to capture in words, at least in English, is the movement of relationship.

For example, on page 168, in the discussion of power with, and based on Jean Baker Miller's "5 Good Things," we write, "When two or more people meet in right relation, *the power arises in the connecting*."

The word "*connection*" is a noun, about a thing, and signifies *stasis*.

The word "*connecting*" is a verb, implying *movement*.

The words "the *connecting*" is a gerund, making an exquisite link between a noun and a verb—and bring to mind *the vitality of movement*.

Finally, the phrase "*in the connecting*" brings an image of even more energetic movement, in this case, of how right relation energizes all who share in it.

We have found that the gerund is the most descriptive way to write about, and talk about, the *movement in relationship*—especially the *movement toward mutuality*. Because this is the best description of core elements of the relational movement at the heart of the Path of Awakening Together—as in phrases such as "*in the arising*" and "*in the relating*" etc.—you will notice it used often in this volume.

## Letter to the Reader

1. These are the only mentions of the Buddha's wife, sometimes referred to as *Bimba*, *Bhadda Kaccana*, and *Rahulamata* (mother of Rahula). The major texts of the Pāli Canon drawn on are the Apadana, the Cullavaga, and the Therigatha. In *Yasodhara, the Wife of the Bodhisattva* (New York: State University of New York Press, 2009), author Ranji Obeyesekere draws on two well-known ancient Sinhalese texts: the Sinhala Yasodharavata (the story of Yasodhara's "lament as a grieving wife") and the Sinhala Yasodhara Apadana (the sacred biography of Yasodhara), where Yasodhara becomes an *arahat* in the Buddha's *sangha*.
2. Modern references of Yasodhara's story:
    - Jacqueline Kramer, "Yasodhara and Siddhartha: The Enlightenment," *Turning Wheel* (Summer 2010).
    - I. B. Horner, *Women Under Primitive Buddhism: Laywomen and Almswomen* (Delhi, India: Motilal Banararsidass, 1930).
    - Susan Murcott, *The First Buddhist Women: Translations and Commentaries on the Therigatha* (Berkeley: Parallax Press, 1991).
    - Deborah Hopkinson, et al., eds., *Not Mixing Up Buddhism: Essays on Women and Buddhist Practice* (Fredonia, NY: White Pine Press, 1986).
3. Janet Kornblum, "Study: 25% of Americans Have No One to Confide In," *USA Today*, June 22, 2006.

## Introduction

1. Melvin McLeod, "Introduction," *Best Buddhist Writings 2005* (Boston: Shambhala Publications, 2005), 322.

2. Jean Baker Miller, *Toward a New Psychology of Women* (Boston: Beacon Press, 1978).

## Book One: Yasodhara's Story

1. Sri Nisargadatta Maharaj, *I Am That* (Durham, NC: Acorn Press, 1982).
2. Ibid., 8.
3. Derived from Dhammapada: The Way of Truth, early Buddhist scripture, Verse 1: "If one speaks or acts with a pure mind, happiness follows" and Verse 5: "This is the law, ancient and inexhaustible."
4. Susan Murcott, *The First Buddhist Women: Translations and Commentaries on the Therigatha* (Berkeley: Parallax Press, 1991).
5. Derived from the bodhisattva vow, cited in Jack Kornfield, *The Wise Heart: A Guide to the Universal Teachings of Buddhist Psychology* (New York: Bantam, 2008), 355.

## Book Two: Introduction

1. Vimala Thakar, "Relationship and Awakening" (dharma talk, Perkins School for the Blind, Watertown, MA, March 1987).
2. Joanna Macy, Molly Young Brown, and Matthew Fox, *Coming Back to Life: Practices to Reconnect Our Lives, Our World* (British Columbia: New Society Publishers, 1998), 51.

## Book Two: Chapter 1

1. Jean Baker Miller, *The Healing Connection: How Women Form Relationships in Therapy and in Life* (Boston: Beacon Press, 1997), 29.
2. Martin Buber, *I and Thou* (Touchstone, 1971).
3. Miller, *The Healing Connection*, 30–34.

4. Giacomo Rizzolatti, Luciano Fadiga, Leonardo Fogassi, Vittorio Gallese, "Premotor Cortex and the Recognition of Motor Actions," *Cognitive Brain Research* 3 (1996): 131–41.

5. Edward Tronick, L. B. Adamson, H. Als, and T. B. Brazelton, "Infant Emotions in Normal and Pertubated Interactions," (paper presented at biennial meeting, Society for Research in Child Development, Denver, CO, 1975).

6. Daniel J. Siegel, *The Developing Mind: Toward a Neurobiology of Interpersonal Experience* (New York: Guilford Press, 1999).

7. Jean Decety, "A Social Cognitive Neuroscience Model of Human Empathy," in *Social Neuroscience: Integrating Biological and Psychological Explanations of Social Behavior*, E. Hamon-Jones and P. Winkielman, eds. (New York: Guilford Press, 2007), 246–270.

8. Richard Davidson and Anne Harrington, eds., *Visions of Compassion: Western Scientists and Tibetan Buddhists Examine Human Nature* (Oxford: Oxford University Press, 2001).

9. Thich Nhat Hanh, "This Is the Buddha's Love," *Shambhala Sun* (March 2006): 52.

10. Thich Nhat Hanch, "Dharma Talk: 'Relationships'—Community as Family, Parenting as a Dharma Door, and the Five Awarenesses," *The Mindfulness Bell*, August 6, 2013, http://www.mindfulnessbell.org/wp/tag/watering-seeds-of-happiness/.

11. Thich Nhat Hanh, "The Next Buddha May Be a *Sangha*," *Inquiring Mind Journal* (Spring 1994).

12. Martin Luther King, Jr., "Letter From Birmingham Jail," (1968).

13. Joanna Macy, Molly Young Brown, and Matthew Fox, *Coming Back to Life: Practices to Reconnect Our Lives, Our World* (British Columbia: New Society Publishers, 1998), 51.

14. Thich Nhat Hanh, *Teachings on Love* (Berkley: Parallax Press, 1997), 55.

15. Thich Nhat Hanh, *True Love: A Practice for Awakening the Heart* (Boston: Shambhala Press, 2004), 5–31.

16. Ibid.

17. Ibid.

18. Gregory Kramer, *Insight Dialogue: The Interpersonal Path to Freedom* (Boston: Shambhala Publications, 2007).

## Book Two: Chapter 2

1. Starhawk, *The Spiral Dance* (New York: Harper, 1979).
2. Harold Gatensby, "Peacemaking Circles," (lecture, Ikeda Center for Peace, Learning and Dialogue, Cambridge, MA, 2004).
3. Samuel Shem and Janet Surrey, *Bill W. and Dr. Bob* (New York: Samuel French, 2014).
4. Ibid., 49.
5. Ibid., 45.
6. Ibid., 92.
7. Ibid., 93.
8. Alan D. Wolfelt, "Helping a Man Who Is Grieving," GriefWords .com,http://griefwords.com/index.cgi?action=page&page=articles%2Fhelping11.html&site_id=2 (accessed October 26, 2014); Lisa Athan, "Men and Grief," Grief Speaks website, http://www.griefspeaks.com/id38.html (accessed October 26, 2014).
9. Louise Hawkley and John Cacioppo, "Loneliness and Pathways to Disease," *Brain, Behavior, and Immunity* 17 (2003): 598–105.
10. John's story, from a conversation with the author, September 22, 2014.
11. Amy Banks, "Relational Neuroscience" (lecture, JBMT Summer Institute, Wellesley College, Wellesley, MA, 2010).
12. Martha's story, from a conversation with the author, July 16, 2014.
13. Macy, *Coming Back to Life*, 52.

## Book Two: Chapter 3

1. Thich Nhat Hanh, "Mindfulness of Ourselves, Mindfulness of Others" (dharma talk, Peace Walk, Memphis, TN, 2002).
2. Sarah Ruddick, *Maternal Thinking: Towards a Politics of Peace* (Boston: Beacon Press, 1989).
3. Jean Baker Miller in "Mother Blaming and Clinical Therapy" by Janet Surrey in *Women-Defined Motherhood*, Jane Knowles and Ellen Cole, eds. (New York: Harrington Park Press, 1990), 134.
4. Jean Baker Miller, *Toward a New Psychology of Women* (Boston: Beacon Press, 1978), 4–6.
5. Miriam Greenspan, "'Exceptional' Mothering in a 'Normal World'" in *Mothering Against the Odds: Diverse Voices of Contemporary Mothers*, Cynthia Garcia-Coll, Janet Surrey, and Kathy Weingarten, eds. (New York: Guilford Press, 1998), 58–9.
6. Ibid., 59.
7. Shelly Taylor, "Tend and Befriend: Biobehavioral Bases of Affiliation Under Stress," *Current Directions in Psychological Science* 15 (2006): 273–277.
8. Sarah Hrdy, *Mothers and Others: The Evolutionary Origins of Mutual Understanding* (Cambridge: Harvard University Press, 2009).
9. Patricia Hill Collins, "The Meaning of Motherhood in Black" in *Double Stitch: Black Women Write About Mothers and Daughters*, P. Bell-Scott, B. Guy-Sheftall, et al., eds. (New York: Harper Perennial, 1991), 205.
10. Anonymous mother, personal communication with author, September 26, 2014.
11. Samuel Shem, *The House of God* (New York: Putnam, 1978), 322.
12. Clarissa Pinkola Estes, *Theater of the Imagination, Volume 2* (New York: Free Press, 2010), audiobook.
13. Susan Kaiser Greenland, *The Mindful Child: How to Help Your Child Manage Stress and Become Happier, Kinder, and More Compassionate*

(New York: Free Press, 2010); Christopher Willard, *Child's Mind: Mindfulness Practice to Help Our Children Be More Focused, Calm, and Relaxed* (Berkeley, California: Parallax Press, 2010).

## Book Two: Chapter 4

1. Thich Nhat Hanh, "Mindfulness of Ourselves, Mindfulness of Others" (dharma talk, Peace Walk, Memphis, TN, 2002).
2. Bhikkhu Bodhi, "Horizontal Friendship," lecture, *Spiritual Friendship*, bodhimonastery.org (August 4, 2008).
3. Ellen Goodman and Patricia O'Brien, *I Know Just What You Mean: The Power of Friendship in Women's Lives* (New York: Fireside Press, 2000), 12.
4. Janet and Kathy's story, from a conversation with the author, June 20, 2014.
5. Joseph Havens, "Relationship as Yoga," Pendle Hill pamphlet (Lebanon, PA: Sowers Printing Co., 1978).
6. Vimala Thakar, *Self-Education* (Navrangpura, Ahmedabad, India: The Vimala Prakashan Trust, 1987).
7. Samuel Shem and Janet Surrey, *We Have to Talk: Healing Dialogues between Women and Men* (New York: Basic Books, 1998).
8. Thich Nhat Hanh, "Chapter 1: Four Love Mantras," in *True Love: A Practice for Awakening the Heart* (Berkeley: Parallax Press, 1997), 5–31.

## Book Two: Chapter 5

1. Diane's story, from a conversation with the author, August 22, 2014.
2. Ellen's story, "About Us: Ellen Goodman," The Conversation Project website, date unknown, http://theconversationproject.org/about/ellen-goodman/ (accessed October 25, 2014).

3. "About Us: Ellen Goodman," The Conversation Project website, date unknown, http://theconversationproject.org/about/ellen-goodman/ (accessed October 25, 2014).

4. Janet's story, written by the author, August 18, 2014.

5. Ann Cason, *Circles of Care: How to Set Up Quality Home Care for Our Elders* (Boston: Shambhala, 2001), 37.

6. Ibid., 37.

7. Ibid., 14.

8. Ibid., 20.

9. Ibid., 7.

10. Ibid., 20.

11. Olivia Hoblitzelle, *Ten Thousand Joys and Ten Thousand Sorrows* (New York: Penguin, 2008).

12. Hoblitzelle, *Ten Thousand Joys and Ten Thousand Sorrows*, 5.

13. Ibid., 2.

14. Ibid., 151.

15. Ibid., 25.

16. Ibid., 165.

## Book Two: Chapter 6

1. "Diversity Program Initiative," Spirit Rock Meditation Center, Diversity Program Initiative, www.spiritrock.org/diversity.

2. Cynthia Garcia Cole, Robin Cook-Nobels, and Janet L. Surrey, Judith Jordan, ed., "Building Connection through Diversity," *Women's Growth in Diversity: More Writings from the Stone Center* (New York: Guilford Press, 1997), 190.

3. The term "relational activist" arose in conversation between Betty J. Burkes and Janet Surrey in August 2014. All other quotations in this story are from the same conversation.

4. Carolyn Boyes-Watson and Kay Pranis, *Heart of Hope: A Guide for Using Peacemaking Circles to Develop Emotional Literacy, Promote Healing & Build Healthy Relationships* (Boston: Center of Restorative Justice, Suffolk University, 2010).
5. Kay Pranis, *The Little Book of Circle Processes: A New/Old Approach to Peacemaking* (Intercourse, PA: Good Books, 2005), 12.
6. "What is Restorative Practices?" International Institute for Restorative Practices, http://www.iirp.edu/what-is-restorative-practices.php.
7. Judith's story, from a conversation with the author, August 29, 2014.
8. Karuna Center for Peacebuilding, accessed September 10, 2014, www.karunacenter.org/.

## Book Two: Chapter 7

1. His Holiness the Dalai Lama in *Buddha's Forgotten Nuns* (documentary), directed by Wiriya Sati (Australia: Budaya Productions, 2013).
2. Thich Nhat Hanh, "The Fertile Soil of Sangha," *Tricycle*, Summer 2008, http://www.tricycle.com/insights/fertile-soil-sangha (accessed October 26, 2014).
3. Thich Nhat Hanh, *Friends on the Path: Living Spiritual Communities* (Berkeley, CA: Parallax Press, 2002), 15.
4. David R. Loy, "The Three Institutional Poisons: Challenging Collective Greed, Ill Will, and Delusion," posted in "The Three Poisons—How Greed, Ill Will, and Delusion Corrupt Our Institutions," by Steven Goodheart, *Metta Refuge* (blog), June 17, 2010, http://mettarefuge.wordpress.com/2010/06/17/the-three-poisons-how-greed-ill-will-and-delusion-corrupt-our-institutions/ (accessed October 25, 2014).
5. Hanh, *Friends on the Path*, 6.
6. Thich Nhat Hanh, *Joyfully Together: The Art of Building a Harmonious Community* (Berkeley: CA: Parallax Press, 2003), 6.
7. Ibid., 6.

8. Ibid.
9. Hanh, *Friends on the Path*, 15.
10. Ibid., 11.
11. Hanh, *Joyfully Together*, 11.
12. Joanna Macy, *Coming Back to Life: Practices to Reconnect Our Lives, Our World* (New Society Publishers, 1998), 195.
13. Eugene Cash in "The Suffering of Separation," by Janet Surrey, *Inquiring Mind* website, 2010, http://www.inquiringmind.com/Articles/SufferingOfSeparation.html (accessed October 26, 2014).
14. Gregory Kramer, *Insight Dialogue: The Interpersonal Path to Freedom* (Boston: Shambhala Publications, 2007).
15. "Foundations of the Work," Work That Reconnects Network website, date unknown, http://workthatreconnects.org/foundations-of-the-work/ (accessed October 26, 2014).
16. Ibid.
17. Ibid.
18. John Seed, Joanna Macy, et al., *Thinking Like a Mountain: Toward a Council of All Beings* (Philadelphia: New Catalyst Books, 1983), 79–90.
19. Larry Yang, "Forgiveness Meditation" (Dharma Seed Talks, Spirit Rock Meditation Center, Woodacre, CA: January 14, 2011).

## Book Two: Chapter 8

1. Vimala Thakar, "Each of Us, a Miniature Wholeness," Awakin.org, July 21, 2008, http://www.awakin.org/read/view.php?tid=579.
2. Meryl's story, from a conversation with the author, September 10, 2014.

# Glossary

## Names and Relations

**Ananda (ah-NAN-duh)**—Siddhartha Gautama's first cousin and closest attendant to him as the Buddha: the Awakened One, formally Siddhartha Gautama

**Channa (CHA-nah)**—Siddhartha Gautama's childhood playmate and manservant

**Devadetta (or Deva)**—Prince, Yasodhara's brother

**Gopa**—An affectionate Indian name of endearment

**Kanthaka**— Siddhartha Gautama's favorite white horse

**Kisa Gotami**—Nun, the Mustard Seed Mother

**Kwan Yin**—Buddha of Compassion (Chinese), "The One Who Hears the Cries"

**Mahapajapati**—Pajapati's name when she becomes an *arahat*

**Mahayana**—later Buddhist texts, written after the **Pāli Canon**

**Maya (or Maya Devi)**—Siddhartha Gautama's mother and Pajapati's sister

**Nayla**—Mother of a child who died, servant of another of the palace royalty, close friend of Yasodhara (fictional character)

**Net of Indra**—Hindu image of the web of interconnectedness

**Pajapati**—Queen, Siddhartha Gautama's stepmother, Yasodhara's mother-in-law, "She Who Hears the Cries" (see also **Mahapajapati**)

**Pāli Canon**—Earliest Theravadan Buddhist texts

**Pamitha**—Queen, Yasodhara's mother and King Suddhodana's sister

**Rahula**—Son of Siddhartha Gautama and Yasodhara; name means "fetter"

**Rohini**—Princess Yasodhara's servant

**Sakyans**—Prince Siddhartha Gautama's and King Suddhodana's family line

**Sarnath**—A city located northeast of Varanasi near the confluence of the Ganges and the Gomati rivers in Uttar Pradesh, India. The deer park in Sarnath is where the Gautama Buddha first taught the *dharma*.

**Shantideva**—Eighth-century Buddhist monk

**Siddhartha Gautama**—the Buddha, Yasodhara's husband, Rahula's father, "He Who Goes Forth"

**Suddhodana**—King, Siddhartha Gautama's father, Yasodhara's father-in-law

**Suppabuddha**—King, Yasodhara's father

**Therigatha**—Verses of the First Nuns, early Buddhist text of **Pāli Canon**

**Vinaya**—Book of Monastic Rules, **Pāli Canon**

**Yasodhara**—Princess, Siddhartha Gautama's wife, Rahula's mother, "She Who Stays" (also known as Bimba, Bhaddakaccana, Rahulamata)

## Glossary of Pāli/Sanskrit Words

***Anapanasati Sutta***—Buddhist discourse: Mindfulness of Breathing Sutta

***anatta***—Basic characteristic of life, no-self

***anicca***—Basic characteristic of life, impermanence

***arahat***—Enlightened being

***bhikkhu***—Buddhist monk

***bhikkhuni***—Buddhist nun

***bodhisattva***—A being bound for enlightenment

***devas***—Heavenly beings, gods

***dhamma/dharma***—Wisdom teachings of the Buddha

***dukkha***—Suffering (First Noble Truth)

***kalyana mitra***—Spiritual friend

***karuna***—Compassion

***koan***—Succinct paradoxical statement

***mandala***—Spiritual symbol, Sanskrit for "circle"

***mantra***—Sacred word or phrase repeated in prayer or meditation

***mara***—Demons, unwholesome temptation in meditation

***metta***—Loving-kindness

***mudra***—Hand movement with symbolic meaning

***nirvana***—Enlightened "deathless" state, Awakened, cessation of suffering

***sangha***—Community of Awakened Ones, can refer to community of spiritual practice

***saris***—silk dress of Indian women

***sutta/sutras***—discourse of Buddha, each sutta is wisdom teaching in the oral traditoin

***Vedas***—ancient Hindu texts